THE ORIGINAL
ALTON DOUGLAS
A Biography

To Bob
Here's to a lot of
Shared experiences !
Cheers

Alton Douglas

THE ORIGINAL
ALTON DOUGLAS
A Biography

Alton Douglas with
Shirley Thompson

BREWIN BOOKS

First published by
Brewin Books Ltd, 56 Alcester Road,
Studley, Warwickshire B80 7LG in 2003
www.brewinbooks.com

ISBN 1 85858 230 X

A Cataloguing in Publication Record
for this title is available from the British Library.

Typeset in New Baskerville
Printed in Great Britain by
Warwick Printing Limited.

To Jo, who made it a story worth telling,

and to Shirley, who made it worth telling the story.

*   *   *

If a man does not keep pace with his companions,

Perhaps it is because he hears a different drummer.

Let him step to the music which he hears, however

measured or far away.

Henry David Thoreau, American writer (1817-62)

*   *   *

Old Jewish Proverb: Sleep faster, we need the pillows.

*   *   *

ACKNOWLEDGEMENTS

(for providing interviews, photographs,
encouragement and numerous other favours)

Keith Ackrill; Neil Allen; The Birmingham Post and Mail Ltd; Birmingham Reference Library, Local Studies and Archives; Douglas Birt; Alan and Alistair Brewin; Jasper Carrott; John Clarke; John Clayton; Mike Gancia; Linda Grant; Vince Hill; Robert Holmes; June Hooley; Roy Hudd; Frank Ifield; Tommy Laughton; Pete Lindup; June Lowndes; Don Maclean; Raymond Mason; Brian Matthews; Major Mills; Dave Mitty; Dennis Moore; Olive Pocius; Maurice and Gwen Price; Richard Price; John Shelley; Win Shelley; Keith and Coletta Smart; Gordon Stretch; David Thompson; Ken Windsor; Terry Wogan.

Our special thanks go to Jo Douglas, for her invaluable contribution, patience, and for additional editing and research.

Please forgive any possible omissions. Every effort has been made to include all organisations and individuals involved in the book.

CONTENTS

Acknowledgements   vi
Contents   vii
Foreword – by Jasper Carrott   ix
A Funny Thing Happened   x
The Kaleidoscope Comedian   xi
Chapter 1   Warm-up   1
Chapter 2   Tidney   12
Chapter 3   Once a Dunce   26
Chapter 4   Dougie Gaiter   35
Chapter 5   The Sackbut and the Bull Fiddle   51
Chapter 6   Comedy Walks   63
Chapter 7   Clubbed!   72
Chapter 8   Dame for a Laugh   82
Chapter 9   Roll of Honour   91
Chapter 10   Nip Along to the Booking Office   102
Chapter 11   The Golden Slot   114
Chapter 12   Flawed by Success   125
Chapter 13   The Odd Couple   137
Chapter 14   The Spice of Life   146
Chapter 15   No – Your Place   157
Chapter 16   Airing My Parts   165
Chapter 17   Alton at War   174
Chapter 18   Lord Ha-Ha   179
Chapter 19   Play and Words   190
Chapter 20   Sing Something, Simple   198
Chapter 21   What's Brewin?   203
Chapter 22   Turn Up the Lights   215
Favourite Things   225
Curriculum Vitae   226
Index   228

FOREWORD

It is perhaps appropriate that this introduction should be called a 'Foreword' because it virtually represents two attributes that Alton and I share. Firstly, 'Forward' is the motto of our beloved city of Birmingham, a place where we were both born and have stayed to make our permanent homes. Secondly, I feel it describes succinctly our attitude to the way we both approach our comedy. As you will see as you read through the pages, both of these common qualities have influenced Alton a great deal in his life and career. From his early childhood in the Small Heath area of the city where his friends and family shaped his attitude for honesty and integrity, to his later days, with his desire to eschew the easy approach to comedy. There were so many comedians telling old gags, trotted out in a never-ending tirade of unconnected one-liners, succumbing to the desires of the lowest common denominator.

You will understand why then, if you have followed his career, that rather than compromise his own standards he retired from stand-up comedy and turned to writing. But, before he did that he had a life in show business that covered many areas including T.V., radio, theatre, pantomime, summer seasons and film.

Through trusted friends, acquaintances and personal recollections he has compiled an account of his life that is both detailed and informative.

His early life was almost humdrum, but that in itself is not uninteresting. As a record of an upbringing in a typical English city it is a life that many of us can share and more than associate with. However, it is his history of theatre and club life that he feels is important to record. The high days of the sixties and seventies when the big cabaret clubs and Variety ruled are but just memories, but Alton's intimate recall means it's all there for us to remember at the turn of a page.

When Alton left the stage, stand-up lost a discerning and talented player, I for one was disappointed but at least it was a bit less competition to worry about! Thankfully he did not turn his back on entertainment entirely. His love of Birmingham and the surrounding areas led him to discover that his passion was shared by tens of thousands of other West Midlanders, hence his many books that recall the history of the region that have sold so well. They are very good indeed, in fact I have collected them all; I even bought one. Yes, they are that good.

By the time you have read this book you will have become good friends with the author. If you're from Brum you will have an extra-added warm feeling of nostalgia and wistfulness. If you're a Brummie, and a comedian, and over 45, you may recognise the odd crack or two!

A FUNNY THING HAPPENED

I stared at a blank sheet of paper for two years, just pausing occasionally for a sip of water. It was Alan Brewin's fault. The aforementioned publisher (known henceforth as 'the appellant') had sent me a contract for a book with the working title: *The Alton Douglas Story* (poor title, great subject). Upon questioning the guilty party his excuse was that, as I'd insisted on trotting out so many anecdotes over the years, this was the only way he could get on with his life. Not having the kind of ego necessary for a project of such magnitude I resorted to developing writer's block. Then a miracle occurred (in truth, *If – The Pat Roach Story* was published). Now, I've collected biographies all my life but this was something special. A beautifully crafted book with an unusual, nay idiosyncratic, feel to it (i.e. just me).

I contacted the co-author, Shirley Thompson, our initial 20 minute meeting lasted 4½ hours and we were off and running. Our working method was quite simple. Shirley would tape the account of my life story (a generous friend said it should have been my mouth). With no prompting whatsoever from me, she would interview a number of fellow conspirators, threading their blatantly libellous transcripts through the tale. Finally, we played a game of literary table tennis, biffing the words backwards and forwards between us, until now, hopefully, *you* become the victor.

If, now and then, I seem to have settled an old score – correct. I'll never get a better opportunity.

Alton

THE KALEIDOSCOPE COMEDIAN

Twist and turn kaleidoscope, the colours whirl and spin,
For the picture's ever changing - first a scribe - then Harlequin.
A thousand different pieces reassemble 'til you see,
Progressing through these pages
Alton's true identity.

K's for Keep 'em guessing hard
A's for Askey – what a card!
Laughter motivates his life, plus
Energy - and Jo, his wife.
Inquisitor in *Know Your Place*, and
Dog named Groucho, loved to race.
Odd couple – a bizarre position,
Singer, compère, jazz musician.
Cricket, an abiding passion.
On stage a showman – height of fashion.
Panto, publications (nostalgic face), thus
Everything falls into place.
To reveal his nature, by and by
Is our intention, at least - we'll *try* ....

Shirley

Chapter 1 –

WARM-UP

Once upon a time, a woman went to the doctor's complaining of stomach-ache. The doctor diagnosed indigestion. Today 'Indigestion' is sixty-five years old.

"Come and see what we've got!" Twelve-year-old Maurice grabbed his father Sidney's hand, hurrying him quickly down the road, on a grey winter's afternoon, to 290 Heather Road, Small Heath, Birmingham.

That was me, of course. In those days, men worked a five-and-a-half day week, at least. So dad came home from work just after Saturday lunchtime, on 22 January 1938, to be greeted with the news that I'd been born that morning.

Alton's birth certificate shows that he was registered as Douglas John Price, on the 1st March 1938, in the sub-district of Yardley. His mother's name is given as Dorothy Margaret Price, formerly Pipe. Ironically, she had only to change two consonants to convert to her married surname. Sidney Neville Price, his father, originally a cabinet-maker, had become a motor pressing inspector by the time his youngest son was born.

In the same year, Hitler moved into Austria and Czechoslovakia, the citizens of England were issued with gas masks for the first time and, in the Arctic, Eskimos complained about a heat-wave. In cricket, Denis Compton scored his first century against Australia, Benny Goodman's famous *Carnegie Hall* concert took place, and in rural America Orson Welles' radio production of H.G. Wells' *War of the Worlds* caused terrified people to rush into the streets brandishing pitchforks, to repel alien invaders. It was also the year that the Prime Minister, Birmingham's Neville Chamberlain, returned from Munich, clutching the notorious 'scrap of paper' that was intended to ensure a permanent war-free environment for mankind. One of the year's top songs, recorded by Slim & Slam, was *Flat Foot Floogie with a Floy Floy*.

The Small Heath of 1938 was mainly a working class area of Birmingham. Two of the main local employers were Singer Motors Limited and the BSA – Birmingham Small Arms (their total workforce was swollen by a large number of 'outworkers', operating from sheds at the rear of their homes). One of the more unusual businesses was that of Clapshaw and Cleave Limited. Situated opposite Small Heath Park, on the site of the original terminus for horse-drawn trams, they manufactured sporting equipment, including croquet mallets and cricket bats. On occasion cricketers would test their products on the best patches of grass in the park and an irate park keeper would dispatch one of his trainees to shoo them off the hallowed turf. Imagine the expression on the face of a fifteen-year-old lad when he was confronted by a demi-god like Don Bradman!

Various authority guidelines disagreed about the actual boundaries, but a rough impression could be formed, by the layman, by place name signs near to Small Heath Station and then in an easterly direction almost next to the New Green Lane Picture House. Coming away from the city centre, the Kingston Cinema was right on the edge and in a southerly line along the Coventry Road, the bridge at Hay Mills formed an indisputable halt.

It's said that, on a Saturday night, at the turn of the century, any policeman finding a drunk in the area would bundle him over the River Cole bridge and let the Worcestershire Police deal with the problem. Sometimes a tug-of-war would develop between the two forces, at the end of which the offender would have sobered up.

Olive Underhill, one of the Price's neighbours, had a ringside seat when Alton made his first grand entrance. "I happened to be out in the back garden when I heard a baby crying. What I was doing in the back garden in January is beyond me. Anyway, my mother said: 'That must be the arrival of Mrs. Price's baby' – and so it was."

At nine months old, Alton began to toddle, so Dorothy asked Olive if she would take him out in the afternoons. She became Alton's babysitter, earning the princely sum of sixpence a week! "He was a lovely child and he always looked so cute in his white knitted cap with a 'pom-pom' on the top. He had a fold up pram and we would go for long walks around the neighbourhood and visit places, like Digby Park, in Somerville Road. I had plenty of time for Alton, because at that time, during the war, we lacked air raid shelters at school, so pupils from Oldknow Road School spent two hours a day of schooling, in neighbourhood homes."

Soon afterwards, Olive and her brother, Robin, who later became the Reverend Robin Underhill, were evacuated to Somerset. They returned home in 1942. "It was then that I took up with that charming little guy again. We spent

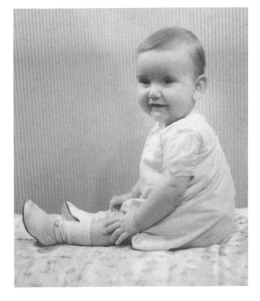

Nine months-old - the last traces of innocence?

our time playing games, what games I can't remember. I do know that Alton had a favourite ball, which was almost as big as his head!" Olive and eight-year-old Alton parted company when she married a GI, Joe Pocius, and emigrated to the United States, in 1946. She explained recently: "In 1983, my father received for his 80th birthday a gift of Alton's book, *Birmingham at War Volume 2*." On reading Alton's 'Dear Nostalgic' letter at the front of the book and seeing the early photograph of him that accompanied it, "I realised that this Alton Douglas could be that loveable little fellow that I adored." She wrote to him, and with her theory confirmed, took a seven-week holiday to Britain in the summer of 1985, to be reunited with the

The photo that brought Olive back into my life, taken in 1940.

boy she used to 'bounce on her knee'. They have stayed in touch ever since.

Maurice describes the location of the family home as "... half way between Somerville Road and Hobmoor Road. There were council houses in the middle, private houses at each end and a sanatorium up the hill, at the top, on the other side of Hobmoor Road." Although they lived in a council house, Maurice endorses an opinion held by several other residents: "It was a lovely area: you couldn't fault it."

Local historian Brian Matthews, a good friend of Alton's, was born in neighbouring Somerville Road, just a year before him. He remained there until the age of four, when they were bombed out, moving into a larger house, just a few hundred yards away, on the Coventry Road. Brian had the foresight, some years ago, to make taped interviews of elderly local residents, for posterity; one, made by Paulina Cleasby, has proved particularly helpful for this chapter; a selection of these recordings may be found in Birmingham Reference Library, together with transcripts to accompany them.

Brian remembers two popular Small Heath landmarks, both on the Coventry Road. The first is Bedder's Fish Restaurant, still situated on the corner of Heybarnes Road and the Coventry Road. It was reputed to serve the best fish and chips in Birmingham! There was also Devoti's Ice Cream Parlour, alongside Small Heath Park. At one time trams used to run along the Coventry Road. "When buses were introduced," recalls Brian, "the old roads were pulled up, so that the Coventry Road could be re-surfaced. The old surface consisted of housebrick-sized sections of wood, covered in tar.

The locals stole these 'bricks' to burn in their grates, as a substitute fuel, as times were hard - especially in winter. There was such a plentiful supply of them that they were sold around the neighbourhood, so that others could do the same."

Another contemporary of Alton's was John Clayton, who would eventually become a good friend, when they joined the local Boys' Brigade. Their friendship lasts to the present day. He was born in 1937, the same year as Brian Matthews. John describes Small Heath as "... a very productive area really – lots of shops. Basically, you could buy anything. There were bakers, greengrocers and so on, none of the big supermarkets or anything like that." C. Urquhart, a generation older than Alton, Brian and John, wrote an article entitled *Early Days in Small Heath*, published in Carl Chinn's publication, *Old Brum*. In the article, he recalled that his mother used to shop for meat on the Coventry Road: "... in Tay's for fresh meat, Furey's for cooked meat, we also used to go to Woolworth's near Green Lane."

John Clayton has other pleasant memories of the district: "My mum and dad went down to a public house called *The Anchor*, which was down by the bottom of St Andrew's Road. As we'd lived there earlier, a lot of dad's mates were down there. If we missed the last tram, we had to walk up from there to Fifth Avenue. People said goodnight and were very polite. It seemed like a very safe place to walk around."

From time to time, during the course of our story, we'll be catapulting you forward into the future – then back again. To avoid a re-entry crisis, and to make the process as painless as possible, we're using 'Fast Forward' symbols, indicated by three arrows >>> - so be on the alert! Also, in *case* you haven't 'cottoned on', the two styles of typeface don't mean that our printer's suddenly had a brainstorm; it simply denotes which co-writer is 'holding forth' at any given time. Direct quotations from Alton appear in italic script. To avoid confusion, although a lot of his friends still call him 'Doug', as he's been known as Alton Douglas for over forty-five years, we'll refer to him throughout as Alton.

To trace Alton's family history, we must first wend our way back to rural Shrewsbury, and from there to Ladywood, in close proximity to Birmingham City Centre. His grandfather, Tom Price, was born at 45 Old Coalham, Shrewsbury, and his paternal grandmother, Lucy Crutchley, was born at 4 Butcher Row - also in Shrewsbury. They did quite well, as they progressed through life.

As Maurice is twelve-and-a-half years older than Alton, he takes up the story at this point; because of the age difference, he is able to recall certain details of the family history. "We've always been a bit vague about this. There were a lot of coal trucks with 'Price' on the side. Whether my dad was pulling my leg I'll never know – but *he* said they were his father's.

"The way he made his money was he had a very sharp mathematical mind. When the coal trains came in, because he was quick, he was bidding for coal while the others were still working it out. They were quite a well off family when they were in Shrewsbury – I would imagine. They had a maid and lived in Moveage Cottages, in Ellesmere Road - the only buildings in the area to be hit by the Germans, in the Second World War. They were too late to catch dad; they'd long gone by then! Alton discovered this when he did some research for his book, *Memories of Shrewsbury* – he found out information that I didn't know." In a 'This Is Your Life' school project about his grandfather, Maurice's grandson, Richard Price, explains: "His Auntie had a cottage in Arthog, near Barmouth (opposite side of the estuary from Farchynys). When they visited her, they treated it as a holiday."

"Arthog used to feature in calendars," recalls Maurice. "The cottages were separated from the gardens, by a road in between. It was in a row of between six to eight back-to-back cottages, just outside the village, on the road to Fairbourne." Alton

Tom Price, at the time of the Great War.

conjures up a lovely Edwardian picture of the family being met at Shrewsbury Station by their maid, Polly Peet, who had a candle for them. They used this to light their way through the tunnels, to get from Shrewsbury into Wales.

The kids used to chant behind the maid's back:
Polly Peet, sweaty feet,
Polly Peet, sweaty feet.

Tom and Lucy had sixteen children, the youngest of whom was Victor J. Price, who later had over ten books published on Birmingham. Sidney, born 5 July 1898, was number six. The Price family moved from Shrewsbury, to several addresses in Ladywood, including Osler Street and Monument Road, but eventually settled at 40 Wood Street, on the corner of Wood Street and St Mary Street.

We don't know the reasons for the move to Birmingham. Grandfather continued his coal business for a bit. The fact that he had a very sharp, mathematical mind is something that all the male members of our family have in common: they can all add up very quickly.

When they moved to Ladywood, one of Sidney's older brothers, Bob, who was married, lived nearby. He and Ethel also had a very big family. Their fourth child, Peter, adopted the stage name of Pete Lucas; like Alton, he became a professional comedian. They met years later, discovering that they were cousins, and that they'd played together as young boys. It *has* to be something in the genes! Several of the Price family sang in the choir at St John's Church, which was particularly handy, being opposite their home at 40 Wood Street. The Reverend Arthur Runnels-Moss presided over events.

Grandfather, Tom Price, was quite a volatile man. One day one of his daughters came in, wearing a big 'picture' hat. He let out a roar and grabbed the hat. Maurice's wife, Gwen, explains: "That was Aunt Dodie's hat. He took it off and flung it down the road. I heard that story many times, because Aunt Hilda, another of Sidney's sisters, used to tell me a lot." According to family legend, on more than one occasion, Tom also threw his dinner up the wall!

There was no early record of people in our family being musical – apart from singing in the choir – that's about it. When Tom was in a temper, or he'd had a drink or two, which he was quite fond of, he'd go in the kitchen and wash his 'jewellery', which was his gold watch and chain and various rings; years later I acquired the watch – through Victor.

Alton's mum, Dorothy's birth certificate shows that she was born at 130 Lowe Street, Wolverhampton, on 17 December 1900. Shortly afterwards, the family moved to 31 Clark Street, Ladywood, Birmingham. Her mother's maiden name was Emily Withington. Richard Pipe, her father, was a Commission Agent at the time of Dorothy's birth. Emily is featured in one of our photographs as 'Nanny Pipe'. Clark Street is situated opposite where the *Crown* cinema was – John Landon's bathroom business is now there. It was less than half a mile from Sidney's new family home, in the same district. A certificate, at the front of a copy of *Alice in Wonderland*, reveals that by 1908, Dorothy was attending Osler Street Infant School, in Ladywood. The book was awarded to her, as a 'Good Conduct' prize. Her school would have been fairly new then; according to Norman Bartlam it was built in 1875.

Research shows that Dorothy had four siblings, three older and one younger. The Census of March 1901 reveals that the youngest Pipe hadn't yet been born; also, they had what Richard rather grandly called a 'boarder', John T. Care, described as a sixty-three-year-old water traveller, from Northampton. As a water traveller (an itinerant water gypsy or boatman), 'John T' was ideally situated, with the Gas Street Basin, the heart of the British Waterways system, right on his doorstep. Space must have been at a premium, as the Pipe's living area would have been quite small. By coincidence, the word 'bordar' was employed fairly frequently in the Domesday Book, 800 years before the Pipe family's census entry. The modern day usage of the word is not *too* far removed from the 1086 definition: 'a lower order of peasant who worked directly for the lord'; ranking below a villain (or 'villein') he had no accommodation of his own.

Richard Pipe.

When you went up to mum's house, you had to go through an archway, with a sweet shop on the corner – and turn sharp left. At the end of the yard were the stables where they kept coal horses, you'd got to lift your washing line up with a prop – to let the horses go under! Her youngest brother, Uncle Vic, was a coalman, so where that all connects up – which came first - I'm not quite sure: whether you put the cart before the horse – or what! For almost seventy years, due to a misunderstanding, mum celebrated her birthday on the 18 December, until she finally discovered the error. Her dad, Richard Pipe, had become an estate agents' collector, by the time my parents married. He appeared very austere and was quite a handsome-looking man, with snow-white hair and very correct in his manner. But he had the most mischievous sense of humour. He'd sit on the top of the tram and when the girls got on he'd drop used matches into their boaters. Or he'd give their pigtails a tug, and they'd turn round to see who it was! And there'd be this benign gentleman sitting there, who wouldn't ever pull a pigtail in his life, you know? So he obviously had a good sense of humour.

Dorothy Pipe inherited her father's sense of humour. She passed it on to *both* of her sons. Even when he became a professional comedian, Alton drew the line at telling Dorothy risqué jokes, although years later his wife, Jo revealed: "Oh, your mum liked that kind of joke! She wouldn't tell them herself, but she certainly wasn't a prude."

Of course, you don't know your mother's like that; you can't imagine that she'd had any life before she was a mother.

Dorothy's great-grandson, Richard Price's summary of Maurice's life, (for the project mentioned earlier), provides an insightful overview of Alton's only sibling. Maurice's grandson makes particular reference to a sense of humour that is very much in evidence, after only five minute's conversation with his grandfather – although it's of a different variety to Alton's. Maurice's storytelling skills, on the other hand, seem quite similar to his brother's, particularly when he 'acts out' (or demonstrates) a scenario.

Richard explains: "As you can see, my grandfather has had quite an eventful life. He has had many jobs and many experiences along the way. You can tell this just by having a conversation with him, for every topic you bring up, he has a story or a joke about it. He also has many hobbies including football, fishing, gardening and some stranger ones like rabbit shows and pigeon racing. Football still plays a big part in his life, he has been teaching referees for nearly fifty years. Three of his pupils are now 'reffing' on the Premier League. At least one has refereed in a Wembley FA cup final. He is now also a shareholder in the Football Association, which is an honorary position and he gets to vote on changes in the rules of football."

Tom Price drank quite heavily and eventually lost the coal business, a situation that was not uncommon in those days. The co-writer's own grandfather, for example, was by all accounts, a heavy drinker, and his father-in-law lost his printing business in Worcester, for the same reason. After forfeiting the business, Tom became an agent for the *Provident Clothing Company*, where he worked for several years. We know, from Sidney's marriage certificate, that by 1920, Thomas had become a coal merchant's clerk. In the fullness of time, his sons, including Sidney, began to find their own niche in life.

As a little boy, dad started work at the age of thirteen, as a cabinet-maker's apprentice. Of course, the first day, they played every trick imaginable. You know the traditional joke: they send you for a William stamp and it turns out to be a bill stamp, you're sent for a rubber hammer – and so on. They got him blind drunk on his first day – he didn't come home! His mother found him - under one of the benches. My dad was never a big drinker after that; he'd have a shandy or something, but he was never a big drinker – it put him off drinking. So it did him a favour. In time he became a very, very good carpenter; he made his own tables. Every member of the family has a piece of furniture that he made. I've got an umbrella stand. My father became a unifying force in later years: he was the one who kept the family together.

Maurice explained that the company where Sidney was apprenticed was 'Walsh's Bedsteads', in Monument Road, Ladywood. He has a wooden tray, which his father made; his wife, Gwen, still treasures a little jewellery box. Maurice confirms: "He was a *wonderful* carpenter – made bookcases – everything."

According to family legend, despite living within half a mile of each other, Sidney and Dorothy's first meeting, unlike many young couples in those days, was *not* in their local neighbourhood. As far as Alton knew, in the romantic tradition of *Brief Encounter*, their courtship began following a chance meeting – at New Street Station. However, more recent research has revealed that, at the time of her marriage, Dorothy was a wood box maker. It seems a pity to discard the former, more romantic tale, but the fact that Dorothy and Sidney lived and worked within close proximity of each other, and had such similar occupations, leads us to the conclusion that that they were far more likely to have met through their work.

Mum and dad got married on 25 September, in 1920, which is a very important date in the book, because you'll find out later that Jo and I got married on the same date – although unaware of the coincidence. We got married suddenly, for reasons that I'll tell you about later – not the obvious! Mum was nineteen when she married and dad was twenty-two. My brother was born in 1925, by which time they'd moved into a council house in Small Heath. They took over the council house which dad's brother-in-law George, and sister, Dodie, had originally moved into, at 290 Heather Road. When they moved from there, George became the licensee of the Lewisham Arms in West Bromwich.

Mum, c 1920.

The lady next door to them, Mrs. Fletcher, was the first person to move into the road, somewhere between 1923 and 1924 and remarkably, lived there until the 1990s. She was known as Cissie Fletcher, until about ten years ago, when I met a relative of hers, who said that her name was really Amy. So like some of us, she had a name transplant.

In the autumn of '38, Alton had to go to Little Bromwich Hospital, because he caught diphtheria.

There was an epidemic when I was eight months old. Mum could only come up and look at the bulletin board: she couldn't visit me. They didn't have Isolation Wards with glass panels, where you could go and look through. She just had to go and look at the boards and see how I was doing. It was a very close thing. But we won't keep the readers in suspense, we'll let them know – I actually lived!

But the Age of Innocence was about to pass, not just in Alton's case, but for the world at large. When the smoke cleared, mankind would never be the same again, either in social attitudes or general mores.

We are particularly grateful to Win Shelley, a member of the Local History Society and local resident, for drawing our attention to a range of material, including a substantial booklet entitled 'St Benedict's Infants, 1913 – 1988.' It contains extracts from the log book entries, combined with photographs and documents relating to the area. Miss E.R. Quinn, it informs us, became headmistress in May 1939, just prior to the outbreak of war, a post she held for twenty-seven years, including the period when Alton was a pupil.

The St Benedict's log book reveals that, while Alton was still enjoying daily tours of the area, courtesy of Olive Underhill, in the chariot that was his pram, thirty-six infant school children were being evacuated, to Charlton Kings, a few miles south of Cheltenham. We know that they were in a separate group from the junior school children, but that the evacuations from both schools were made on the same day. This was the first wave of protective measures.

For the inhabitants of Small Heath, and their fellow Britons, the Second World War was about to begin in earnest. Miss Paulina Cleasby, a retired teacher and former pupil, born in 1902, gave forty-one years service to the junior branch of the school. She recalled that momentous event in 1939, during a taped conversation in 1980, with Brian Matthews:

"We were evacuated with those children who wanted to be evacuated, into Herefordshire, on Saturday 1st September 1939, two days before war was actually declared. We walked down to Tyseley Station, with our gas masks, food and belongings. The parents said goodbye at the school. I was in a little village called How Capel, a few miles from Ross-on Wye, with about thirty children – and my friend, Miss Haycocks, was with us. The children were in various cottages and farms." They remained there until Christmas, although some pupils returned home earlier.

Brian has studied copies of maps that the Germans used in the war, to locate the old B.S.A. works on the Coventry Road - for bombing purposes. They had aerial maps of the railway lines and were instructed that, coming from Elmdon, they should use certain railway lines as landmarks - quite easily done - they glistened in the moonlight! The Luftwaffe turned left when they reached the River Cole, from which point, additional railway lines guided them to their target; being an armaments factory, it was heavily damaged.

Like Brian, John Clayton was also a victim of the bombing raids – but twice over! "The first years, up to about five, I lived in St Andrew's Road. We moved because we were bombed out of *two* houses in the road. So we moved into Fifth Avenue in 1942."

Alton's own wartime experiences stimulated his initial interest in the subject, as he says in *Birmingham at War Volume 1*:

My father was Deputy Head ARP Warden for Small Heath, my brother was in the Home Guard and mum, eternally aproned and headscarved, was really everyman's mum. Wearing a Mickey Mouse gas mask and siren suit and armed with a tin machine gun, I crouched under the stairs at 290 Heather Road, Small Heath and personally brought down more German planes than anyone else in the whole wide world.

His family, like so many others, had been supplied with an Anderson Shelter, but sometimes, during the worst of the raids, especially around 1941/42, they couldn't reach the garden in time. So on occasions when the family sheltered under the stairs, being reassured by a fully 'kitted-out' Alton that he was destroying half of the Luftwaffe, their next-door-but-one neighbour, Mr. Tennant, would suddenly complete the picture by appearing with his trusty harmonica. The idea was to cheer the family up, by playing a rousing tune; the fact that his repertoire was mainly limited to *When They Call the Roll Up Yonder*, must have been a little worrying! Although their house didn't receive a direct hit, they were nevertheless surrounded by families who did. Understandably, a feeling of uncertainty pervaded Alton's early years.

Houses were sometimes taken out, quite close to you: right opposite us, two houses were totally demolished. If you looked at a bombed house in those days, it was just as if a giant had bitten into it: you'd see half of say, a first-floor bedroom. I remember seeing one with a dressing gown hanging on the back of the door, and a lopsided picture, just above the mantle-piece. Mr. Farmer, a neighbour, was walking down the road one day when he heard the whine of a bomb. He and the man he was with dived into an entry. The man fell across Mr. Farmer. Mr. Farmer told him to stop mucking about and pulled him off - and the bloke was headless!

>>> In 1985 I filmed a programme for children's' television, for ATV, in the road outside our house. Then we went through the house and we filmed into Mrs. Fletcher's back garden next door, where she'd still got her Anderson Shelter – she kept her coal in it.

The large plate glass windows of Bedder's Fish Restaurant were blackened – for obvious reasons. Brian recalls: "When the war ended, St Benedict's schoolchildren were given a small razor blade each to scrape off all the black paint, and were rewarded with a special fish-and-chip meal. As supplies were scarce, the owner of the ice cream parlour used slithers of firewood, up-ended into eggcups of coloured ice, to make halfpenny lollipops. A year or so after the war ended, Mr. Devoti was once again able to obtain the correct ingredients to make ice creams - which he sold for a penny."

A copy of an extract from St Benedict's Admissions Register, kindly supplied by Win Shelley, shows Admission Number 510 as the last entry on one particular page. From this we discover that on the 1st February 1943 (three years and four months after that first 1939 evacuation from the school) Alton Douglas (a.k.a. Douglas John Price) began his infant school career, in company with eight other neighbourhood children. Just a year or so before, however, a memorable incident occurred, which you're unlikely to find anywhere on the CVs of the two gentlemen concerned!

In those days, people would quite often put a long blanket with fringes on it, over the kitchen table, then put a tablecloth over the top of that. We were in a neighbour's house, when mum looked under the table, this one day. I'd be about three, or certainly pre-school age. I was playing with a little boy – excuse the term – but it's appropriate in this case! We'd found that each of us had a whistle, and we were taking it in turns to blow it! I won't mention his name, because he went on to have a very distinguished career in banking. Mum was completely horrified! She dragged me up the road. I'd got to go to the hospital and have my mouth washed out with carbolic soap!

Chapter 2 -

TIDNEY

They named me after my father. Ridiculous name for a kid – "Daddy".

St Benedict's Road School was at the top of our road. The school touched on two roads: Heather Road, and St Benedict's Road. The bit on our road was the Junior School, and the other half, on St Benedict's Road, was the Infants' School.

An entry by a former pupil, in the St Benedict's Infants' Book, focuses on the period 1939-1966. It reads as follows: 'Miss Quinn was head throughout the whole period. A perfect lady, loved and respected by generations of children, parents and staff.'

By the time Alton reached school age, in 1943, he became increasingly able to appreciate his father's stories, which contained plenty of humour, pathos and colourful characters. Despite all the savagery and mayhem that existed during the First World War, Sidney had managed to salvage such tales, about his own experiences. His young son's imagination was fired by these graphic, often witty descriptions of a military past, combined with subsequent sagas about local characters and events.

I think we ought to stress that men in those days, in the Great War, and later in the Second World War, never talked about the gory side of war; they always dwelt on the fun and humour. They never even dwelt on the fact that they had to sleep under wagons, in France, for example.

Sidney was in the 453rd Company Army Service Corps. It was their task to supply a range of equipment to different branches of the army; a 'Royal' prefix was added to their title later. During the First World War, Sidney was always involved with horses. A sepia-coloured army photograph features him in the centre, with two favourite horses, one on either side. One of the most enduring of Sidney's tales, concerning his wartime experiences in France, also provides our chapter title.

They had this glorious character called 'Icky Todd'. Now it was Dicky Todd really, and 'Icky' had a speech impediment: he'd obviously got no sibilance. Also, he couldn't consistently say certain consonants, so he became 'Icky Todd'. Dad had wonderful memories of him, with the horses. It was Icky's job to look after them. If a horse was sick, he would throw a pill to it, saying: "Catch it Tambo, catch it Tambo!" Which became the regimental catchphrase.

Icky Todd, who, coincidentally, was also a Brummie, was on sentry guard and he would say: "Alt – oo tose tere?!" One night, after getting no response to the regulatory three inquiries, he fires, and of course, everyone in the camp comes rushing, and they find that he's shot a cow! The sergeant calls him a 'tilly tod' (or Todd?). Then Icky said this line, which dad treasured for the rest of his life: "Tidney, he talled me a tilly tod. If I tought he meant what I tought he meant, I'd tuddy well till him!" That became a family line: whenever anything went wrong, or somebody was nasty to us, we'd all say: "If I tought he meant what I tought he meant, I'd tuddy well till him!"

The name 'Tidney' seemed to stick. Nancy, one of the two horses photographed with him, had been acting strangely for some time. One day, in November 1917, she reared up dangerously, lashing out. The next thing Alton's father knew, he woke up next to the inert body of his favourite horse. To save him, one of his fellow soldiers had no choice other than to shoot Nancy. As an act of consolation, before burning her body, they cut off one of her hooves and filled it with cement, to preserve it. Sidney, who had been very upset by the whole incident, brought the hoof back with him from France, as a keepsake.

>>> Around 1930 dad made Maurice a toy fort, at his parent's house in Ladywood. Then they transported it back on the tram, to Small Heath. It was incredibly heavy and when they arrived home, dad opened the hinged compartment at the bottom, which was made to house model soldiers – and there was Nancy's hoof! It was used as a doorstop for the next forty years!

Dad, somewhere in France, 1917 Nancy is on the right.

Another inter-war reminder lay in store for Alton's father. Having crossed the Channel and re-entered 'Civvy Street', Sidney was driving his motorbike and sidecar, near a popular local tourist spot, known as the Lickey Hills, in Rednal, Birmingham. Suddenly, to his amazement, he spotted Icky, as 'large as life' - standing at a bus stop – (Icky at the Lickeys)!

It's evening; it's growing dark, so he stops. "Icky!" "Tidney!" "Want a lift Icky? OK then, hop on the back!" He says: "Dust a minute – dan I det de wife?" So he calls to his wife and this huge woman comes out of the shadows – with three children! Icky climbs on to the back of the bike, and she gets into the sidecar with the three children. They go careering off down the Bristol Road, with the bike listing heavily towards the pavement. And as far as we know, that's Icky Todd riding out of dad's life, because we never heard any more reference to him, after that. But dad always felt very affectionate and protective towards him.

'Tidney' had a best friend, known affectionately as 'Uncle Ralph', who had been in the navy. He lived in Allestree in Derby; Alton and Ralph Wolstenholme continued to maintain contact for many years. Unfortunately, a ship's mast had fallen on Ralph's arm, when he was a young man; the injury had been incorrectly re-set – with bizarre results:

For his party trick he would grasp something, and you'd watch his elbow move round to the front!

Although Sidney had been a skilled cabinet-maker, he was unable to earn a reasonable income from his trade. So when World War Two was approaching, he applied for a job at the Castle Bromwich Aeroplane factory, where he became a foreman. Then he went to work at Singer Motors Ltd. Afterwards, for a while, he became, ostensibly, a storeman at Butlin's Holiday Camp at Clacton, having been secretly instructed to keep an eye on a spate of thieving. Once this problem had been resolved, his delighted employers moved him back down to Edgbaston Reservoir in Ladywood - strangely enough, where he had spent the latter part of his childhood. He looked after the stores and solved further pilfering problems. Eventually, he returned to the factory in Castle Bromwich, where he'd worked previously: by this time it had become Fisher and Ludlow Ltd.

Due to the smaller age gap between Sidney and Maurice, the two men had a different relationship to the more paternalistic one that existed between Alton and his father. As Maurice recently explained: "Sidney and I were friends. We worked at Castle Bromwich together, we went in the car together in the mornings, and came home at night. When my mother was in hospital, one of the neighbours wrote and said that my father and I were like two brothers."

Alton's memories of Sidney, from a young boy's point of view, combined with Maurice's perspective, (closer to that of a friend or younger brother), have furnished us with a broader picture of Sidney, than might otherwise have been possible.

Sidney's experiences in France, as a young man, stood him in good stead. During the Second World War, he was appointed Deputy Head ARP Warden, for all of Small Heath. Owing to these duties, he was absent from the family for substantial periods of time. He'd be working during the day, but doing ARP duties at night. Maurice recalls that the Head Warden for Small Heath was a Councillor Johnson.

Dad bought a caravan in Coleshill to put us in, if he felt things were getting bad. This friend of his had a cottage around the corner from the caravan. But dad used to put us in the caravan if he was worried about the raids. I was a bit young to be formally evacuated I suppose. The raids would be in 41, 42.

Maurice elaborates: "The friend of my father's, who Alton is referring to, also used to work for him. When my father was on duty, he used to take us there and pick us up in the morning, rather than leave us in Small Heath. The one night, we were in the house at Coleshill, and my father had just gone outside, to get the car, to go back into Birmingham. A plane came over and dropped a bomb. As a result of the explosion, a brick damaged my father's car roof, right on the corner – at the back.

"About ten o'clock, a police sergeant came and knocked on the door. He said: 'We've found an old well down the garden, and either it's subsided, or we think there may be a delayed-action bomb in it!' So they evacuated about twelve of us, who were all in the house at the time, to Coleshill Town Hall. We were really their exercise for Air Raid Precautions. They dished us out with blankets. At seven o'clock in the morning there was a big bang and the whole house had gone! After that it became a maintenance yard, which is still there – in Coleshill. If it had gone off, none of us would be here – delayed action!"

Dad was deaf in one ear, and one night in 1941, when we were safely in the caravan at Coleshill, he was sleeping at home, because of his ARP duties - (on his good ear). He woke up in the middle of an air raid to find bombs dropping, two houses just opposite had been totally demolished; whistles were blowing and there were flashing lights. "Blimey," he muttered, "you'd think they'd tell someone if they're going to start a war!"

Maurice was, initially, a member of the Army Cadets, at Stoney Lane Barracks. "I was a fourteen-year-old, training in the Local Defence Volunteers, (which later became the Home Guard), because I was an Army Cadet." At the age of sixteen, he officially joined the Home Guard. As one of its trusted members, he was asked to perform a rather unusual, but important task: "Leaving my job at Castle Bromwich Aeroplane Factory one night in thick fog and a total blackout, I acted as guide and walked in front of the bus all the way to the *Fox and Goose* at Ward End. There the fog cleared, so I boarded the bus, only to be charged the full fare from Castle Bromwich."

Meanwhile, young Alton was getting into 'hot water'.

We found a lorry in a garage just round the corner from us, one evening, in Somerville Road, and we got in it. We were sitting in it – like kids do – it was unlocked. We were turning the wheel – pretending to drive it. We weren't running it off - we didn't move it.

The garage owner caught us, dragged us up the road to our house, and he gave dad one helluva sherakin! Dad said: "I'm ever so sorry. I'll make sure it doesn't happen again. I'll tell him off." But this man went on and on and on. So dad went back into the house, and came back carrying a police helmet. He said: "It's OK, I've got the message now. We'll go and have a look at your vehicle now, and see what damage has been done." So we went outside and the man's offside light wasn't working. So my dad said: "I think you'd better go on your way!"

Mum, Dad and I, c 1942.

Sidney hadn't hired the helmet from a theatrical company; it was a bona fide part of his equipment, because he was a Special Constable during the war.

On one occasion, he found a man absolutely stoned out of his mind, propped him up against a hedge, and went off to find a phone box, because in those days they didn't have phones in police cars. He rang the station for help with this drunk, came back, but the man had disappeared. So dad spent twenty minutes in the middle of a blackout, trying to find him. Then all of a sudden, he looked down and there were two feet sticking up, exactly where he'd left him. The man had fallen backwards through the hedge, and the hedge had closed behind.

In 1943, Nanny Pipe, Dorothy's mother, came to nurse her, because Dorothy had developed phlebitis. Alton remembers the bed being brought downstairs, for that purpose. Unfortunately, it developed into a form of 'relay nursing', because after a couple of days, Nanny Pipe fell down the stairs and broke her leg. So Alton's mum got out of bed,

Nanny Pipe and Mum just before the exchange system came into operation, 1943.

nanny got *into* bed, and Dorothy had to look after her. As explained in the opening paragraphs of this chapter, this was the same year when Alton began his school career, at St Benedict's Infants' School.

One of my first memories of school was of a boy having a slight accident. They put him by the radiators to dry off! With the smell and the steam we all had to move out of the classroom, into the cloakroom, until the caretaker came along and mopped up everything!

Some time in 1944, Miss Quinn, the headmistress of St Benedict's, took a group of small children, including Alton, down to the Coventry Road, a few hundred yards from the school. They lined up on the pavement. A little while later, a car drove towards them.

A man was sitting high up in the back, with his feet up on the seat, wearing a Homburg, smoking a cigar and holding up two fingers – to make a V. And Miss Quinn's jumping up and down in great excitement, and she's saying: "Look children – here he is. Here's our saviour!" And my friend Brian Matthews turned to me and said: "That's not Jesus Christ!"

Gwen recalls making a birthday cake for Alton, when he was about six. But the *classic* tale that went into the family repertoire, and was trotted out at intervals to taunt him – in the best possible sense – was an occasion when he brought a little girl called June Summerfield home from school.

I was probably five or six. She sat on the settee at home, and apparently mum came round from the kitchen and caught me, kissing the hem of her dress, which, of course, after the incident described at the close of the previous chapter, must have reassured her quite a bit. June's visit became part of the family history and I often wondered what happened to her.

Around 1945, Alton had to go to the Birmingham Schools' Clinic in Yardley Green Road, where he was instructed never, ever to eat rhubarb, although no one in the family can remember why.

I was a very weedy lad. I had sunray treatment, because I was so thin and scrawny. I suppose, because I had a bad start with diphtheria. But I'm still a bit spindly now – my arms and legs. I had to miss quite a bit of school, because of having to go to the clinic for treatment – to build me up. Being forbidden to eat rhubarb was a bit upsetting, because we had a big rhubarb patch, at the bottom of the garden. We also had loganberries, which I could eat. Dad kept chickens, as many people did in those days. I had a little white chicken, which was always called Rupert – and he was always the first one to be killed by a cat   or die with the cold. I had a new Rupert each time!

Brian contributes more Prime Ministerial information, on pages 32 and 33 of the St Benedict's Book, by noting, "...Winston Churchill was made Honorary Freeman of the City on 31 October 1946." Maurice recalls that the great man also visited nearby Somerville Road School. He has good reason to remember the occasion: "I know that Churchill visited Birmingham, because I was in the Guard of Honour, at Castle Bromwich Aeroplane Factory."

One of Sidney's sayings, which has stayed with Alton throughout the years, was: "If you don't understand what someone says, at least look intelligent!" His mother had her own, idiosyncratic sayings. At the time, he assumed that everyone's mother used similar expressions, but now feels that they were probably more unique.

If you said that you didn't feel very hungry, and you'd just have a snack, she'd say: "Would you like a lightly-toasted feather?" Or if you weren't very well, she'd say: "I'll rub your chest with half a house brick!" Or describing someone's injuries, she'd say: "He'd got his head in a sling." Now where these sprang from I don't know. Perhaps they came from her father; we've established that he had a good sense of humour, although I was always puzzled by a line from a friend's mother, "He can't come out today, he's got one of his heads."

When dad bought his car we used to go out at night, on the way back we'd sing:

Show me the way to go home
I'm tired and I want to go to bed.
I had a little drink about an hour ago
And it's gone right to my head.

No matter where I roam,
On land or sea or foam,
You will always hear me singing this song
Show me the way to go home.

Readers who recall the Forties and Fifties, will probably realise that this was a popular song of the period. As a child, the co-writer used to sing it, in company with her three sisters - in suitably drunken voices!

In any neighbourhood, there will always be certain individuals who, because of their actions or attitudes towards other members of the community, become an integral part of it. Heather Road stretched for some distance, but Dorothy, in an unassuming way, became a hub of the particular section, where she and her family lived.

If anyone died, mum would be asked to lay them out. I never found out, until years later, that she'd shown great acts of kindness to people. We had a family, just a few doors away, who were very poor. Every so often, my mother would sneak out when it was dark and leave a bag of tea or sugar, or half a pound of butter on the doorstep. Then she'd scuttle back fast, before anyone could see her. One of the few similarities that I can see between mum and I is that if I give money to charity in the street, I can't bear to be seen wearing a flag or a sticker.

Dorothy was very hospitable, making people feel very much at home, as soon as they arrived. According to Alton, she'd hear the doorbell, put the kettle on, then return to see who it was. She was also the sort of person whom people felt able to confide in.

Her youngest son had a passion for reading, from an early age. He joined the library, travelling to the one in Green Lane, which was the nearest, on a number 15 bus. Alton recalls saving his pocket money until he'd collected seven and sixpence then going into Birmingham, either to the Midland Educational, Hudson's or Cornish's, to buy a book about 'Romany' or 'Nomad'. The books' two principal characters were rural adventurers, who roamed the countryside. Alton originally bought several copies, although he has none left now. Curious to discover exactly what it was about the series that had first attracted him, he and Jo recently visited a specialist bookshop in Hay-on-Wye.

The woman there had one or two. I looked at them: they were incredibly childish, and didn't invoke any memories of happy days. But the bookseller said: "Of course you'd have liked them; they were always on Children's Hour." So that's where I must have heard them – then gone out and bought the books.

Despite his father's gift for telling entertaining stories, in general terms, Maurice remembers Sidney as, "Quiet and unassuming. He was very hard-working. His charge-hand, who used to work with him at Castle Bromwich, said: 'He was the straightest man I've ever known.' I said: 'If they can say the same about me...' "

Sidney also had a fetish for polishing shoes – a possible 'throwback' to his army days. Maurice recalls: "He used to say to me: "Come on, let's have your shoes!" He had an old tin box in the kitchen, up on a shelf, which he used to get out every night." After they were married, before visiting 'Tidney', Maurice and his wife, Gwen, always made sure that their shoes were gleaming! Both brothers describe him as a family man, who kept the further-flung members of the family in touch.

Maurice and Gwen's wedding with me looking a bit out of it. Bournville, 15th May 1948.

Sidney continued to work in car manufacturing, where his skills were much in demand. His meticulous nature was reflected in his work. "At one time he had worked at the Austin," explains Maurice, "building what they called 'Specials'. If someone wanted a special car, four of them built that: a hearse – or something like that. If Lord Austin wanted a car – *they* built it. He was a carpenter: some cars were partially built of timber, you see? They got an extra ten shillings a week for doing that.

"He never had a day's illness in his life. He went to the doctor's with a cough and the doctor said: 'Do you smoke?' He said: 'Yes, sixty or seventy.' The doctor said, 'Oh, that's only ten a day.' Sidney said: 'No, sixty or seventy a day!' He came out and never had another cigarette. Now, how he did that I'll never know." According to Gwen: "They told him he'd got nicotine poisoning." Sidney made sure that his young son didn't follow that *particular* example.

Dad caught me smoking in the shed, at the age of eight or nine. He said: "Oh don't waste your time on cigarettes. We can do better than that!" He gave me a cigar and I puffed away at it – I was sick for two days. I never smoked again.

From Maurice's comments about his father, it is self-evident that he held him in very high regard: "I always looked up to him - he was great" - sentiments that Alton echoes:

My dad was a real hero to me. I remember one day, someone was on top of me, punching and fighting me. I couldn't see any sun: the light was all blocked out. All of a sudden, dad walked down the road, found this boy, pulled him off me, and went round later to tell this boy's dad that he couldn't stand bullies – and I've grown up with a hatred of them too.

John Clayton recalls hard times: "I can remember that, at a very young age, you couldn't get coal; you had to go down to Saltley Gasworks, with a trolley. We used to get three bags of coke, because it was so short. I think that was *after* the war, because my dad was involved in the air raid stuff; he was too old to go in the army; he'd been in the First World War, you see."

I suppose by today's standards and mainly because of the war, we would have been considered quite poor. But we didn't realise it and in any case, everyone around us was in a similar plight. If you want to talk about real poverty, consider the case of my sister-in-law, Gwen. The first time she came to our house, we all had poached-egg-on-toast for tea. Now Gwen admits that she had to watch us, to see how we ate it, because it was the first time in her life that she'd ever been given a whole egg! We kept chickens, because dad thought it was his duty to feed us. He'd kill a chicken – and we'd also have eggs.

Douglas Birt, who now lives in Tamworth, became a close friend of Alton's. He has very pleasant memories of Small Heath, having moved in 1946, from a less salubrious environment, close to Birmingham City Centre. In a recent letter, Douglas explains how much he appreciated his new surroundings: "After the restrictive war years, we moved to the open aspects of Heather Road, i.e. houses with large gardens and a local park. Firstly, Digby Park, which I would walk through daily on my way to school. Also, Heybarnes recreation ground, with the river running through it, and a circus occasionally; Eatonways charabancs (not coaches), dreaming of rides to the seaside, and the Singer motor factory where Alton's dad worked. The allotments on Hobmoor Road were magical, and for sixpence you could get a handful of sweet peas for mum. Finally, watching people tending their gardens, cutting the grass, growing flowers, and the huge loganberry bush in Alton's garden; the temptation was too much, too often."

Doug recalls their very first meeting, when he was ten. "We moved into 293 Heather Road. My mother and father were very strict people. They had four children at that time. We were told: 'Don't you dare go outside the gate!' Of course, I would walk to the gate – I wouldn't go outside, but I could see this other young lad across the road. There was an entry between the houses – and a motorcycle. As far as I can remember, that's the first time I ever saw him. I think he was just standing there. I was a little bit wary to say anything. It might sound a little bit odd – but although we were from the inner city, it wasn't the inner city like it is today. We were well brought-up children. But I still had a bit of a complex in those days - that he was a bit more upper class. He was in the front garden, but his gate was open."

Doug hung back, but after a couple more encounters, he and Alton began to speak to one another. "I don't know whether it was he, or one of the other lads, who had some roller skates. And of course, you start to talk then – just say 'hello' – and things like that."

Doug formed the impression that Alton was a little reserved. During the five years the Birt family lived there, the two boys became good friends. They visited each other's houses, rode into each other's gardens, and were sometimes invited inside. One or two of the other lads, eventually joined their little 'gang'. "I'd say there were about five, but I distinctly remember, Donald Huxley was the 'cool dude', as it were; then there was Derek Miller. There was another rather reserved, chubby lad, I can't remember his name; he lived eight doors up from Alton."

This was Norman Hartland. The first time I met him he was in tears: due to his weight, his bike had snapped clean in half!

Douglas remembered Alton's father – without any prompting. "My impression was that he wasn't a manual worker; he seemed more like the office type." Alton makes the point that although Sidney worked manually, like Dorothy, he was rather 'genteel': one of his friends called him 'Gentleman Sid.' Sidney's workplace was very convenient, whereas Doug's father worked in West Bromwich, as an industrial cleaner, so had a greater distance to travel.

He recalls the Price Family car: "It was a Ford, but it only came out occasionally, because of petrol rationing. A couple of times, they took my sister and I for a Sunday afternoon ride - she remembers it well. Of course, this was absolutely 'top-notch'; it was me, more than anybody else, he would take. We thought it was brilliant!"

He remembers one particular trip up Bristol Road - "round the 'Lickeys' – as they used to call it. Again, it was a Sunday afternoon drive, and I think we approached places like Blackwell, then came back home. To be honest, I think they did it to be *kind* to us." Alton is absolutely certain that Sidney would not have done it to be patronising, describing such actions as: "just his way."

Doug remembers Maurice well: "To me, in those days, he was a very large man, very burly. He didn't look like a manual worker either. What I remember about him most was that he had a motorcycle. They'd just had their first child and they had a sidecar fitted to the motorbike." He agrees that the Prices were a 'spick-and-span' type of family. Whereas Sidney loved polishing shoes, Doug recalls that Maurice "...was always polishing his *motorcycle.*"

We used to listen regularly to 'ITMA' ('It's That Man Again', starring Tommy Handley) and 'In Town Tonight', on the wireless. Every time there was any music, dad, Maurice and I used to drum on the arms of the settee or armchair and drive mum completely barmy!

At the bottom of Heather Road, where it meets Somerville Road, was Mr. Hill's cobbler's shop. I'm sure he was the nicest man in the world, but somebody spread the rumour that he kept little boys' ears in his cellar! So all the little lads – I can just see them – used to tiptoe past, because we were terrified of our ears joining the collection!

By the summer of 1948, a Brave New World was emerging; the war had ended three years previously, and people were gradually beginning to rebuild their lives. Alton had just received the heartening news that he'd passed for Saltley Grammar School and Sidney was negotiating to buy a sweet shop, on the corner of Bankes Road and St Benedict's Road. Dorothy had ensured that her son's school uniform was ready for when he began the next stage of his school career, in early September.

Being of a cheerful disposition, Sidney always went into work whistling, but on Thursday morning, 19 August, he was uncharacteristically quiet. Ironically, on the very day when we were preparing material for this chapter, Maurice phoned Alton to say that Channel 4 was televising the classic film, about life in the RAF, during the Second World War - *The Way to the Stars.* The distinguished cast included Michael Redgrave, John Mills, Bill Owen and Stanley Holloway. Although Sidney rarely visited the cinema, Maurice took his father to see the film, on the evening of the 18th. Sidney was still an active fifty-year-old, so neither of them could have possibly known that it would be the last film he would ever see.

Understandably, Maurice still recalls the sequence of events vividly, although initially he was only given sketchy and rather confusing details. Gwen interjects: "He didn't rush that morning, because your mum said to him: 'You're taking your time aren't you Sidney?' He said, 'Yes, I've decided, I'm going to use the car. I've arranged to pick some of the fellows up.' At five to eight he parked the car, and at eight o'clock he collapsed. He went to the workshop and they said he sort of 'zigzagged' down. Somebody said: 'Sit down a minute Sid. I'll get the kettle on and I'll make you a cup of tea.' Then, quite out-of-character, he said, 'I'll go to the surgery and get some tablets.' The fellow that lived down the road, who used to work with him, told us all of that."

By this stage it was obvious that something was wrong with him, and that his headache was becoming progressively worse. He collapsed on the way to the works' surgery; fortunately two of his friends had remained with him. According to Maurice: "He lost consciousness at the surgery. They took him to the General Hospital. Mum got a call at 11am. to say it was very serious.

"They phoned me up at about half past ten in the morning, shortly before they notified mum, and said my dad was in hospital. I'd got a motorbike at the time. I went to the General Hospital. They said: 'Do you think there are any tablets in the house?' Because they couldn't find out what the problem was. I said: 'Yes, phenobarbitone – probably about three hundred.' So they said: 'Whose are they?' I said: 'They're mine; when the doctor used to give them to me, I wouldn't take them – even though I suffered with terrible migraines.' They said: 'Do you think they're still there?' I said: 'Well, I'll go and find out.' I went back home to check that the tablets were still there – which of course they were." The timing was unfortunate; as Maurice was obliged to check the tablet situation, he returned to the hospital shortly after his father died, which meant that Dorothy was entirely on her own, during Sidney's last few moments.

In fact he'd had a cerebral haemorrhage, and he died at five minutes past four in the afternoon . As they wheeled him down the corridor, mum heard the death rattle in his throat, which haunted her for the next quarter of a century.

Maurice subsequently went down to Fisher and Ludlow's surgery, at the request of General Hospital staff, to see if he could discover *exactly* what had happened: they wondered if Sidney had suffered a blow to the head. It wasn't until this point that he learned the *full* details of what had actually transpired. Maurice also made a point of thanking the nurse at the Castle Bromwich Aeroplane Factory, who'd been so kind to him. "She said *she* knew he'd had a stroke, all the while," he explains. "What the police were playing about with – going to the house – she didn't know. But of course, that's hindsight, isn't it?"

Alton was playing happily in the garden that afternoon, with his friends, totally unaware of the sea change that was about to affect his life.

All of a sudden the house seemed to fill up, with my brother and his wife, my Uncle Ted, and my mum. Uncle Ted came out in the garden; I was playing with two friends, Douglas Birt and Derek Miller. He sent them home. I still get choked today – remembering it. We walked down the garden, by the Anderson Shelter, and he said: "Everything in life has its own timespan. It can be quite short with some people, and unfortunately your dad has come to the end of his." So I burst into tears and ran back into the house, and mum was weeping.

Gwen confirms: "He showed Alton the plants, and explained about them growing and dying. Oh he was a lovely man - Uncle Ted." He was also a policeman at Steelhouse Lane police station and Sidney's best friend-cum-brother-in-law: his wife, Effie, (born 1908) was one of Sidney's sisters. After Sidney's demise, Maurice and Ted got into the habit of playing a weekly game of snooker together, at the police station. The manner in which Ted explained Sidney's death, to ten-year-old Alton, denotes an intelligent, rather sensitive individual. Alton's response, given the traumatic circumstances, seems to have been rather mature, for a young boy, especially as only two hours had elapsed, since he'd been given the news of his father's death.

I had to go back to the boys and tell them why they'd been sent home. I went to Derek Miller's house and his mother didn't believe me. She said: "That can't be true. I waved to him this morning!" Everybody knew dad, I suppose, because of his wartime activities "I've spoken to him this morning. He's alright – he's fine." I said: "No, he's died."

According to Alton, his mum would have insisted that he explained to his friends why they'd been sent home. He also makes the point that nowadays, we'd probably say it was good therapy for him to have done so.

I'd been to see the film 'Sanders of the River', that afternoon, with Paul Robeson in it, and I can't stand the song 'Sanders the Great' - even to this day. When I hear them sing it, it brings it all back.

Douglas Birt still recalls these events vividly: "It's funny how you *sense* things. You suddenly realise that there's someone else there – and that something's going on. Being lads, we were charging around the garden. I was asked to leave. I can't remember the *exact* words, but it was something like: "He's got to come in – for the time being."

I just said, "Thank you very much" - and went home. It wasn't until the next day that I was told by my mum: 'Mr. Price has died -there's no better way to put it.' I was not to go over the road, and not to cause a nuisance. Not to bother them, not to go to the door, and so on - to be polite. It was maybe another day or a couple of days after that, my mother said: 'I want to speak to you.' She told me: 'He won't be going to the funeral. He's going with you on this little holiday - you'll enjoy it.' "

Alton stayed with Gwen's family, in Bournville Park, over a four-day funeral period, with Douglas Birt to keep him company; her father, who was the park keeper, had a house on the edge of the park. In those days, children didn't normally attend funerals.

The police came along, took the gate off the hinges, and lined up outside the house. When the procession reached the Singer - which was at the top of Heather Road – (they turned left to go to the cemetery) the workers were lined up outside the factory. There was a policeman at every crossroads, to stop traffic coming, and they were lined up outside the police station. Although Sidney was a Special Constable, and hadn't risen to any great rank, it shows the esteem and great affection that people felt for him.

Alton's final day at St Benedict's Junior School, only the month before, had not been a pleasant one: a group of boys who hadn't managed to pass for the Grammar School, and were therefore going to Marlborough Road School or Oldknow Road School, decided to vent their feelings of frustration and jealousy on him. Alton, (possibly through misplaced feelings of shame, at being a victim) couldn't bring himself to confide in Dorothy. He simply said that he had a bad headache.

They found out that I'd passed for the grammar school and they bullied me. They went round doing what they called 'pilling' – where they grabbed your - (don't ask)! They said, "This is what they'll be doing to you at the grammar school" - and they beat me up.

I went home for my lunch and I was so terrified I didn't go back to school on my last afternoon, which would have meant going up onto the platform and getting a certificate. That has remained with me; it haunts me to this day - the shame of not going back to school that last afternoon.

Chapter 3 -

ONCE A DUNCE...

It was a big rambling school – in the biology class we used to dissect elephants. We called the headmaster 'Nancy', because he'd line all the naughty boys up and let them cane him.

I remember very clearly my first public laugh. At school, we were reading 'Pygmalion' - I was the Hungarian, Nepommuck (in 'My Fair Lady' they changed the character's name to Zoltan Kaparthy – a big improvement). At one point I should have 'let out a hollow laugh'. Knowing that it was the wrong laugh, I deliberately did a deep-throated "He-he!" And the whole class erupted. That was the first time I ever got a big laugh – I'm sure that was an important pivotal moment for me.

September 1948 marked the start of Alton's first year at Saltley Grammar School. Coming just a fortnight after Sidney's death, it proved a particularly harrowing time for him. Saltley was the same grammar school that his brother and cousin Ruby had attended. It must also have been an emotionally charged period for Maurice: he and Gwen had been married only four months before. There was a tradition at Saltley, whereby pupils went into the same House as other family members who might have preceded them. So Alton went into Kenrick House – the same house as Maurice and Ruby. With characteristic honesty, Alton reveals that he was near to the bottom of the bottom class, all the way through. Hardly an easy position to maintain!

Maurice was still involved with the Birmingham Referees, who were not only concerned with football, but also ran their own cricket team. Alton participated as a scorer, for some of the matches, in company with Denis Howell, who was also a Birmingham football referee. A pattern emerged: Alton would invariably keep the tally for his team, whilst Denis kept score for the opposition.

He said to me once: "I'm going to buy you tea – you're my lucky talisman. Every time I see you I get promoted, or something good happens." Shortly after, he became an M.P. and then in time, the Minister for Sport and Recreation! They sent me for a coaching course at Warwickshire County Cricket Ground: I was coached by Derief Taylor, the West Indian opening batsman, who played for Warwickshire. His son is now Lord Taylor of Cheltenham. But as with so many things in my early life, I failed to fulfill any promise. I wasn't a very good cricketer, and that fizzled out. But I did meet my heroes, Tom Dollery and Eric Hollies.

Maurice continues to be a football instructor, to this day. When Alton was a young man, his brother refereed local football matches, in the Works' League; they had their own private grounds. Denis Howell was a friend of his: "I've known him since we started as referees in 1948. He took the referee's course just before me. Derief Taylor, Alton's coach, was a football referee too."

I asked Maurice, who had initially arranged the cricket coaching for his younger brother, about the contradiction between Alton reaching a sufficiently high standard to warrant coaching, yet describing himself as never having been a good cricketer. His reply was surprising: "Alton was a brilliant cricketer; he used to enjoy it, and he was a good bowler. But he wore glasses and he worked out that only two top-class cricketers had worn glasses, so the chances of his getting anywhere were virtually nil; so he packed up cricket. There's a story about us going to see a cricket match between Worcester and Warwickshire. We went on the train to Worcester. When we returned to the station, we realised that he'd left his brand new blue gaberdine school mack at the Worcester ground. We went back and looked for his mack – which we never found. He can tell you about the Worcester player who helped him look for it."

It was Roly Jenkins (Spin Bowler). >>> I did a BBC television programme called 'The Gentleman's Game' with him, in the late 70s. (On reflection, wearing glasses didn't do Geoff Boycott or M.J.K. Smith any harm)!

Everyone knew how keen I was. I couldn't afford any of the equipment, because I had a widowed mum. The Referees Cricket Team therefore supplied me with a bat, pads and gloves, and sent me along. My mother used to pay a guinea for a lady's ticket, and this enabled me to become a member - (I was under eighteen at the time and could therefore go in on her ticket, to watch the county team). Cricket became an absorbing hobby and my great hero was the captain, Tom Dollery. >>> When I was researching one of our books, I went to Edgbaston Golf Club, and asked them about some photographs. They said: "Oh, you need to see our Mr. Dollery." I went cold from head to toe! I said: "It's not Tom Dollery?" They said: "Yes, he's in charge." Oh dear! Anyway, I spent a whole hour talking to him. His wife made us a pot of coffee and we had the most wonderful hour! I sat there, with this man who'd been a god to me. At that time he was an elderly man - but he'd seemed wonderful to me, as a little boy- and still did.

I joined the Boys' Brigade at the age of twelve and there I met the man who had a massive influence on me. He was really Arthur Garbett, but they called him 'Doc'; he'd been the one who ran on with the wet sponges – sticky tape – whatever, at football matches, so he was always known as Doc. He interviewed each of us and asked us why we had decided to turn up that day. He was forming the 12th Boys' Brigade Company at the Methodist Chapel in Blake Lane. I said: "Well, I've just really come to see what it's all about." He was impressed, because everybody else had just said that they'd come along to join. So he made me a squad leader and I very quickly became a Lance Corporal. We selected boys for our squad. One of the boys I selected was John Clayton, who I'm still in close contact with, to this day. He lives down in the South, and became a painter.

John recalls: "We 'hit it off' straight away - we just seemed to get on well together. He played side drum in the band. I played bugle. I just fancied one, and got very upset because I didn't get one at first. Doc Garbett went out specially, and hunted one down for me. I was really looking forward to playing it." John learnt to play by 'trial-and-error': "It's basically only made up of five open notes; most bugle music is. Once you'd learned how to blow the thing and go up and down, there was a little bit of technique. Alton said: 'Why don't you take up the trumpet?' I did, and then he put me in contact with people from the Birmingham Symphony Orchestra." John is just one of a substantial list of friends, who have made a point of mentioning the encouragement that Alton has given them, over the years.

I learned so much from Doc Garbett, including the fact that it wasn't wrong to be an independent freethinker and that it doesn't preclude you from also being a team player. It just means that you can approach problems from an unusual angle, instead of always running in tram-lines. He also instilled old-fashioned values, such as honesty, loyalty and reliability, into all of his lads.

Douglas Birt remembers that Alton's house was *far* different from anything that he was used to. "It was fully carpeted and soft furnished – beautiful. It had a cottage-type suite." (This may have had basket-weave upholstery). "Silly things that you notice; the bread came un-sliced in those days: his mum would always put a breadboard on the draining board of the sink, and then cover the breadboard with a lovely, crisp, clean towel – and cut the bread on that. It struck me as rather quaint. Although as a ten-year-old, I don't remember having too much conversation with her, she struck me as a *lovely* woman: really, really nice." We can't help wondering if Dorothy was in service at some stage; her refined manner and certain practices that she had, like the one with the bread, seem to suggest the possibility, particularly as Maurice recalls a reference to it, in the distant past.

*I love Doug's description of our house. To me it was just **our** house - and didn't everyone's dad make an oak table? We had a painting of 'The Haywain', by that bloke, Constable - but I don't think it was an original!*

It seems quite a coincidence that Mary-Rose Benton, author of the excellent book, *Family Values*, was living only six doors away from the Birts. She lived at 281 Heather Road, from 1943 to 1953, and sent Alton a copy of her book, out of the blue, a few years ago. She had previously been treated rather badly, but at the age of ten, was fostered to the neighbouring Williams household.

12th Birmingham Boys' Brigade Band, with our intrepid hero on the right and Billy McMichael on the left of the front row, Blake Lane, Small Heath.

Douglas Birt was in the Boys' Brigade for a while. There was also a boy, in my squad, called Billy McMichael. He, along with his brother, Kevin, and sister, Christine, had an act called The Three Merry Macs. Christine played the accordion, one played the drums and the other played – I can't remember exactly what - and they all sang.

As an adolescent thirteen or fourteen-year-old, Alton went through phases of having crushes on certain girls. Christine was among the first:

I had a mad crush on her. I thought she was the most wonderful thing – in this little kilt. I worshipped her from afar. >>> In 1963, she had a record in the Hit Parade. Her name had become Christine Campbell, and she had a hit with 'Wherever I Go'. The juvenile relationship had never developed in any way at all, but she found it very amusing when I met her at the BBC and told her about it.

The Birt family lived in Heather Road from 1946 - 1951. Douglas Birt confirms that Alton had a crush on *another* budding performer - his sister. Like Alton's mother, her name was Dorothy. "She was a Betty Fox Babe in pantomimes, for a long time, performing under her own name," he explains. "Eventually she left and went round theatres all over the country." She performed in seaside shows, as a chorus girl, rather than a solo artiste. Dorothy remained in the business until she married, in her twenties. She was four years younger than her brother, having been born in 1940, and two years younger than Alton. He seems to have liked girls with a bit of personality, *especially* if they were interested in showbusiness," explains

Christine Campbell (in 1963).

Doug. "Of course, my mum doted on her; she was always having her photograph taken, by mum and dad: she was very attractive." He thinks his sister may not have realised that Alton had a crush on her. Alton agrees with his friend that, " … it wouldn't have been 'cool' to pursue girls directly."

Doug recalls other neighbours: "I remember the Bloomer family. Diane and Freddie Bloomer left an indelible mark on my memory. Diane was a beautiful girl, very polite and sensible. Freddie was a tall handsome sportsman, once again, another grammar school boy, like Alton - (I was envious). When Freddie was otherwise engaged I would do his paper round for the day and receive one shilling. Mr. Bloomer was a chauffeur and drove a Humber Super Snipe motorcar. Diane always rode her cycle with her pet dog sitting in the basket on the front."

Alton can pin-point the start of his showbusiness career, to about the age of thirteen:

I became a drummer in the Boys' Brigade, and also started a little band, with a boy called Ray Pritchard on piano and a lad playing the mouth organ. We played at a dance in a Scout Hall. I remember the very first quickstep. I gave a hefty beat on the bass drum and the whole cardboard front fell out!

Doug confirms: "Alton was always a bit of a showman. There was a redundant chicken coop in his back garden, where he and three or four other members of our 'gang' used to stage improvised performances. It was about 3 feet high, and maybe 4 or 5 feet across. He didn't call it a 'show', in those days. It was completely enclosed and we crawled into it from the back: when I think about it now – all those spiders and things! He got the neighbours to come into the back garden; they had to pay a penny each, through this little slot: he was dead keen that they paid the penny. He was a really good organiser and knew *exactly* what he wanted to do." Doug recalls hiding behind a curtain and that each performer had his own particular lines to say. "Alton made sure that we had a couple of days rehearsal beforehand."

At the age of fifteen I produced Heather Road's Coronation Concert.

It's an interest that has a familiar ring: the co-writer and her sister Caroline used to organise and perform in neighbourhood shows with their friends, from the age of nine or ten. Each of us had a specific job, ranging from performer, to ticket seller. As evidenced in other biographies, if someone is interested in the Performing Arts, it's often apparent from an early age.

At school, Alton had the cane on two occasions: once for talking, and the other, courtesy of Mr. Shakespeare, for playing football with a girl's netball.

John Shakespeare was a teacher who seemed to absolutely hate me. He taught P.T. and wrote on my School Report – he knew my passion was cricket: 'A keen cricketer of no particular ability' - it really destroyed me. Also, I couldn't do a forward roll. I was terrified, for some reason, of going over on my head. He lined all the boys up and

Alton, Coronation Party concert producer, looks for the nearest exit, 1953.

got them to get their towels out. I had to run through this column of boys while they hit me with their towels. That was his idea of punishment. But he discovered my bad eyesight, and realised what my problems might have been. After that, his attitude towards me changed for the better.

There was a girl at school who was expelled for some kind of sexual activities behind the bicycle sheds. I remember there was a queue one day - for whatever it was. I joined the queue out of curiosity – as kids do. I could see they were using her as a trampoline - bouncing up and down on her. I got bored, standing there waiting, and just cleared off and played cricket. I didn't know what it was about anyway, so it just vaguely puzzled me. We had no sexual education at all; it just didn't exist. Incidentally, that girl ended up as a heroine to all us lads. We all thought she was great – although she got expelled!

While attending grammar school, Alton dated Marjorie Badham – Jack Badham's daughter. Jack played for Birmingham City Football Club. The co-writer's husband David, who's something of a Football Oracle, explains: "Jack was '12th man' and would stand in as Full Back or Centre Half, when either of these players was injured. He often played as Number 5 and took part in the Cup Final in 1955 against Manchester City - which Blues lost." By sheer coincidence, Maurice sometimes plays bowls with Jack Badham's son, also named Jack.

Having no sisters meant that Alton was a little naïve, as far as sexual matters were concerned. How were you supposed to know - for heaven's sake - unless someone told you?

I went out with Marjorie, in the way that kids do - a totally innocent relationship. I had a crush on another girl in the same road – Finnemore Road – a girl called Pauline Davis – and again – unrequited love. The same applies to a girl named Wendy Pardoe, a beautiful girl, who lived in Heybarnes Road; again, she would never know about it. I realise now, that I was probably an early prototype of today's stalkers! I'd linger around outside their house – hoping to catch a glimpse of them.

Alton reminded me (I can just *about* remember) that in those days, you never passed a phone box without going in and pressing the B button, to see if any money came back! His favourite cinema was the *Era Cinema*, in Bordesley Green, a single-storey cinema with just a sloping rake – no balcony as such. When his brother took his future wife to the cinema, he offered to pay for the best seats, although, as things turned out, it was a bit of an anticlimax! A cinema visit was quite a novelty for Gwen, coming from a Salvation Army background. As she recalls: "In the Era Cinema it was just one step up to the balcony, and if anyone wanted to come past, everybody had to stand. Then they had to stand again, to let them come back."

The Era, one step to Paradise.

*I also used to go to the fleapit – which was the New Green Lane Cin[...]
Ivy, in Cherrywood Road, had an Outdoor, and she would put their [...]
window. She was one of dad's sisters. Her daughter Ruby was the one w[...] [...]
Saltley Grammar School with my brother. Because she displayed posters or
'advertising cards' on the door, she was given complimentary tickets for the fleapit. So
I used to go there – free.*

*I loved films: Westerns and Randolph Scott in particular. My other big hero was
Johnny Mack Brown, who is long forgotten by people. Funnily enough, he often wore
black, which good guys didn't normally wear.*

The co-writer used to enjoy going to the Shirley Odeon on Saturday
mornings – we'd come out pretending we were the characters. I mean - kids
do that - don't they?

*That's it – yes. You'd ride up the road, wouldn't you- with your mack on one
button – like a cloak? And you'd be slapping your thigh!*

I think that's a vital part of it; you could pretend you were the character
– and get into the role. Especially if you were that way inclined – a budding
performer.

*Yes, I was in love with June Allyson. I was always falling in love with different
actresses – as well as real-life people. I got involved in the normal sexual exploits that
young boys get involved in. I remember sitting with a girl on the settee at home once,
and I put my hand somewhere in the direction of her non-existent bust. She said:
"Don't, don't - I'm like that!" I thought: 'God, I've given her a baby!' I worried for
days afterwards – I didn't realise what she
meant by 'that'. I qualified for the title of
'Full-blown Idiot' – even in those days.*

*I remember a thigh-clutching
episode. I put my hand on this girl's
thigh, and she gave out with a clarion
call of a typically modest Birmingham
maiden: "Ay yow – tits fust!"*

Every Thursday, Alton, in
company with school friend, George
Terry, made the journey straight
from school, to the *Birmingham
Hippodrome.*

*We'd queue in Inge Street for the
cheapest seats, to see people like Larry
Parks, who played Al Jolson in 'The
Jolson Story', with his wife, Betty Garrett,
Al Martino, Jimmy James, (who was my
all-time favourite), Ted Ray, Jimmy
Young – yes, the same one!*

June Allyson.

>>> In the 60s, Harry Cohen, who had the tailor's shop, across from the *Hippodrome*, told Alton that every so often, on a Tuesday morning, a heavily stained pair of dress-suit trousers would arrive, for cleaning and pressing. And Harry would say to himself: "Oh, I see Hutch (singer Leslie Hutchinson) is on the bill, with Tessie O'Shea!"

I took my School Certificate and didn't get a single pass. For the one and only time in my life, I stood on the bridge at Belchers Lane and thought: 'Shall I jump off?' I decided not to. Oh - terrible that was – I had to go back and tell mum. Then I took the School Certificate for a second time, got five passes, and was vindicated.

An author in search of a comma, 1953.

The end of Alton's final year at Saltley Grammar was in sight, although he still had no definite career plans. He'd had a vague idea about being a vet, but that fell through – because he couldn't stand the sight of blood!

The common denominator on all my school reports was 'he talks too much.' Then one day, a little old wise teacher called Mr. Probert, who was the History master said: "I wonder if we're missing the point about you? I wonder if you're one of those people who're going to talk for a living?" And I loved him for that, because I knew instinctively, from that minute onwards, that I was going to be doing something that involved a great deal of talking. But what?

Chapter 4 -

DOUGIE GAITER

I said to the army doctor: "I feel so silly standing in front of you, without my clothes." He said: "Well let's get off the bus and we'll talk about it!"

After leaving Saltley Grammar School Alton applied for a job at the Motor Union Insurance Company, Cherry Street, in the centre of Birmingham. He has no idea why; it was probably in response to a newspaper advertisement. Although with hindsight, it's a little embarassing to recall, his mother went with him.

She went to town with me and waited in a café or restaurant somewhere, while I went for the interview. I got the job and became a clerk at the age of sixteen, on £2-17/6d. a week. That's where I met Jo. She was already working there, because she's much older than me - six months!

Jo recalls their first meeting: "A very tall boy came for an interview. Coming through our office, he jumped down the last step – we knew he had the job – from the look on his face! So Alton joined the MU, as the office junior, and at last I didn't have to go out and buy the cakes from Kunzles, or take the petty cash to the bank."

I was a tall and incredibly thin, spindly character – wearing glasses by this time. They sent me as the bodyguard with the caretaker from the place, to the bank where he took the money every day. I'm the bodyguard!

Always ahead of his time, Alton eventually became Jo's 'toy boy'! According to Jo "When he first came to the Motor Union, he was just somebody who'd moved into the office. I didn't get any particular impression of him. All I was thinking was, 'he's going to take over my job and I can progress further up.' " After a while she began to notice him during tea breaks – (the fore-runner of coffee breaks). "We got talking and found out that we both liked theatres and cinema. I'd found somebody else who I could talk to, on my level."

At that stage, such conversations were in the company of others. She was a junior clerk, or, to use her words, 'general dogsbody': answering telephone calls and doing the typing. Unlike modern insurance offices, there was no restaurant or canteen, where they could relax, during the lunch hour. "This was a very small office. Someone came in, brought a tray of cups of tea, and we'd just have a break. Everybody was talking together. I used to go out in the lunch hour. I'd got my own friends – and Alton was meeting his."

Four or five months later, when Alton was still sixteen and Jo was seventeen, they started going out together in the lunch hour. "The idea of having a coffee together was just gradually coming in then. We went to the *Forum*, in New Street, just a short walk from the office, to see *Deep in My Heart*." The film, starring José Ferrer, was the story of Sigmund Romberg the songwriter. They continued to date and gradually became an 'item'.

Jo was the only child of Elsie and Cecil Ward. On her paternal side, the family had a grocery business, on the corner of Winson Green Road and Heath Street. Over the years, we've had numerous letters from people, who remember the shop, 'Ward's the Grocers'.

Jo explains: "My father's side of the family, the Wards, were originally farmers from Weedon, near Daventry. They came to Winson Green in the late 1800s and opened the grocery shop, later adding wines and spirits. My Uncle Stockley (dad's brother) kept the shop until the mid-50s."

Stockley used to do things like putting a pig's head in the window, which would be smoking a cigarette. They'd have a little boy, crouched down, puffing away, so that smoke came out of the pig's mouth. All politically incorrect! Every child who went in to do the shopping was given a boiled sweet. A lady wrote to me, saying: "I remember once he gave me a square of chocolate," - she was thrilled with that. Jo's Aunt Ellen, Stockley's wife, was a very liberated woman. There was a woman, a neighbour, who had killed her own daughter. For many, many years, until they left the area, Ellen went to visit her in Winson Green prison, which was very forward-thinking - for that time – to visit a woman who'd killed her own child.

Her father, instead of electing to join the family business, studied, and became an engineer. Jo's mother's family, the de Vantiers, were antique dealers. Originally, the French Protestant family, who were Huguenots, had fled to England to escape persecution; anglicising their name via de Wantier, to Wantié, and then to Wanty. Jo's maternal grandparents died before she was born.

"Dad was with the 2nd City Battalion (1stW.W.) He caught malaria and dysentery and was in hospital for two years." He was, reputedly, injected with horse blood, due to a shortage of the human variety and was subsequently told that he would never make 'old bones'. Ironically, he lived to the ripe old age of 89, attributing his longevity to that decidedly odd transfusion!

On marriage, rather than join the family business, her father chose to go abroad as an engineer, for the Rop Tin Corporation, in Rop, near Lagos, in West Africa. His young wife worked as a part-time teacher and secretary; they lived there for thirteen years. "Dad worked in the tin mines and mum helped the missionaries teach English. She was the first white woman to go there. They went out by boat, first-class; their clothes and accessories were bought by the Rop Tin Corporation, from Fortnum and Mason." Every two years, they were allowed six months annual leave. Jo's mother became very superstitious, having witnessed curses of various kinds, whilst in Africa.

They returned to England in 1936, Jo's dad had appendicitis and the doctor told him that quite often, wives conceive afterwards. Sure enough, Jo was born in 1937! Although he'd been named after Rhodesia's founding father, Cecil Rhodes, her father hated the name and adopted the nomenclature, 'Cyril'. He started a driving school, but this was brought to an abrupt end by the war. Despite the fact that cash was in fairly short supply, Jo's parents managed to send her to private school: Miss Marshall's School in Harborne, followed by Stamford House, in Edgbaston. Afterwards, she attended the British School of Commerce, before joining the Motor Union.

"Being an only child I was quite bossy and was nick-named 'Swanky Lanky Liz' - after the comic character. I was very much a tomboy and enjoyed ice-skating, cycling, tennis (I won the house cup one year). From the age of eight, I loved anything to do with cars: I helped my dad repair them. When I was quite small, he used to pull me on a piece of carpet, under a car, to release the nuts to change the oil. I used to log in the hours worked and calculate the labour charges. He taught me to drive as soon as I could reach the pedals, on Weston-super-Mare sands."

Jo recalls that around the time they visited the *Forum Cinema*, "Alton was writing songs and learning to play the trombone. The first photograph he gave me was of him posing, Glenn Miller-style, with his trombone. Little did I know at that time what the future was to hold for us. So here I was, going out with someone who was very romantic, always writing me poems and leaving me notes at work."

At the time, The Glenn Miller Story had a big influence on me, and I decided to take up the trombone. I was already playing the drums, although not very well. I had trombone lessons with Denis Wick, who was the principal trombonist with the City of Birmingham Symphony Orchestra. He was such a good trombone player, Gordon Jacobs dedicated the First English Trombone Concerto to him. One of Denis's pupils had been Chris Barber, who'd been a bass player, but wanted to learn trombone; he had great success with Chris, but a diabolical failure with me!

I wish Glenn Miller would stop copying my poses, 1955.

Jo inherited a love of the theatre from her parents and used to visit the Birmingham Hippodrome most weeks. She remember the old Variety bills, where numbers 1,2,3 and so on, were displayed at the side of the stage. "They'd start off with a juggler or whatever, then a singer and possibly a comedian. They'd perhaps finish with a dance act, at the end of the first half. Often, a singer would start the second half." The Top of the Bill was usually the penultimate spot, because quite often the audience would have to leave, to catch the last bus or train.

Jo continues to visit her lifelong friend, Rosemary Wilkes, in Malvern. They first met when they were nine-year-old schoolgirls. Rosemary's aunt and uncle, Amy and Tom Troman, were landlords of *The Queen's Tavern*, opposite the stage door of the Birmingham Hippodrome, in Inge Street. "They had well known artists staying there, like Johnny Ray and Norman Wisdom – (before he became well known). It was only just an ordinary pub and Pro digs. We used to see the shows free, on Monday nights. I remember seeing *The Loose Screws* which was a dancing act: two-thirds of the act became Mike and Bernie Winters. >>> Years later, Alton worked with them many times and shared with them a love for the music of Duke Ellington.

Jo became familiar with a range of variety acts, long before she met Alton. From about the age of eight to thirteen, she began to write, requesting photographs and autographs, culminating in quite an extensive collection!

I found Jo easier to laugh with than anyone I'd ever known – and still do. Add to that the kind of looks that send the hormones pumping around my body. It was enough for me! I mean, she was tall, and shaped like Sophia Loren. >>> Later, I realised that she had a tremendous capacity for hard work, and in times of crisis, she had an ability to mount an almost terrier-like defensive, of family and friends – in the face of adversity – whatever. I also discovered that she never had a watch that worked properly, and a diabolical sense of direction. I mean, how else could you explain the fact that she finished up with me? And if we finish the book, it will demonstrate that her cooking's not too bad either!

Ironically, Alton and Jo's mothers grew up in neighbouring streets, in Ladywood. "My regret is that I didn't meet his dad," explains Jo. "Alton did say to me:'Be careful, mum hates vulgarity.' I needn't have worried, when girls get together, she had the same sense of humour as me." She recalls the first time Alton invited her home for tea, to meet his mum. " You know you want to make a good impression – well I did. I kicked a cup of tea all over the floor! However, his mum and I liked each other from the start – I'd always been able to say anything to my mum and dad – and here was another!"

Alton and Jo went to Sunday shows at the *Birmingham Town Hall, Windsor Theatre*, Bearwood, *Dudley Hippodrome, Coventry Hippodrome*, featuring bands such as Sid Phillips, Johnny Gray, Frank Weir, Eric Delaney and Carl Barriteau. "We also went to the *Birmingham Hippodrome*, seeing variety bills, and to the cinema. My social life hadn't changed – I'd met a boy who loved the same interests as me –we even played tennis! (I couldn't get him to come ice-skating though). We went out more and more; where most young people went dancing, we combined our likes: love of the theatre and big band music." Their lunch hours were frequently spent visiting city centre record stores, such as Murdochs in Corporation Street, Dale Forty in New Street, Lewis's and Walker Brothers. They listened to records together in the booths provided – and even bought some!

In 1954, Pete James was demobbed from the army, and came to work at the Motor Union, having been in the 5th Royal Inniskilling Dragoon Guards, as a trumpet player. Knowing that Alton played the trombone, and that he was due for National Service, Pete wrote to the bandmaster on his behalf, applying for Alton to be sent to the same regiment, which is how Alton came to be in the Dragoon Guards. Jo recalls: "We were having a bowl of soup in Woolworth's cafeteria in the Bull Ring, in 1956, when his mum came in with his call-up papers for National Service, which was for two years. Off he went to Catterick camp for six weeks square bashing."

The very last week I'm due to leave, we're in the filing room, fooling about – you know! The way you do at that age, when you're courting. Somehow or other we set the fire extinguisher off – and there was foam everywhere – can you imagine?

Jo elaborates: "Alton and I had to keep our romance secret, because the branch manager would have sacked us if he'd found out. In the 50s, firms were quite strict in that way."

We were hauled off to see Mr. Botteley, who was the manager of the Motor Union. He said if I hadn't been going to join the army the following week he would have sacked me. But within a week, he'd not only kept Jo on, but had also given her a pay rise!

On Alton's first leave she, Maurice, and two of Maurice's children, Keith and Margaret, went to meet him at New Street Station. "He came towards us wearing this huge beret – I'd never seen him in a hat before."

The initial six-week's training at Catterick was pretty horrendous. People know the old stories about breaking the ice to shave in the morning. We were in a billet with about eighteen blokes. The heater in the middle of the room would become so hot it became transparent! I didn't take kindly to army service, particularly the first part of the training. I always remember a hod carrier from somewhere up North, who sat bolt upright, in the early hours, and shouted: "Do we have to press pants for't mornin'?" Everyone shied their boots at him. We spent five minutes the next day, sorting out whose boots were what. We were given a little kit with needles, cotton etc. It was known as a 'housewife'. You had to do all the normal things like coiling your bootlaces into circles, bull your boots with a heated spoon, and all the rest.

Rather than the tough drill sergeant, beloved of comedy writers, Alton's arch-tormentor was a Lance Corporal. Having been put in charge of the squad, he was out to prove himself.

He'd come in, with his nose against yours. Wearing glasses – I was a "dozey, four-eyed bastard" - naturally. The six weeks dragged through interminably, with initial injections, where the arm would blow up like a football. Then you'd be forced to march, to get it out of your system, which was agony; the biggest of blokes would be fainting all over the place.

Although it was no picnic for Alton, at least he had the thought of the forthcoming band and his music, to distract him from some of the unpleasantness. For some recruits, however, army life was so intolerable that they resorted to 'working their ticket', employing all manner of tricks.

One man decided to cut off all his buttons, on his flies and his shirt and everywhere. He stood there flapping, on the Parade Ground. Another fellow followed the instructions that he was to Blanco all his equipment – and he did: he blancoed his shirt, his boots, his trousers – everything! They usually got shoved off to somewhere like Aquaba – hundreds and thousands of miles away.

Alton recalls a particularly enterprising newcomer, who eventually got kicked out of the army, ostensibly, because they found that he had one leg fractionally shorter than the other (this would undoubtedly have been evident from his initial medical). The *real* reason was that he'd been overheard, regaling a comrade with tales of how he'd worked his way through college - by becoming a male prostitute!

We had showers after PT. After we left another squad went in, and the wall collapsed and killed one of the blokes.

I had such thin ankles, my trousers didn't fit too well in my gaiters. As I did an about-turn on the parade ground, my trousers came out and flapped. So all the lads christened me 'Dougie Gaiter'. I was 'Dougie Gaiter' to everybody – for those first six weeks.

It's a wonder he didn't go permanently bald. Alton was reluctant to part with his dark locks, so the sergeant major prescribed three haircuts in one day!

*They would always say: "Am I hurting you?" You'd say: "No." Then they'd say: "Well I should be –I'm standing on your f*****g 'air!" I was shocked by the language - and by how many times the 'f' word was used as an adjective. I mean, I'd only ever heard it used infrequently, and then as a noun.*

They used to 'back-squad' you if you didn't do very well: they'd put you back into another squad and you'd have to go through it all over again. I'm sure they were greatly tempted to do that with me, but they couldn't because the British Army in general was very short of trombone players – however bad they were.

Then I joined the band. We had some decent little billets actually – just two in a room, but quite cosy. I shared with an oboe player, Johnny Dawson - if you can imagine the excruciating sound of oboe and trombone duets. It must have been torment for everybody!

>>>Johnny was in the early stages of his musical career. He actually developed into a very fine musician and eventually became the bandmaster

of the Green Howards. In a strange twist of fate, after spending his life as a staunch socialist, on demob, he became the licensee of the *Conservative Club* in Richmond (near to Catterick Camp). Sadly, he died far too early, at the age of fifty-eight.

Alton was posted to Germany in the January of '57, to Sennelager, near Paderborn - a predominantly Catholic region of West Germany, to become an essential part of the British Army of the Rhine. There was still a lot of post-war enmity. Alton recalls that some Germans would cross the road to avoid British soldiers, or spit on them, if they came near.

The regimental band played for a range of events.

We played for parades, of course, and also in the Officers' Mess - sometimes to accompany artists. In Germany, conditions improved enormously. We went into the old German army barracks, which were centrally heated. We'd had a little fireplace in our room at Catterick and we had to get our own coal. But in Germany they were beautiful barracks and we were put in the end one. (The band is always in the end – because of the racket!) Life there wasn't too bad, but I still didn't take well to the army. In fact, the perfect clue is that they say, 'every serviceman can remember his army number' – I can't.

It was a Cavalry Regiment. Alton was never officially a 'bandsman', but remained a 'trooper' all the way through, because bandsmen got a little more money than the average conscript. He was the only National Serviceman out of a band of forty-three. As a trooper, he was paid at the lowest rate.

As well as our other duties, we also had to do Trumpet Guard. It's a different mouth/lip embouchure for trumpet, than it is for trombone. I did a Trumpet Guard – my very first one. The officer said, "OK trumpeter - sound Reveille." (Imitates an atrocious rendition). And there was this bemused silence. "I think you'd better do that again." (Repeats diabolical performance). He was absolutely stunned. Then he started laughing – so much that he sagged against the wall; I can see him now, with the tears dripping off his chin. He laughed and laughed – then he put me on a charge!

The band played for a Queen's Birthday Parade at Dusseldorf.

The sergeant major in charge yelled his orders out (staccato bellow). We heard this tittering start, and it spread all around, until the whole arena was in uproar. (Repeats staccato bellow). Then I heard this word being

"Trumpeter, Charge!"

used, and I said to John Shelley, one of the clarinet players, who was going out with a German Naafi girl. "What's that word they keep saying?" He said: "It's 'hund' – it means dog!"

The regimental band returned to England, for several engagements: they played at the White City Tattoo, with the massed bands, which was really impressive. Jo recalls watching the event on black and white television (colour sets wouldn't become available until several years later). "I remember his mum and I, together with Maurice and Gwen, sitting on the floor on our hands and knees, and Maurice pointing at the screen with a pencil. Alton looked so smart in his regimental uniform, marching and playing trombone. On reflection, we could hardly see him – but from the excitement in his mum's lounge that Saturday evening, he seemed to fill the screen!"

I was in the front row, the tallest member of the trombone section, so army logic dictates that I'm going to be the one on the inside, who marks time (moves on the spot) while everybody else marches round. So, as I marched in the mud, I gradually became the shortest in the trombone section.

One afternoon, the band coach was broken into and two or three instruments were stolen. Now when the massed bands march, they invert - then march back - through their own ranks. So the trombones invert on the front row - come back - and as we get to the clarinets, I look – and the first bloke who's had his clarinet stolen – he's playing the branch of a tree, and I start to break up. Then I looked at the next chap: he's got nothing – he's just miming! By which time I've gone completely - I just can't blow a note! But as guardsmen, the Americans, (who probably had the

Rehearsals for the SSAFA Searchlight Tattoo at the White City Stadium, Summer 1957. if you want to follow me, with your pencil, I'm on the extreme right of the front row.

biggest impact of anybody in the entire Tattoo) appalled us, because they pu̯ɹ. *Banana Boat Song – and **danced** as they played.*

Another engagement, on the floating bandstand at Scarborough made newspaper headlines! Members of the band were required to row out to the bandstand, in order to take part. As chance would have it, due to a shortage of space, Alton wasn't actually playing: they had no room for a third trombone player. This proved very fortuitous for a woman who accidentally fell into the local pool. Alton and a civilian dragged her to safety; the rescue was mentioned in the local paper. In this case a tragedy was averted, but disaster was just around the corner - plus further headlines.

When we got to Folkestone, we were on the open-air bandstand, playing away, and a woman backed a car into the crowd – reversed it by mistake! We had to stop playing, run off, and lift the car off the bodies. There was a dead person – I'd never seen a corpse before. A young girl was very badly injured. She was taken to hospital. We all collected some money for her, to buy a teddy bear. I always remember the headlines in the paper. It said: 'The Kindest Band in the British Army'. >>> Years later, I went back to Folkestone, to appear at the Lees Cliff Hall, with John Boulter. My publicist, George Bartram, put a piece in the paper: Was the girl still living there? Would she like to come and meet one of the original bandsmen? But nobody ever turned up.

Returning to Germany, the band did broadcasts with several celebrities, including Lorrae Desmond, the Australian singer. >>> Forty years later, she could be seen acting in the television soap, *The Country Practice*. George Martin, billed as 'the casual comedian', also came over. He undoubtedly had an accurate musical ear, because he walked in, just as the band was warming up and said: "The third trombonist's a bit sharp." Alton would be the first to confirm - he was!

>>> I was appearing at the Flamingo Nightclub in Northampton, fifteen years later. George Martin was in the audience. I reminded him afterwards about having met him in Germany. I asked him for any advice and he very wisely said: "You embarrassed a man who was on your side, by ridiculing him. Don't ever pick on someone who likes you." Obvious – but it needed saying. By a coincidence, his brother Bill was a fellow warm-up comic, years later.

Trumpet Major Herbert, who was also a skilled exponent of boxing and fencing, was the most active man I ever met: he couldn't cross the room without leaping over a chair on the way across. He died a few years ago, after having a long series of heart attacks, so there's a moral in there somewhere.

That's rather like people who go jogging all the time isn't it? They reckon it causes more problems – it can be counter-productive?

Well Bernard Manning said: "I get all the exercise I need - walking behind the funerals of people who jog!"

As the only National Serviceman in the band, Alton supplemented his paltry wage, doing anything – virtually – to make money. This included writing poems for other young soldiers to send to their girlfriends or wives. He used to play table tennis, because he could earn a bit of extra money if he won. Sometimes he would press trousers, or clean boots. His fellow soldiers, as bandsmen, were at least two pounds a week better off - a massive difference. Jo was unaware of the extra time he was putting in: "Every time he came home there'd be presents and things. I could never understand how he could afford it, because the money they got was nothing: twenty-eight shillings a week, for eighteen months and then £3-00 for six months. I had clocks, a camera, ornate make-up cases and souvenirs of places he had been to with the regimental band."

One of the men came into the billet after having a few drinks one night. He saw this man walking towards him, raising his fists in a threatening manner. So he lashed out at him – and fell into a full-length mirror!

A fellow bandsman was, to put it mildly, a bit on the 'light-fingered' side. He collected souvenirs from every place we visited. Unfortunately, one night in Cologne, the hotelkeeper saw him filling his pockets with glasses and ashtrays, so he picked him up by his lapels and threw him against a wall. He broke - like a pane of glass. It took us the whole of the next morning to pick the shards of glass out of his hide!

One evening in a bar, the barman overheard a group of German 'hot-heads' planning to murder a British serviceman – any British serviceman. We made a fast exit, pursued by about twenty Germans, who quickly gained ground on us – until we turned a corner and ran into a military police unit! After an impressive display of baton twirling, the 'enemy' was swiftly dispatched.

Listening to *Two-way Family Favourites*, the popular Sunday request programme between Britain and Germany, provided some comfort for Jo: "It made me feel closer to him, because by now, we were romantically involved, and writing to each other several times a week. I promised him that I would keep an eye on his mum. She lived on the other side of town to me, but I went to see her every weekend and in the week too." Alton's friend, John Clayton, visited Dorothy, every other Sunday. Maurice and Gwen, despite their additional family responsibilities visited as often as they could and so did his cousin Ruby. Meanwhile, life for Alton, in Rhineland Germany, continued to be an education in itself!

We were on a bandstand, where we all sat in tiers, t-i-e-r-s- not the other one – with the trombones at the top. We'd been there quite a long while. It was a hot day and they used to bring a crate of ale out for us. The trombone player next to me was absolutely bursting. He looked around – couldn't get off the bandstand of course. There was an E-Flat Brass Bass in front of him. So he decides to ... into that – (I don't know how you can express that). Just as he's halfway through, we hear "Click-click-click" – the bandmaster tapping on the music stand. Of course, he has to finish. The man in front lifts up his bass and blows, and you can hear all these gurgles and bubbles coming out!

While we're on about peeing, we were stationed with the Welsh Guards in Scarborough. One of the fellows came home to the barracks - a bit tiddly, and decided to pee out of the window, right onto the officer of the day, who was marching past. That caused a bit of a problem! We were always lucky though, because, being a band, we were on the move. So if they wanted to take some kind of retribution against us, they'd got to follow us around – which wasn't totally practical!

We played at a Schutzenfest, a shooting festival in Brackweder, and they billeted us out with a German family named Wiehenstroh. The youngest daughter, Elke, chose fellow-trombonist George Brigden and myself, to go back and stay with them – it was a bit like a slavemarket! We stayed at the house overnight. Poppa Wiehenstroh was one of the organising committee of the Schutzenfest. Their son, Paul, a polio victim, was confined to a wheelchair. He said to me one day: "I am a Jehovah's whiteness!"

We sat at this dining table. It was a very formal family setting, with a very Prussian atmosphere: grandma at one end, father at the other, George and I next to each other, the girls and mother ranged opposite. They served a banana on a plate, with ice cream around it - like a Banana Split, but they served the banana still in half of its skin.

The atmosphere remained formal, until grandma happened to glance across, noticed, and started to giggle, father looked across and started to giggle. And the whole family giggled.

Then eventually George and I started. Everybody was sitting there, wiping the tears from their eyes, because George was the only one who hadn't got a banana skin still left on his plate! He said: "I thought it was a bit stringy!"

On a more sombre note, Alton and his fellow bandsmen played at a young dispatch rider's funeral. He'd been riding his bike, came round the corner, and in the high wind, a telegraph pole had been knocked over. The telephone wire decapitated him.

We played in the pouring rain. There were tears streaming down my face. I thought it was the saddest thing ever. His young wife and child were at the graveside, and we were playing Chopin's Funeral March, which, even for an old jazzer like me, is a very moving piece of music.

One morning we were at the Hook of Holland, and four of us were struggling to lift the crate that you kept the wooden music stands in, which was incredibly heavy. This little guy came along; who was as wide as he was high. He didn't speak

The flower of England's youth, looking for a porter, the Hook of Holland, 1957. If you must know, I'm the fourth from right.

English, but indicated that he wanted us to lift the crate onto his back. So four of us lifted it onto his back, and he ran the whole length of the platform, carrying the crate that we couldn't pick up properly between us - like a little beetle with a house on its back.

The dance band had been chosen from within the ranks of the military band. They decided to buy a tape recorder between them, the idea being to make it available to people in the evening, if the band weren't playing; people could also listen to themselves rehearsing.

A fellow called Charlie Carmichael borrowed it one night, and the next morning we came to use it. During the course of that morning, the microphone was dropped and broken. Sergeant Mick Clifford decided that he would blame Charlie Carmichael, who'd used it the night before. Charlie wasn't there at the time, but the sergeant said we were going to present him with the bill. I said: "I don't think that would be fair." He was absolutely livid with me for daring to disagree with an N.C.O. So he marched me outside, and said that if I didn't keep my trap shut he'd belt me. Great big massive man, and I was this thin, spindly, nineteen-year-old, terrified of everybody. But it didn't matter, because by the time I'd got back into the billet they'd rounded up Charlie Carmichael and everybody had told him about this. So I was a bit of a hero for a while.

An idiot trombone player on parade once, at one of the big parades, got one of his spurs caught in the other and fell forward – straight onto his trombone. I got into terrible trouble over that - and I had to pay for my trombone.

Lieutenant Colonel Ansell, a blind officer, arrived to carry out an inspection, (which seemed a bit ridiculous to Alton). He organised the jumps for the *Horse of the Year Show* and was, by all accounts, a brilliant man, with a wonderful history behind him. He'd been blinded in the course of service.

He came to me and said (mimics officer's voice) "I understand you're leaving us shortly. What do you intend doing in Civvy Street?" I said: "Well I'm hoping to be a librettist." He said: "Don't be so bloody impertinent!" I'm still puzzled.

Alton was inspired to become a librettist after meeting Bill Briggs, a character in the regiment, who played the piano, and was shortly due to go to Officer Training College. He and Alton started writing parodies of songs. The bandmaster heard about their talent and roped them into broadcasting. Alton's first appearance as a comedy artiste of any sort, another pivotal moment in his career, was in camp concerts, or broadcasts, in Germany.

The following example of Bill and Alton's early collaboration, is a parody on *These Foolish Things*:

A pair of cellular green unterhosen,
A bottled ship that needs a mate and bosun,
A bowl of mouldy stew,
These goulash things remind me of you.

Balaclava Day Parade, Athlone Barracks, Sennelager, 27 October 1957.
No prizes for identifying the tallest trombonist in the centre.

Well, Bugs Bunny seems to like my playing, Regimental Dance, Balaclava Day, 1957.

For the uninitiated, 'A pair of cellular green unterhosen,' were army issue underpants - which raised a big laugh from the other soldiers. At this point, in 1957, he decided to change his name, for songwriting purposes. Until then, he had always been known by the name his parents had chosen for him - Douglas Price. But a metamorphosis was about to take place: Alton, Glenn Miller's Christian name, became Doug's adopted first name too, whilst his Christian name became his surname. 'Alton Douglas', he reasoned, was a far more dramatic and memorable name for an up-and-coming entertainer/songwriter, compared with the more mundane 'Douglas Price'.

Len Scattergood, yours truly and Bill Briggs ensure that British Forces Broadcasting has a limited life.

Bill and I wrote a full scale musical version of James Barrie's 'The Admirable Crichton'.

>>> *The day I was demobbed, I bought a copy of 'The Melody Maker', to discover that the Barrie Estate had commissioned Dave Lee and Herbert Kretzmer to do exactly the same thing. It ran in the West End, starring Kenneth More and Millicent Martin, for six months.*

I used to do an impression of James Stewart; we did an excerpt from 'The Glenn Miller Story'. (Mimics James Stewart beautifully)! "W- Willie Schwartz could play that part on clarinet." Also: "Well ladies and gentlemen, we're going to play 'A String of Pearls', by Jerry Gray." I did that impression on broadcasts as well.

I don't know if you know, but bandmasters are addressed as 'Mister', and are not entitled to a salute – unlike other officers in the British Army. But the new people joining the army – the 'nig-nogs', didn't know about this, and they would see our bandmaster, Mr. Vince, approaching and salute him. We used to play the game, dodging from billet to billet, watching him; because he always returned their salute, which was most definitely not 'de rigueur'. He also had a Humber car. He used to get out of it every morning and walk round and round the car, admiring it.

Mr. Vince was certainly an impressive looking man. Alton recalls a particular instance, on the bandstand at Folkestone, when their 'leader' walked onto the stage, then turned, with panache, to face the audience.

*There was a gasp from the female members of the audience – well I **trust** it was mainly the female members - because he looked remarkably like Errol Flynn; and with his sword and all the rest if it, it **was** Errol Flynn. If anybody wants to see him now, to discover just how good-looking he was, there's a film of the Thomas Hardy book,*

'Far From the Madding Crowd', with Alan Bates and Julie Christie. There's a scene shot in the chapel, with him conducting the orchestra.

Band Sergeant Major McCoig spent half of his life trying to get Alton to sign on as a regular soldier, because they were short of trombone players, and the other half, absolutely hating him! But suddenly, his entire attitude changed, when Alton started doing broadcasts, towards the end of his service career.

He discovered I was the biggest character in the world, and he couldn't look at me without smiling! He used to say: "You're a fackin' scream Topper – fackin' scream!" (I've no idea why he called me 'Topper'; it's a thing Londoners did). I became his favourite person in the world – for the last two months of my army service career - after being the most hated. I can only think that he found the broadcasts amusing and the songs we wrote, because all of a sudden, instead of being this awful wretch who caused him so much terrible personal pain...

Comedian and broadcaster Don Maclean, a friend and fellow performer of many years standing, recently commented that he had always imagined that Alton would eventually become a comedy *writer*, as opposed to simply a performer. Interestingly enough, it was at this *early* stage in Alton's career that he gave serious consideration to that type of career: a librettist - a supplier of words. Shortly afterwards, the temptation to diversify became too great! As our book will show, a great deal of water was to flow under the bridge, before he would gravitate, once more, towards the genre of wordsmith and author.

The close of Alton's National Service days, apart from a short interim period, would herald the beginning of a showbusiness career, which lasted many years.

Back in England, Jo managed to ease feelings of loneliness, by leading a very busy life.

A less self-sufficient person might easily have felt isolated, but as an only child, she had been accustomed to keeping herself amused. Firstly, there were the visits to Dorothy, who was only in her 50s: "It's embarassing when I think about it, because she would have been a lot younger than I am now. I used to say: "Don't touch the hedge. I will cut the hedge or mow the lawn." Jo also had a number of friends to keep her company: "We'd go to the theatre, the cinema, ice-skating."

Alton included poems in his correspondence to her: "He's always done that - even now, with birthday or Christmas cards – something appropriate, or topical." Some of the letters, written to his co-writer during the creation of this book, are an entertainment in themselves! Jo comments: "A friend of mine, Linda Park, has just had her 50th birthday. So I got him to write a poem – and she was 'over the moon'."

Incidentally, readers will have noted that when Alton imitates someone, explanatory comments are often included, in brackets. In the course of writing this book, I've been treated to a one-man, highly entertaining cabaret act: one moment I'm talking to Donald Sinden, the next Jasper Carrott - or some deep-voiced Russian - so why should you miss out on all the fun?

If anybody wants to read the best description ever of National Service, which fits my service days and those of everybody I've ever met, there's a book entitled 'Brasso, Blanco and Bull', by Tony Thorne – it's hysterical. It's everybody's service career.

On my last day with the band, as Mr. Vince shook hands with me, he said "And don't think I haven't noticed that you never once called me 'Sir'." I felt a mixture of despair and elation that my one childish act of defiance had been uncovered.

Jo recalls: "Looking back it wasn't an easy time, but at least he wasn't fighting a war. Demob day came and we prepared for tea and celebrations at his mum's, in Heather Road."

As I came down the gangplank at Southampton, I heard this chanting, coming from above. I looked back and there, leaning over the side of the boat, was at least half the intake from my initial six weeks' training – and they were chanting – yes, you've guessed it: "Dougie Gaiter, Dougie Gaiter, Dougie Gaiter."

And with that, the thinnest pair of legs in the British Army marched into Civvy Street.

Chapter 5 –

THE SACKBUT AND THE BULL FIDDLE

I used to play trombone in a circus band, but I got tired of them feeding me buns.

This stage in Alton's life marks the beginning of what might best be described as a 'three-tier career' situation: commerce, followed by showbusiness, and finally, many years later, the world of books. For those who're intrigued by our title, a 'sackbut' is a Yiddish word for a trombone, and the 'bull fiddle', another term for a double bass!

I came out of the army, went down to the Labour Exchange, and without any problem at all, immediately got a job selling Catholic bibles. Or – in my case – not selling Catholic bibles.

Jo explains: "Alton found the adjustment to Civvy Street quite difficult. He could never have gone back to a nine to five job (he always hated working in an office). His job selling Catholic bibles lasted about three days, which, on reflection, isn't bad for a Methodist!" More angst-ridden times followed - in quick succession.

At the age of twenty, the police picked me up in Selly Oak, smashed out of my head, and threatened to take me to hospital and use a stomach pump on me. I felt so degraded, that from that day onwards, I've been a teetotaller.

"I was still at the Motor Union," recalls Jo. "Like most couples who had been apart, we fell out, and got back together again – several times. It wasn't easy, because we had become independent. However, the making-up was great!"

Alton used to be very shy until he was in his early 20s, but when he was demobbed, he resolved to change the situation. "Even at times when we fell out," recalls Jo, "it was only because he was unsure of himself. I still think that boys take longer to grow up, and I felt perhaps a little bit ahead of him then. It must be terribly difficult to do National Service and then come back again. For two years they've had everything found for them. How are they going to adjust?"

I go back to the Labour Exchange and tell them that unfortunately I've been guided in the wrong direction. They send me for an interview at the Britannic Assurance Company, where I get a job immediately as an agent. My area was Sheldon and Yardley.

In conjunction with his newly acquired job, Alton persevered with writing songs, taking them to music publishers in Denmark Street, London, off Charing Cross Road (better known as Tin Pan Alley). Often, Jo would accompany him, then wait, in various restaurants or cafés, frequented by singers and songwriters, to see how he'd got on. So while he went for interviews and explored various other options, trying to fashion a career, she was there in the background, patiently supporting him.

During their stay, they registered as a couple - Mr. and Mrs. Johnson. Jo observes: "It's ironic that Alton had spent two years in the forces and could have been asked, at any time, to die for Queen and country. All he would have had, in a war situation, would have been a pair of wooden handles - (in battle, musicians always became stretcher bearers) - but the idea of being involved in unmarried sex was frowned upon. Life was like that in the 50s; things that would be considered perfectly normal now, in those days came under the heading of 'Forbidden Fruit'." They combined trips to London with seeing the shows, as always, taking notes for future reference.

Alton continued to explore other avenues. He and John Clayton resumed their interest in music together, which had begun in the Boys' Brigade. In 1959, they formed a rehearsal trio with Dennis Whitmore. Any performances were on a purely voluntary basis - just as well - some might argue! "We played at a school in Washwood Heath," explains John. "Dennis had all of the orchestral sheet music. We played stuff from Glenn Miller, right through to *The William Tell Overture*. Alton played the trombone, I played the trumpet, but Dennis used to play alto sax, clarinet and violin. We had a really good time and a good laugh – but we must have sounded absolutely terrible!

"We ran the trio for a couple of years. Dennis had a car; he always put all of his stuff in a little aluminium trolley, which he made himself. We not only played in *that* band, there was another, a classical/military band, in Blakeland Street, on Sunday mornings. Alton had a Vespa scooter, when he went to work for the Britannic. When we first started off, Alton was probably a better musician than me, but he couldn't transpose quite as well. I think he probably

John, Alton and Dennis obviously thrown out for creating a disturbance.

52

*The George
Harris Quartet.*

learned to later; that was in our early days." Fortunately the next visit from one of Alton's timely male 'guides' or mentors, was about to take place.

I was home one day; there was a knock on the door. It was a character called George Harris, who ran a small, local band, playing at dances and parties. He was stuck for a musician, somebody had been taken ill, and he said: "Could you play with the band?" I stayed with him for the next ten months. I only had an old Indian valve trombone then – I called it my 'Bombay Bugle' – if you think I was bad on the Slide Trombone… Then a drummer, Sid Millard and I formed our own band, which quickly became 'The Alton Douglas Quartet'. >>> Sid eventually became a professional wrestler, under the name of 'El Sid' – guess who christened him?

It wasn't always the same line-up, because over the years you get through quite a few musicians. I remember we had a West Indian tenor player called Hughie Forbes. A man asked if he could play Happy Birthday. Hughie stood up and played the wildest version ever – really way out. This fellow grabbed him and said: "You're the only white man in the band!"

I bought myself a double bass and taught myself elementary fingering, so that I could pluck away, doing waltzes, and so on. I also started warbling the odd number (I choose my words carefully!) Our engagements came from various sources: a regular three-line 'ad' in the 'Birmingham Mail', several bookers (especially the Paula Bailey Agency) and, of course, 'word-of-mouth'.

For the first two years or so, after forming the band with Sid, transporting their musical equipment (including the sackbut and bull fiddle) to engagements, resembled a scenario from a Buster Keaton movie. The journey was made in two stages: firstly, Alton would strap the double bass on his back, then head for the venue on the Vespa, praying that his sense of balance hadn't deserted him! He'd return for Sid the drummer, who rode pillion (behind him) with various other musical bits and pieces, strapped precariously to the two of them. There must have been sighs of relief all round, when Alton eventually graduated to a small Hillman car.

Maurice remembers: "He used to hire a room to practise, with his group: he was very professional in his approach. If you booked anyone for a wedding, or a group, years ago, all they said was: 'Where are we next Saturday or Sunday?' Now with him, the band used to book and pay for a room, then rehearse, to become more professional."

John Clayton risks a spin with me, c 1960. It's amazing that our friendship has survived for over half-a-century!

"Strangely enough, although he had his dance band, I never once went with him," recalls Jo, "because that's what I hated. I'd seen other bands' wives sitting there, straight-faced and thought: 'If I were a musician, I couldn't work under those conditions.' I mean, if you were a decorator, you wouldn't take your wife with you, so that she could sit and watch you put the paper on the wall!"

At this stage, such freedom of expression was crucial, particularly as Alton was trying to develop *The Alton Douglas Quartet* into more of an entertainment and was therefore 'fronting' the act. It was essential, that he should feel free to experiment and develop the presentational side of their performance.

Billy Lowndes used to be one of Alton's theatrical agents. His widow, June, recalls: "That's how we met Alton – at a 'do' somewhere. He stood at the front of the band. My husband loved bands: he was brought up on going to the Palais de Danse, which his step-father, Cyril used to manage. He loved music and everything to do with it; he played piano himself – not as an entertainer – but he'd got a nice touch on the piano. We were at this place, dancing around and we kept passing Alton. My husband started having a little 'Hi again!' – coming round: Billy said something to him as we passed and Alton would say something back to him. Billy said: 'I like his band.' "

I've always tried to learn (and adapt) from other people. I read that the society bandleaders, such as Ambrose, would chat to the clientele as they danced past, so I thought…

John Clayton remembers meeting Alton again, at the *Tower Ballroom* in Birmingham, some time after he had formed the quartet. "I was working as a cocktail bar attendant. He auditioned there and I was amazed - the band was so good! I believe they offered him a 'residency', but he turned it down." Alton wasn't earning sufficient money from musical engagements, at this stage, to make a living, so he continued to work for the Britannic. As the previous agent had been quite a character in his own right, Alton found himself on a steep learning curve!

I was offered the job, despite my commanding officer Vince's slightly backhanded comment when he wrote in his report: 'He has considerable talent, and when he overcomes a certain shyness of manner, he should have a good future.' Maybe in spite of it, I got the job. On one of my first 'calls', an elderly man came to the door, with a towel around his shoulders. He said: "Where's the Britannic fella?" I said: "I've taken over the round now." He said: "Oh – well he used to cut my hair every month." So for the next nine years I cut his hair. I also found that I'd inherited a lady who played tennis with the agent. So once a month I used to play tennis, on a regular basis. I always remember one family who were incredibly poor. They'd each have one piece of cutlery - one would have a knife, one would have a fork, and one would have a spoon. There were still some really poor people around.

While Alton was doing his monthly 'Jack-of-all-trades' number, he was also selling new insurance policies and collecting weekly premiums. No thought was given, at that time, to the danger of carrying large sums of money around. At the end of each week, his takings amounted to about a hundred pounds.

I'd never seen a hundred pounds in one go: it was a huge amount of money.

One lady, one of my regular customers, started a monthly catalogue club. She asked me to join. She said to her mother, when she first got the catalogue, "You need one of these mum." And her mother didn't speak to her for a week afterwards. So she said: "Mum, tell me how I've offended you." She said: "Well it's that thing in there. You told me I need one, and I always make sure I wash!" She looked at it – and it was an aerosol spray!

He made the mistake of warning a girl on his round, about her current boyfriend, whose violent reputation had preceded him. She reported the conversation to him and for the next twelve months, on the advice of a policeman friend, Alton was obliged to ride around with a tyre lever under the front seat.

I should have heeded the words of Lord Chesterfield: "Advice is seldom welcome; and those who want it the most, always like it the least." Or, better yet, the American screenwriter Aaron Sorkin's. "Walk softly and carry an armoured tank division!"

By this time he'd got his Hillman. Within a week of having the car, he had an accident - he hit one of his own policyholder's cars.

He stopped in front of me and - wallop! It would have to be one of my own clients. When I'd been with the company for a while, I achieved a certain sales figure and became one of their top salesmen. I was awarded a silver coffee set, which I've still got.

Although both were working very hard, Jo and Alton found time to get engaged. She recalls: "We were going to London for holidays and seeing so many shows. One of the most memorable was the *Judy Garland Show*, at the *London Palladium*. There were numerous stars in the audience: Capucine, George Sanders, John Le Mesurier, Hattie Jacques, come to mind. But when Judy called Dirk Bogarde to come up on stage and sang *You're Nearer*, while he sat at her feet, the audience went wild. That was really something to remember forever."

This would be the late 50s and right up until the middle 60s. We saw 'My Fair Lady' ten times I should think. We saw Rex Harrison, and then we saw George Bernard Shaw's original choice, as Professor Higgins, which was Alec Clunes, the father of Martin Clunes (from 'Men Behaving Badly'). We saw the First Night of 'The Rattle Of A Simple Man', with Edward Woodward and Sheila Hancock. We went to see Van Johnson in 'The Music Man', and Topol, in 'Fiddler On The Roof'. When I actually put an act together, I did an impression of him singing 'If I Were A Rich Man'. Topol went away to fight the Six Day War, and they auditioned Alfie Bass for the part; also, Alfred Marks and Harold Berens, who became a friend of mine. Alfie Bass got the part and took over for a while.

Jo and Alton took a holiday in Bournemouth. Kathy Kirby came out, as the star of one of the shows, sang three notes of *Secret Love*, then fell flat on her face.

They drew the tabs and pulled her off by her ankles. Tom Mennard the comic had to come on and flannel for a bit, until they could get another artiste to take her place. Of course, I didn't realise I'd go on to do pantomime with Tom; he became a friend - ten years later.

Meanwhile, life for *The Alton Douglas Quartet* was not without it's problems. He recalls one occasion, when a New Years Eve booking went sadly awry:

They rang me up and said: "You've got a coloured tenor player in your band. We don't allow coloured people into our club; would it be possible not to have him?" So I got on my 'high horse' and told them what I thought and cancelled the booking. Hughie Forbes won't know that – even to this day. The irony was that he got a job for New Year, with another band, and the three white blokes ended up not working!

There were, however, many lighter moments:

We were tuning up in the dressing room and the entertainment secretary said: "Right lads, let's have you on stage!" I said: "Can you hang on for a minute? We couldn't tune up before, because there was a girl singer on stage." And he said: "Now come along lads, you've known about this booking for over a month!" On another occasion, a fellow said to me: "Excuse me mate, do you play requests?" And of course, me being a wag, I said: "Only if we're asked. What do you want?" He thought long and hard and then he said: "Oh - anything!"

We had a guitar player called Ted Gotch. A note came up which said: 'Could you please turn the guitar down?' So Ted turned it down to half-volume. Ten minutes later, another note came up: 'I have asked you, will you please turn the guitar down?' So

*Ted turned it off and played acoustically. After a further ten minutes, this man strode up to the bandstand, grabbed yours truly, on **bass**, by the collar and said: "I've asked you to turn down that f******* guitar!" Johnny Parker was in the middle of a drum solo (Skin Deep) – going at it like mad – and a little old lady came up and said: "Could you play the Blue Danube?" And he said: "What the hell d'you think I'm playing?"*

```
┌─────────────────────────────────────┐
│ Big Night Out ...                    │
│ IN THE HEREFORD LOUNGE, BULLS HEAD   │
│ Coventry Road,                       │
│         "Stars & Garters"            │
│                  ★                   │
│ ★ ON TUESDAY                      ★  │
│ Featuring B'hams Brightest Biggest Small Band │
│   THE ALTON DOUGLAS QUARTET          │
│      with The Fabulous JENNY         │
│ plus .. The Lovely JOANNE   plus .. A Guest Artist │
│ CONCERT    ★   DANCING   ★   BUFFET FACILITIES │
│ Admission 3/6              8-30 - 11-0 │
└─────────────────────────────────────┘
```

Alton committed faux pas on two main occasions - (at least - those are the ones he admits to)! The first was at a Jewish Social Club.

We did a Negro Spiritual called 'Jesus On The Main Line Now', which was a touch 'infra-dig'. The other was when, without in any way being aware of it, during a Spot Waltz, a man won a prize. I said, "Give him a big hand," - and of course, he turned out to be an amputee!.

On the writing front, in 1961, Alton wrote a sketch called *Everything and the Kitchen Sink*, which became part of the *Leeds Rag Review*, at the *City Variety* in Leeds. He also wrote a play, a one-act black comedy, for four characters, called *A Lawn for Spindlethrift*. It won the *Illyrian Theatre's* playwriting competition and the Tamworth Drama Festival. Subsequently, the first piece about him appeared in the *Birmingham Mail*, written by John Daniels called *An Author In Search Of An Audience*.

I met a character called Tommy O'Hara – a very fine piano player and organist. I'd advertised in the Mail for a composer, and we started writing songs. We had a couple of songs recorded by a French singer, Jeanne Patou, who heard our songs and liked them. On one of them, I duet with Jeanne – a song called 'We're Just Good Friends', I affect the most atrocious cockney accent – I can't imagine why!

I developed throat trouble, so I went to a singing teacher called Michael Lambert, who I met at the same music studios where I was writing with Tommy. He taught me how to sing 'Bel Canto' style – and how you support

Jeanne Patou.

the voice on a column of air – a bit like a Ping-Pong ball on a waterspout; and how to change the colouration of your voice, as you go through the range. Michael became yet another influence for good in my life.

Jo was already accustomed to the idea of members of the same family being involved together in business, so it was a natural progression for her to help Alton with his career. She was twenty-five when she started a dance band agency. "It only came about because Alton was doing so much work, with the band. I was taking the calls, at my parents' home, because he wasn't on the phone." Nowadays, with a wide range of sophisticated phone systems available, such an arrangement sounds rather primitive, but at the time it sufficed.

By this time, *The Alton Douglas Quartet* was becoming very popular. "I was passing the dates he was booked, on to another band," recalls Jo. "I can remember it so vividly. I suddenly thought, 'Well, why can't I be an agent? Why are we losing money?' But it wasn't as easy as that. You had to go to the Law Courts, fill in forms, then a police sergeant and a female police officer came to your home, to make sure that everything was in order: that you weren't running a brothel, or white slave trafficking! They gave you a license, which you had to renew every twelve months. I ran the agency for twenty-five years."

Jo tried to make the business uniquely hers. To ensure commitment from the bookers, she would visit their houses and collect a deposit - rather like the 'down-payment' on a holiday! During recent interviews, several people have commented upon how well she ran the agency. "I loved it, and of course, that brought me, more or less, into what he was doing."

Alton reckons that towards the end of the band's life, he actually had the *perfect* band, although one of its members, Paddy Ryan, did trot out a line that was pure Spike Milligan!

I had Adrian Barnby on piano; he had previously played for Carol Levis's Discoveries, accompanying all of the acts, and a bass player called Aloysius 'Wish' Donaghy; when he sang, it gave me a chance to play bass again (badly). Our drummer, Paddy Ryan, also sang. I remember saying to Paddy: "You know when you sing The Green Grass of Home? You get the verses in the wrong order." He said: "Oi've noticed that!"

Rob Pryke, who was a local councillor, and also owned a nightclub called 'The Moat House', rang us up one day and said: "I'd like to book the band, as long as you ask that tall bloke who plays the trombone if he'd mind not singing."

Maurice echoes the sentiment: "As an entertainer, Alton was brilliant. He was resident at the *Tardebigge*, at Bromsgrove, every Wednesday night. The *professionals* from television used to go there that night, because he was there – to entertain. But he was an entertainer – he *wasn't* a singer. You could enjoy the night – even if you didn't dance."

Performing in front of other people isn't easy - for the majority of people. Maurice comments: "One of Alton's first bookings was for me, with the King's Norton Referees Association, at the *King George V*, on the Bristol Road. I booked him for a dinner, and I realised how similar we were. I do referee lectures now. I sit there, swinging my legs - but it *is* an act!" It's been the co-writer's experience, having been actively involved, for many years, with the Performing Arts, (both as a teacher, and as a member of various musical and dramatic societies), that it's a very *unusual* person who doesn't experience some degree of nervousness. But the adrenaline rush that ensues can be harnessed to *enhance* a performance. Maurice agrees: "Without it I don't think you're any good. I've given football coaching to over three thousand people, over the years, and I still get as nervous now as when I started. I get books out and swot it up beforehand. I just stand there and talk to them; but I've only just put the book down! Alton wasn't a 'natural' - was he?"

Despite my almost overwhelming shyness, I started cracking jokes with the band, because I wanted to turn it into something more than just a dance band. I thought about the chap sitting in the corner, who couldn't dance at all. Who was catering for his needs?

We did an afternoon fête at a mental hospital. All the patients were dancing in front of us. There was a little fat guy, dancing with a long tall man. All of a sudden, the little guy hit the big fellow in the stomach, and he jack-knifed over. Nurses came running up and said: "What did you do that for?" And the little guy said: "The Lord told me." And the big fellow straightened up and said: "Oh no I didn't!"

Alton related this tale, at a dinner one evening, where one of the guests was Ted Drake, who played Centre Forward for Arsenal and England, during the 1930s, and was famous for scoring seven goals in one particular game.

Ted said: "I can tell you a story about that. We played football at a fête, at a mental hospital. I looked around, and there were a lot of children. So I put my cap on the table and said to the footballers: "Stick a couple of bob in each lads, we'll buy them some ice creams." I got my cap with the money in and went over to the ice cream seller and said: "Fifty ice cream cornets please." He said: "Bugger Orf!" Ted said: "Come on mate, I want fifty ice cream cornets!" He said: "Bugger Orf! – and if you don't bugger orf, I'll get your nurse to take you back to your room!"

Some years later, I was speaking at a Ladies' Luncheon Club in Pedmore. A lady stood up and said: "I must tell you, I had Alton Douglas and his quartet, for my twenty-first birthday!" I stood up and said: "Whatever you were thinking she meant – you're right!"

The quartet auditioned for an agency in London called *West One*, which handled Jimmy Young and several other 'high profile' artists. The only positive outcome was that they were given three or four days' work, playing in Selfridge's, to advertise a new fabric called 'boggle-woggle', plus some work in Manchester, with Pete Murray.

We rehearsed in London. We were all walking along Old Compton Street, after rehearsals had finished. Prince Monolulu, the racing tipster, came toward us, with his headgear – feathers – and so on. He saw me, ran across the road, spun me round and threw his arms around me. He said (West Indian accent): "Great to see you man, oh wonderful, wonderful!" I sort of reeled away. But I won that many 'brownie points' with the lads from this, that I couldn't admit I'd never clapped eyes on him in the flesh, and I'm sure he'd never seen me either!

We did an audition for 'Opportunity Knocks', at the Midland Hotel in Birmingham. Because we were a band and we'd got to go off to an audition at Skegness for the 'Derbyshire Miners Holiday Camp', they put us on first. So we were in the room, setting our equipment up, and Hughie Green walks in on his own. As there were four of us and only one of him, I felt obliged to speak first. I said: "Good morning Mr. Green." The bass player looked at me: "Look at his eyes – we're dead!" We never heard another word from 'Opportunity Knocks'. The lads reckoned that my attempt at friendliness killed our chances. Anyway, we went up to the holiday camp that afternoon; auditioned and got the job – to play for dancing in the ballroom.

In 1967, Alton gave up his job at the Britannic and began his first summer season with the band, at the *Derbyshire Miners' Holiday Camp*, a booking that was to put him on a fast learning curve, and prove a highly significant turning point. Tommy Laughton, camp compère for that season, and now a features' writer on the *Northamptonshire Evening Telegraph*, provides the following, first-hand account of their original meeting, and Alton's subsequent 'metamorphosis':

"I *liked* Alton Douglas the moment I first met him. That was at the *De Montfort Hall* in Leicester, early in 1967. Nottingham agent Jimmy Haynes, who at one time had been the biggest theatrical booker in the Midlands, was auditioning acts for a pantomime being staged at the concert hall, by Leicester City Council. Scores of performers were auditioning, including a very young comedy double act, Paul and Barry Harman, who later became well known as *The Chuckle Brothers*.

"Among the other acts was a four-piece musical and comedy act – *The Alton Douglas Quartet*. The outfit had begun life as a conventional dance band, but by the time I met him Alton was already showing a strong flair for comedy. Neither of us was signed up for the Leicester panto. Our paths crossed again when I arrived at the *Derbyshire Miners'* for the 1967 summer season.

"The band played music for dancing in the ballroom, but were also taking part in all the revue shows in the camp theatre. These included a minstrel show, an olde tyme music hall, a pantomime, variety shows and revues. By now, Alton was much more than just a musician. He sang, danced, took part in comedy routines and sketches, and was one of the best all-round performers in the company.

The Alton Douglas Quartet meet The Kinks, Derbyshire Miners' Holiday Camp, 1967.

"But his big moment of the week came late at night, every Saturday, in the *Golden Butterfly Club* – the camp's nightclub – which was also open to the general public. *The Alton Douglas Quartet* performed a one-hour slot and rapidly gained a strong following among holiday-makers, Skegness people and pros from other shows. Alton would devise a new one-hour show every week – a mixture of comedy, song, music and all-round entertainment. But it was Alton himself who held it all together and around whom it all revolved. The success of these late night shows was one of the factors that convinced him it was time to break away from the band and go solo. So at the end of the season, Alton Douglas, all-round entertainer, hit the clubs.

"During those early days, Alton would sing and dance, tell jokes, play the trombone and perform character numbers like *If I Were A Rich Man*, from *Fiddler on the Roof*. But he didn't have the 'all-round entertainer' tag for long. His flair for comedy was so strong that within weeks he was doing very little singing and trombone playing in his act, and had become Alton Douglas – comedian.

"It was during that period that my friendship with Alton was cemented. He often refers to the 1967 summer season at

Wish, AD, Adrian and Paddy meet guest star, Eddie Calvert, Golden Butterfly Nightclub. Eddie had a No.1 hit with his trumpet feature, "Oh, Mein Papa".

Skegness, as the catalyst that enabled him to make the transition from musician to comedian."

True-to-form, Alton was keen to learn from fellow artistes. Tommy explains: "Alton already had a strong interest in comedy and an established, although small repertoire of original material, by the time I knew him. We would spend many hilarious late nights in his chalet, over glasses of Coke and cups of coffee, swapping jokes, gags and stories, and talking about comedy in general."

Julian Jorg, one of the resident artistes at the camp, was an enormous, obese man, but a fine singer. I saw the way he could work an audience. I once asked Julian how, weighing as he did about 25-stone, he could cope with sexual gyrations. He muttered: "Has't heard o' t'rocking chair?"

*A visiting show came round, advertising cigarettes, with a comic called Bernie Landy. I watched him and I knew this was what I wanted to do: I'd **got** to become a solo entertainer.*

On the very last day, it's a showbusiness tradition to play pranks on people. The band duly selected the most likely man, to play a prank on; in this case, Michael Buckmaster of the *Buckmaster Puppets*.

If you can imagine a man with a miniature stage erected in the theatre. He is balancing over the top of the stage, with both his hands occupied, operating the strings for his puppets - there can't be anyone in the world more vulnerable! And in the half-light, he sees me standing there, with an enormous pair of garden shears. But worse is to follow. I don't do the obvious. One of the lads in the band lowers the Buckmaster trousers, and using the shears, I trim the hairs on his legs!

Tommy concludes: "Thereafter, I would often stay with Alton and his wife, Jo, when I visited the West Midlands, and he would visit me at my home in Stamford, when working in the East Midlands. We kept in constant touch and I always regarded Alton as one of my very best friends in 'The Business', until we lost touch and drifted apart, in the mid-1980s."

When the 1967 season ended, Alton took a decisive leap into the unknown: packed the band up, put an act together, and became a comic. At the same time, he offered Adrian Barnby the job of accompanying him on the piano, but Adrian (according to Alton, very wisely) turned down the offer, and returned to his original job.

On the last day of the last band engagement, I thought of the words of Wilf Shaw, the Deputy Manager of the Britannic. When I'd handed in my notice he'd said to me: "You'll never make it in showbusiness as long as you've got a hole in your arse."

Chapter 6 –

COMEDY WALKS

I'll try and be brief. I do have a tendency to go on a bit – some nights I go on for so long, I have to finish my act on the way home.

At first it looked as if Wilf Shaw was something of a seer. Getting to stage one, i.e. a paid job, seemed like conquering Everest.

As mentioned, Alton put a comedy act together, incorporating the trombone. One of the numbers in his repertoire was *Bir Mir Bist Du Schöen.* For years, his co-writer thought the words to the first line of the song were 'My dear Mr. Shane'!

The first thing I realised, of course, was that if nobody laughed, the silence is deafening! Because with the band, if I did a gag and nobody joined in, at least the band would back me up with laughing. But now, of course, I was on my own.

Alton did several 'shop windows', events organised by clubs, where acts were invited to come along – singers, comics and so on – and do a free spot. Comedy magician Mike Gancia, a long-standing friend and colleague of Alton's, is one of several artistes featured in our book, who experienced their fair share of them. The entertainment secretaries made up the audience, and they would book you - or not - as the case may be.

Everybody starts with these, and in my case it was always 'or not'. I must have done a dozen and nobody in Birmingham even asked me how much I charged! I remember an act called Desi Arnold, who used to finish off playing the guitar, and his guitar amplifier would explode. And they queued up round the building to book him.

So in desperation I thought, 'I'm going to try my luck in London.' I knocked on doors to see if anyone would give me a start as a comic. I was given just the one opportunity, after visiting the Paul Wingrave Agency in Charing Cross Road. A man called Philip Hankinson offered me a shop window at the 'St Pancras Reform Club', on the next Sunday, which seemed to be the most unpromising thing in the world! So I came back, talked it over with Jo, went back to the 'St Pancras Reform Club' – and it was a sheer delight – from start to finish! There was a man at the front who heckled me in a nice way, a funny way, and it was all very jolly. I came home and the next day I had a phone call from Philip, to say could I come straight back? Astor Productions, owned by Bertie Green, wanted to talk to me about a deal. They had the 'Astor Club', which was at the back of Berkeley Square.

Alton went down there, met up with Philip, then they went to meet Bertie. The man who'd been heckling him turned out to be Harry Dawson, the main booker for *Astor Productions*. They signed Alton up for a one-year deal, whereby they would pay him three thousand pounds. If they achieved that figure by the end of the year, they would sign him up for a further year; if they didn't, he was back on his own. It was a significant leap, in a relatively short space of time.

There was also a lady in the audience, called Bettina Merson, who didn't mean anything to me at the time, but she became important later on. So I'd gone from a situation where I had nothing, to a contract with a West End agent, Philip, and a West End manager, Harry. The first place they put me into was a nightclub called 'The Best Cellar', in the heart of Leicester Square; two doors up from the Odeon, where all the Royal Film Premières are held. I was booked as a compère there. I started gradually doing other dates, as well, for Astor Productions.

Alton began as a compère at the *Best Cellar* in January 1968. A variety of acts would appear in the show, for a week, after which the bill would change. One of the 'weekly' artistes at the *Cellar,* Gillian Burns, did particularly well, going straight from an Astor show, to playing the part of Nancy in *Oliver -* also in the West End.

As things turned out, over the year, I did seven or eight months at the 'Best Cellar'. Sometimes they'd have me 'doubling out' for early shows in East End pubs,

Bestcellar
20 Leicester Square . London . WC2
Whitehall 4825

Our excellent
CABARET
TWICE
Nightly
at 9 pm and midnight

DINE
IF
you wish
Complete Dinner
3 course 18/6
This is ridiculous!

DRINK
IF
you wish
Lounge Bar Prices
Whisky 3/9
Lager 3/– etc

We are
OPEN on
SUNDAY
from 7.45 till
midnight
CABARET
at 10 pm

**2
BANDS**
to Dance to
from
7.45 to 3 am

Entrance
Sunday to Thursday
7/6
Friday 10/6
Saturday 12/6

There is
NO
place like the
Bestcellar

Twice nightly

Week Commencing JANUARY 8
The Gorgeous Bestcellar Girls
THE MAORI HI-LINERS – One of New Zealand's most
    sensational Vocal Acts
ALTON DOUGLAS   – The One-man Comedy
AL TORRINO   – Popular Singer

Week Commencing JANUARY 14
The Bestcellar Girls
SILVERS   – A Brilliant Vocal Trio
LINDA KAYE   – The Dynamic Young T.V.
    Radio and Recording Sing-
    ing Star
ALTON DOUGLAS   – The One-man Comedy

Week Commencing JANUARY 21
The Bestcellar Girls
LORNE LESLEY   – Sensational International
    Cabaret Artiste
LORRAINES   – Highly Successful Song
    and Dance Act combining
    Glamour and Talent
ALTON DOUGLAS   – The One-man Comedy

№   0533

*Please keep this programme because every week we have
a draw and the winner receives an invitation for a
champagne dinner for two. The winning numbers will
always be exhibited at the cash desk.*

for four pounds and a collection; on more occasions than one all I'd have was the four pounds. I also doubled with nightclubs like 'The Blue Angel', 'The Poor Millionaire' and the 'Eden Roc'. Because you'd got to dump your car and rush to your 'double', one week I paid more in parking fines than I earned. I'd go to the police pound and they'd say, "It's just over there Alton."

Musical entertainer Linda Grant describes Alton's act in glowing terms: "He would go out on stage and be instantly likeable to most people – I would say. He looked very smart; his stage clothing was impeccable: Alton was always in fashion; whatever people were wearing on stage, whether it was a high-lapelled thing, or otherwise, he always looked immaculate. He didn't look ridiculous. I mean, he's a handsome guy! In showbusiness, you have to look the part; you've got to make the audience like you within the first minute, or even less than a minute. I think that he had that ability - unless he'd got a really hard audience, that couldn't care less, or were determined not to be entertained! His strengths were also that he had a head full of gags, and that he could handle most situations."

I remember a girl in London, who threw a rose on the stage one night, and I was quite flattered by this. I picked it up and went over afterwards and spoke to her. She'd been in several nights and she said (broad cockney accent) "I've been watchin' you darlin'. I'll tell you what we could do. I earn enough for the two of us – on the game! I could keep you. Because let's face it, you're no fackin' good at this!" I said: "I think I'll try for a bit longer. I've only just started!" We stayed friends for the whole of the run, although I didn't avail myself of her services. But I realise now how, in her way, she was paying me an enormous compliment!

The one question you never ask anybody in a West End nightclub is: "By the way, what do you do for a living?" You never ask that question under any circumstances! In one particular nightclub where I was appearing, I noticed that every Friday night two men in smart suits, with briefcases would come in and they'd open up all the ledgers, and sit at the back, poring through them. I said to the bandleader: "I suppose they're the club's accountants?" He said: "Not quite. They tot up the club's takings for the week and then take out their percentage: it's 'protection' money."

He only played the *Astor Club* itself a few times, because it wasn't a good venue for comics; the club hostesses were employed to encourage clients to buy drinks, so a comedian on the premises was about as welcome as an undertaker at a wedding!

The girls were very good to me there - they knew I was an Astor act. I was coached by a lady named 'Phil', who taught me stage deportment and the rest of it, every afternoon. So I got to know them all, and they would keep the punters quiet while I was on, which was very nice. But we had this heckler, when I was on one night - and I absolutely nailed him. Bertie Green came to me afterwards and said (cockney accent) "If I were you mate, I'd get out as quick as you can!" I said: "Why?" He said: "Don't you know who that was?" I said: "I've got no idea!" At that moment the heckler

65

appeared in the doorway. He said: "You're a cheeky bleeder you!" I said: "I was only doing my job!" He said: "Answering me back like that – do you know who I am?" Well there's a silly side to my nature, which says, "Always do the opposite to logic." So I said: "Yeah, 'course I do!" Anyway, he took me to the bar and he bought me a drink – and it turned out to be Ronnie Kray.

Alton's diaries provide an essential record of the comings and goings of his career, which might otherwise be too complicated to follow. We find, for example, that in March 1968, he arrived at the *'Ace of Clubs'* in Worksop, for a week of doubling with the *Carlton Club*, at Chesterfield, to be greeted by the Irish tenor, Josef Locke.

(Irish accent): "Hello there young Alton. I don't drive so can you take me about for the week?" So I did. He'd had a problem, to put it mildly, with the Inland Revenue, which meant that he could only appear over here for a few weeks each year.

The hypnotist, Zaraeda, was also on the bill. On the opening night he and Alton became involved in a long discussion, during which Alton couldn't help but reveal a little of his scepticism.

*He gave a sort of half-smile, which should have started alarm bells ringing in my head, but being thick, it didn't. On the last night, I finished my act, and I can see even now, just as if I'm watching a video replay, exactly what happened. I can visualise the microphone stand, with the clip at the top, and as I replaced the mike, I slid it straight back into a 'ghost-holder', just a fraction to the right of the real thing. And of course, it smashed to the ground! Terrible finish to anybody's act. I go back into the dressing room and everybody there is falling about laughing, because Zaraeda had told them on the **first** night, exactly what I was going to do!*

After his act, Zaraeda was challenged by a man who'd heckled him all the way through. The man yelled at him: "If you were a real hypnotist, you'd have shut me up in

Josef Locke.

no time!" Zaraeda said, "I'm sorry, sometimes you sense that the other person's will is stronger than yours, and there's nothing you can do."

So the man shouted: "You're a charlatan, a fake – I'll make sure everybody knows!" Ozzie Zaraeda just shrugged, turned away from him, clicked his fingers, and the man crumpled to the floor. As I drove away from the club afterwards, I saw this poor innocent being supported by two of his friends, and being walked round and round the outer perimeter of the car park!

Speaking of hecklers, Josef Locke had a most unusual method of silencing them. Instead of using the sort of heckler-stoppers that we might use, like "You tell them goldfish, you've been round the globe!" Or, "There's a man with a chip on his shoulder – oh sorry – it's his head!" Or, "Will someone come and collect tonight's booby prize?" Josef would just say, (Irish accent): "Excuse me sir, you're with a very attractive young lady. Every time you speak out of turn, you insult her." It worked far better than any of the clever lines that we used.

>>> By a strange quirk of fate, when they later turned a fairytale-like incident, supposedly from Josef Locke's life, into the film, *Hear My Song*, Alton was surprised to discover a *host* of connections between himself, and six performers featured in the film.

Apart from having appeared on the same bill as Josef, I'd also worked with his doppelganger, referred to in the film - a singer who used to sing his songs, wear a mask and call himself 'Mr. X'. I worked with this act several times in Olde Tyme Music Hall. I don't want to disillusion anybody, but it certainly wasn't Josef Locke!

My old pal, Harold Berens, had a part as the bandleader. Also, in the opening segment, another friend of mine, Phil Kelly, was featured. The voice for Josef Locke, in the film, 'Hear My Song', was supplied by Vernon Midgley. I worked with him many times, and his sister, Marietta, in the London hotels. They were the offspring of Walter Midgley, the famous operatic tenor. The final coincidence about that film is that John Dair, who appears in the opening sequence, was Chairman of the Olde Tyme Music Hall, at the Edgbaston Cinema in Monument Road, Birmingham.

During spring of that year, Alton did his only day's work as a television extra, for a series called *The Public Eye*, starring Alfred Burke. He recalls standing on a Stratford street with Les Wilson, whom he describes as 'the world's worst-dressed policeman'. The scene was shot in black and white. Les resembled a character from the Stanley Holloway song, because he wore a navy blue tunic, black trousers - and dark brown boots.

A woman came up to him: "Excuse me officer, could you tell me how to get to the market?" Les, after a couple of policeman-like flexes of the leg muscles, said: "Madam, if I were you, I should ask a policeman!"

Part of the *Astor Productions* contract, was that Alton should also appear at service camps abroad. The base for this was Wiesbaden, West Germany. None of the performances actually took place there, but artistes would make a tour of the bases, from that point, performing at a series of venues. His diaries show that between 5 –7 April 1968 inclusive, he was in Naples, Southern Italy, appearing at *The Flamingo Club*, and the *Allied Officers' Club*. Alton found working to American audiences extremely difficult

We got to the 'Flamingo Club', and I couldn't find a way of surviving! What do I do? How do I get through my act? I don't work 'blue', and I'm certainly not American. Then I suddenly remembered: "In England," I said, "we have a thing called 'pantomime'. If the comedian puts his hands in his pockets, the audience are supposed to tell him that that's not the way to behave, and they shout out: 'Pockets!' So would you do the same, if you see me put my hands in my pockets?" So, if you can imagine, all over this room, for the next twenty minutes, great big tough warriors, standing up and shouting: 'Pockets!' 'Pockets!' It was the greatest success they'd had at the club – simply by using a bit of pantomime.

On the Saturday night they said (American accent): "Could you introduce the Top of the Bill?" I knew they had a tradition of Tony Bennett, Frank Sinatra, Dean Martin - the biggest names went over there. So I said: "Who is it?" They said: "We're not telling you." I said: "You have to tell me – I'm the compère!" They said: "You go out there and tell them that the Top of the Bill is coming on stage." At that point I should have realised who it was, when I saw the accompanist, Benny Payne, slide onto the piano stool. I said: "Ladies and gentleman, I don't know who it is, you don't know who it is – the Top of the Bill –." And out walked Billy Daniels singing "That Old Black Magic…"

It was in the West End that Alton first encountered Jewish Humour, and developed a tremendous liking for it. Bertie Green and Harry Dawson, being Jewish, would often tell him gags. So he built a successful Jewish routine into his act, which got him a lot of laughs.

Spike Mullins, the scriptwriter who later wrote for Ronnie Corbett, in 'The Two Ronnies' (where little Ronnie Corbett sits in the armchair and does a routine) said to me: "I've got a record here by a comic you'll absolutely love. I'll give it you as a present, because I know you like Jewish humour." The comic was unknown – and that was Jackie Mason; that was my first introduction to him.

One Sunday, Alton worked with a girl called Jane Fyffe. She was rehearsing, with Sir Donald Wolfit for the West End musical, *Robert and Elizabeth*.

We became friends. She and her brother, Robert, used to come and see me at the 'Cellar'. He went on to become Dame Hilda Bracket of 'Hinge and Bracket' fame.

I worked with an act called Lara. Actually, his real name was Alan Kemp. He was a drag act - the most beautiful, gorgeous woman, when he was made up. In between shows we'd go off into Soho and have a meal. Men would look at us:'What's that beautiful-looking woman doing with that awful-looking man?'

>>> to the late 90s: a friend of Alton's, Brian Thompson, visiting a restaurant abroad, was amazed to find a picture of his friend on the wall. He said: "That's my mate, Alton Douglas. That's an *old* picture of him!" And this fellow said: "Oh yes – my friend Alton!" It was Alan – he'd got a restaurant in Portugal.

During the course of his career, Alton has encountered a vast range of people, whose personalities and lifestyles seem to cover the whole gamut! Joan Rhodes, who had a successful 'strong-woman' act, was among the more flamboyant characters. At the end of the week, she gave him a picture of herself, bearing the legend: 'To Alton, in memory of our week together, in a cellar, with the rats!'

I was in a show with Bobby Hanna, who recorded, the following year, the theme song for the western, 'Soldier Blue', also Lorne Lesley, who's married to David Dickinson (the presenter of 'Bargain Hunt'). I worked with so many names - just give me an hour!

*Monday nights, at the 'Best Cellar', were traditionally the quietest night of the week. One in particular, was an extreme example of this – we had an audience of one. Somewhat inebriated, he insisted that we did the full show. Despite an Equity ruling that if the cast outnumbered the audience, the performance would be cancelled, with a line of five dancers, Ricki Renèe, the Canadian drag act, and myself, we did a ninety-minute show for a solitary watcher. At the end of it, by this time, much the worse for wear, he demanded his money back. Due to the 'Best Cellar' being a basement club, it was one of the few times in my career, when I heard the bumps as a customer was thrown **up** the stairs!*

Regarding working conditions, Jo explains: "Very rarely did you find private dressing rooms. Alton would often have to share with a line of dancers. Occasionally he caught them peeking!" During this period, as on many other future occasions, she was back home in Birmingham for much of the time, but would visit him, whenever possible: "I'd got my agency then and I was working as a PA at Heathcote and Coleman, a firm of accountants. Right from childhood, I wasn't one to stay in. I used to go

Jo checks the prices, Leicester Square, 1968.

out and about. I missed him, of course, but with the telephone – there was always something to say to each other – from both angles. I went down two or three times, at the weekend, so I met the people in the show." They would enjoy a late evening meal together, after the performance. "We had beautiful steak, baked potato and salad, all for under 4/11d -(25p), in a steak bar next door to the club. There was an old man in there (reputed to be a moneylender) who always wore a black, wide-brimmed hat, counting large quantities of money, in full view of everyone. How times have changed. Imagine that happening today!"

Alton became friendly with a man called Harold, who came in almost every night during one week. They visited the same restaurant, mentioned by Jo (between the club and the Odeon) for a late-night steak and a chat.

On the final Saturday of the week he was in London, there were a lot of Welsh Rugby supporters in. They'd been to a match in Twickenham and had decided that I was the 'Patsy' for the night. They hammered me with every line they could think of. But, I always remember Eric Morecambe saying: "The thing that makes a good 'ad-libber' is fear." Well, fear came to the rescue. I managed to quieten them – much to the delight of the audience - but not to their delight.

So they made it quite clear that they were going to kill me, after the show. But the bloody side of my nature came in again. Instead of escaping, I thought, 'I'm not going out of the stage door – I'm going out the front way' - and they're all waiting to 'take me out' – at the top of the stairs.

Harold was in that night. He said, "Let me take your trombone case" - and he charged up the staircase with it. I'd got my suit over my arm, because I was going to another nightclub. He charged towards them, and the minute they saw him, these twenty-odd rugby supporters disappeared, like snowdrops in the Sahara. I should mention that his full name was Harold Sakata. If that doesn't mean anything to anybody, look at the cast list of the James Bond film -'Goldfinger'- at the name of the character who plays 'Oddjob'!

Because of his deal with Astor, Alton had to take anything that was going, so he found himself doing stag shows - for example.

You just begin – and then sort yourself out. My material just wasn't crude enough for stag audiences. Combined with that, is the fact that I can never quite adopt the reverential manner that such occasions demand. In one northern nightclub, as a stripper finished her act, and walked stark-naked, except for a pair of high-heeled shoes, through a roomful of gawping men, I couldn't resist: "Just think lads, two hours ago she was shopping in Woolworth's!" The organiser looked at me, more in disbelief and pity than in anger: "Ee, tha's spoilt t'atmosphere!"

Another of my comedic colleagues was reprimanded at a strip show with: "It's nothing to laugh at you know – this is artistic!" To add a touch of sophistication, how about the other side of the coin – a comment heard at a Hen Party? As the male stripper made his entrance, a woman in the front row yelled: "Good God, we've seen your face – I just hope you've got a big cock!"

He was booked at *Caesar's Palace* in Dunstable. Unfortunately, after the first night, the entire show was sacked. They later discovered that the club had been offered Frankie Howerd - he'd suddenly become available, (there wasn't an established *name* on the first bill). An act called *Three Hits and a Miss*, which had won *Opportunity Knocks*, was to have been on the show, with Alton, plus a snake act. The latter staged a bizarre protest: incensed at being sacked, she cut a rabbit's head off and skewered it to the door of the dressing room.

I contacted the 'Best Cellar', and the owner said: "Oh you come down. I'll sack the compère we've got this week!" So I went down there and did another two or three weeks. Every time I was out of work, I went back to the 'Best Cellar'.

The deal with *Astor Productions* was the only time in his life when Alton ever had a manager – and it was to be his last. He wanted to be his own man. Having always been a free spirit, he felt far too restricted by having important decisions made for him.

We came towards the end of the first year and I realised that we were fifty pounds short of the three thousand pounds they promised me. I went to the 'Astor Club', to Bertie Green, to try and get out of my contract. I had visions of me being found in a gutter somewhere, or having my kneecaps shot off – or something like that!

I explained to Bertie that I really wanted to be out of it – I wanted to be in more control of what I did. He looked at me, and thought for a moment. Then he opened a drawer – (I thought: 'This is it') - took out my contract, and without a single word, he handed it to me. We shook hands.

But what an experience - with all those colourful characters – and such a range of situations to contend with! In later chapters we consider the importance of having the right comic in the right place, a situation that was often difficult to achieve as a comedian must, of course, earn a living. Strangely enough, despite some of the negative aspects, this West End environment was, with hindsight, to prove more suitable for Alton, than many other subsequent venues.

Several people featured in the book have mentioned occasions when my material went over the heads of audiences. I think because I was working fast, one-line, fairly sophisticated comedy, I found my spiritual home in the West End – that was where I was best suited; in a floorshow with dancers, and audiences that listened and were mainly made up of business people, and so on.

Now at last I was on my own - but which way to turn? The next phase of my life had begun. I stared at an empty diary.

Chapter 7 –

CLUBBED!

I don't have to appear here, you know. I could go back into Show Business

At first I floundered for work. Strangely enough, after a while, the very working mens' clubs that had rejected me, in 1967, came to my rescue. Because of the publicity I had been getting, working for Astor Productions, they started to make inquiries. Financially, although I was never really a 'club' act, they kept me going.

Oddly enough, through those difficult early days, I never doubted my ability to get work. The German philosopher, Arthur Schoepenhauer, said "The more intelligent the man is, the more pain he has. The man gifted with genius suffers most of all." Well, that should give you some idea of the depth of my intellect because deep down I am quite a happy soul. In any case, someone infinitely wiser than me, once said "Worry is a misuse of the imagination." Over the years I have developed quite a simple philosophy: only worry about the things you can change. However, occasionally that principle is put to the test...

At one Black Country working mens' club, Alton walked out onto the stage, looked down, and a woman was breast feeding her baby at a front table.

I said: "Well, I knew they served all sorts of drinks here, but... " I was immediately led off the stage by my arm, and banned from working there, for life. As the entertainment secretary correctly pointed out, "Yo shouldn't 'ave said nothink. Babby's gorra be fed."

At Hilltop Social Club in West Bromwich, I was introduced with the clipped tones of a boxing MC. "Ladies and genelmen - hintroducing – all the way from Brummagem – first time in the club – an artist...." I couldn't resist chipping in with: "Weighing in at sixteen-stone." As I came off he chided me: "Hey you – you spoilt your introduction!"

The magazine, *Entertainment Review* carried some wonderful comments about acts including: 'He was a good vocalist, but I wish he hadn't put the mike so near to himself'!

A singer in the north found to his dismay that the pianist couldn't read a note of music. After a lot of discussion they settled on half a dozen numbers that they thought they mutually knew. The pianist played an opening chord, the singer began "I left my heart in..." but stood frozen to the spot as the accompanist launched himself into - "San Francisco open your golden gate...."!

I played in a typical officers' mess: oak-panelled walls, gleaming regimental honours on display, everyone in evening dress. One of the other acts was also a comedian. Halfway through his act, the C.O. came running round to me. He said: "You'll have to get him off – he's far too blue – far too blue!" I said: "I can't go on in the middle of his act!" He said: "You'll have to. Look – the ladies are changing colour!"

In another club, the other act on the bill hadn't turned up. I was changing my clothes to go back on stage again, to do a third spot – to try and fill in. The committee was in the corner, discussing how they were going to split his money between them. All of a sudden the door opened and this flushed, dishevelled character stands in the doorway, with his tie under his ear. He said: "Good evening gentlemen, I'm the Mind Reader. What time do I go on?"

A concert pianist friend of Alton's was booked for a circuit of working mens' clubs, having never appeared in one before. He arrived at a northern club, only to find a piano, leaning drunkenly on its side; it was an upright piano, not the concert grand to which he was accustomed. It was in a terrible state, with a beer glass on top of it, and stains all down the front. He said to the entertainment secretary: "What sort of music do they like?" He said: "Just give them your normal stuff. I've got to warn you though, they don't clap!" My friend said: "They don't clap? How will I know if I'm going well?" The secretary replied: "*You'll* know if you're going well or not!"

Well, the rougher the club, the bigger the snobs, so he gave them the Warsaw Concerto. His hair's all over the place, his fingers are flying like mad. He comes to the end, he pauses – total silence - and he's facing the wall. He fearfully turns his head to the left. And the entire audience is sitting there with their thumbs up!

Quite often in social clubs, the billing would present a problem. Maxine Marquis and Alton arrived at one venue, to find that they were billed as 'Horton Douglas and Maxine Mackworth.' The Irish tenor Phil Kelly, 6-foot 4 and built like a well constructed external building, found that he was billed as 'Phyllis Kelly – female vocaliste'. Dickie Valentine told Alton that he discovered that his contract had been pinned on a working mens' club notice-board; the committee said they did it because people didn't believe that they'd paid that sort of fee to a singer!

I died the 'death of all deaths' at 'Darlington Band Club'. I walked out of the club at the end, with my suit over my arm, and my trombone in my hand. I put my hand on the door handle and thought: 'At least I've got away alive' - and a voice shouts out (northern accent): "And you're no bloody good on the trombone!"

In another working mens' club I said: "Please give a big hand to our drummer – an excellent musician – he not only keeps time, he's also done it!" Silence. Guess why?

At this point I'm wearing contact lenses on stage. I always take them out, and put my glasses on, to drive home. So I'm standing in the loo, after my act, between two men, up against the wall, attending to business. I'm in the middle of them,

73

remember, and they obviously don't recognise me. The one fellow says to the other: "What do you think of the comedian then?" The other bloke says: "I suppose he was alright – if you like laffing!"

One of my ambitions was to appear in pantomime, so at the first opportunity, I went to see the impresario, Bunny Baron. I knocked on his door and naturally, they hadn't got a clue who I was. I said: "I would like to be in pantomime." Bunny said: "What experience have you got?" I said: "I haven't got any, but I just want to do pantomime." He said: "I can't use you, I need people who're experienced." I said: " I'm disappointed in you. I'd always heard that you gave a chance to young artists. I thought you'd be the ideal person to approach." He said: " You're a cheeky sod! Come in here!" So I went into the office. He sat down and said: "Gordon, go and get one of Clarkie's wigs!" Almost independently, in came one of Clarkson Rose's wigs (he was probably the most famous Dame in the history of the British Theatre). It was a little ginger thing, which looked like a dead rat! They stuck it on my head and he said: "Go on then. The only part I've got in panto this Christmas is a Dame. Do a Dame's voice."

From somewhere I conjured up a cacophony that sounded like a cross between Mrs. Thatcher and Donald Duck, "Oh what a terrible day I've had!" And Bunny said: "Right – Hastings – this Christmas! Go in the other office – talk money with Gordon. See you there!" And he cleared off, and that was it – that was my audition!

Gordon typed up a contract, 'on-the-spot': there was no *discussion* whatsoever about money - fifty quid – end of story! It was the start of a relationship with Bunny that lasted for a couple of years.

Stars and Garters, readers may recall, was one of the most popular television programmes at that time, with Tommy Bruce, Kim Cordell, and a singer called Julie Rayne. The compère, Ray Martine, had subsequently become a major star, in his own right. He was therefore too big for them to hire for a tour of the show, so they booked Alton as compère instead - because he was relatively cheap.

It was there that I met Harold Berens, who was the guest act with the show. Harold, in the forties, had been the highest paid comic in England, starring in a radio show called 'Ignorance Is Bliss'. Wonderful, master of dialects, a very good actor, and we became firm friends.

When the tour finished, he was appearing at the 'Cresta Club' in Solihull, and I invited him for

CIVIC HALL BARNSLEY
Manager : John C. Simmons
Phone 6727-5728
MONDAY, MAY 13th and week—NIGHTLY at 7.30
SPECIAL O.A.P. MATINEES WEDNESDAY & SATURDAY at 2.30 p.m. — 4/-

Astor Productions Ltd. present

THE STARS FROM
STARS & GARTERS

TV, RADIO STAR
KIM CORDELL

TOMMY TOP HIT PARADE RECORD
BRUCE

TV AND RECORDING STAR
JULIE RAYNE

THE TV's Funny Comedy Entertainers
LYNTON BOYS

ALTON ONE MAN COMEDY ENTERTAINER
DOUGLAS

Guest Star : FILM AND TV COMEDY STAR
HAROLD BERENS

PRICES STALLS 6/- CIRCLE 5/- (All Bookable)
FULLY LICENSED BAR SERVICE TO TABLES

tea at my mother's. She said: "He's Jewish, isn't he? What does he like?" I said.
he likes Russian tea." But none of us was sophisticated, in that sense, in those days,
so mum didn't know what Russian tea was. So I said: "It's tea with no milk and a
slice of lemon." The day arrives. Harold is due. We hear the click of the gate. We look
out and Harold is walking up the path, carrying a lemon, thinking 'I'm going to see
these people, and they won't know the drill.' What he doesn't know, is that in the
kitchen, mum's got two pounds of lemons!

I appeared at the ill-fated 'Penguin Club' in Birmingham, which used to be at the
back of the Holte Hotel, by the side of the Aston Villa Football Club. I appeared there
for a week, with the pianist, Winifred Atwell. Her husband Lou, asked me afterwards
if I'd like to go back to Australia with them. He said: "You're going to make a fortune
out there, because your type of humour would be ideal for the big clubs we've got in
Oz." But I felt my fortunes lay here and I didn't take up the offer. So that fizzled out.

I remember doing 'Gino's', in Cardiff, which was quite a grotty little club. It was
always full of pimps and prostitutes, and gangster-like people, the scum-of-the-earth.
There was a police inspector in there one day and I said: "Why do you allow them to
congregate?" He said: " Well if we want them, we know where they all are!"

In April '69, Alton appeared in Sunderland.

I was in digs with Guy Mitchell, who had been a massive star in the 50s – had lots of
hits like 'She Wears Red Feathers', 'My Heart Cries For You', 'The Roving Kind', 'Singing
The Blues'. The Geordies used to chant for "Spoogie! Spoogie!" and we realised that means
'Sparrow in the Treetop'. I did one or two shows with him, but he had a very bad drink
problem. We found him flat out on the carpet one morning. It turned out that he'd got a
bottle of 'Green Goddess' - or something similar – and drank it all in one go. Another day
we couldn't find him, so his manager, Billy Wright, (not that one), and I, went searching
for him; we found him at ten o'clock in the morning, sitting on the steps of an off-license,
waiting for them to open. Despite that, he was a lovely man. I went to see him at a
nightclub, on one of the nights when I wasn't working, and he was so thrilled. He got me
to join in a medley of hits (hand on shoulder à la Flanagan and Allen). We paraded back
and forth across the cabaret floor – (Guy drunk - and me far from word perfect). He gave
me his record afterwards, and signed it on the back. I still treasure it today.

Guy was about forty-four, during this 'downhill' period, but fortunately,
the story has a happy ending. >>> He gave up the hooch, became
religious, started recording Country and Western songs, and lived another
thirty-plus years, until the age of seventy-four.

I appeared at 'Cleopatra's' in Easter Compton, Bristol. The compère was Kenny
Baker, the little tiny guy who played R2D2 (pronounced Artoo Deetoo) in 'Star Wars'.
He was a Brummie – from Sheldon. Kenny said: "I could do with some gags." So I
wrote him some material, I can only remember a few of them. He used to come out
*and say: "'Allo, I'm the new waiter here. I serve the drunks **under** the table!" I wrote*
him some 'cod' song titles: 'I'm Looking Under A Four-leaf Clover', 'Climb Every
Mushroom', 'This Could Be The Start Of Something Small'.

One city I seemed to go back to regularly, for weeks, was Liverpool. It may seem strange that the so-called 'home of comedy' would import a 'Brummie', but I think the reason was that most of their comics were doing roughly the same gags, and, not being reliant upon jokes, my material was something different.

I was booked for a week at the 'Cresta Club' with Diana Dors. We knew each other quite well, because she'd been part of the Astor Productions stable - she was one of their acts. She'd just re-married, and I met her new husband for the first time. He shook hands with me and he said: "I'm Alan Lake, and if anyone calls me Mr. Dors, they get a knuckle sandwich." So, as I wasn't particularly hungry that week, I had no difficulty remembering his name!

Diana had a tendency to put on weight, and by this time she'd become quite a challenge for the average bathroom scales. It coincided with those baggy gaucho trousers that were all the rage. She was standing at the bar, with her back to us and I came round the corner with the compère, John McVay, brother of bandleader, Ray McVay. He took one look at this sturdy image and said: "Christ! It's Lee Marvin in drag!"

June Lowndes, whose late husband Billy was one of Alton's agents, recalls: "Billy put him into the *Cresta Club*. Alton didn't like to go up north because they were completely different up there; they were really rough. Although they were wonderful venues, they had a completely different sense of humour. There was a lot to do at the *Cresta*, because it changed weekly. There were about four acts on every time, and we had the band to contend with; there was occasional squabbling, and some big 'let-downs' by artistes. Billy and I worked hand-in-hand really, for a period of six to eight years. We were up all night sometimes – ringing people, organising things."

June met a wide range of artistes at the *Cresta*. "I'll tell you what we *did* have there. I've never seen anything like it in my life – a man with no arms! He used to come and sit on a stool and he would use his feet to shoot at targets. He did all kinds of things with his feet. In the interval, when we were at the bar and he'd finished his act, he'd stand there and pick his own pint up, off the counter, with one foot and drink it out of the mug he was holding. We took it as normal because he was so relaxed about it. He used to shoot at a target with a gun and everything; just leaning on a chair.

"We had a fellow called *Jumping Jack Flash*. He was an Australian; again – a wonderful shot. He used to leap and he'd end up by jumping or shooting. He would measure up the distance between himself and someone sitting in the front row, then land at their feet, incredibly accurately - amazing people really! He used to go up quickly to the person concerned, and say: 'Please don't move – just sit there; nothing's going to happen to you.' He whispered so that the rest of the audience didn't hear at all. And whoosh! He'd land at their feet!"

June, as one would expect, became very familiar with Alton's act. "He was very sophisticated really – that's why he was no good to go up to the north: he wasn't rough enough. He was extremely smart – impeccable – and obviously tall – with quite a presence – and 'clean'." Don Maclean makes the point that he and Alton were of the 'Jack-the-Lad' school of comedy; in the Jimmy Tarbuck sense that you went on dressed as smartly as any singer, and people couldn't tell that you were a comedian until you began to speak.

June commented that in terms of comedic style, however, "Jimmy Tarbuck could be quite saucy; we booked him for private functions, at places like the *Belfry*. You couldn't really compare him to Alton. I don't know whether you remember, having been to the *Cresta* yourself, that there were always a lot of women fainting there?" (I resisted the urge to say that I hadn't realised that Alton had that effect on people!) "They found out it was something to do with the *air* in the actual building." Guy Mitchell, whom we mentioned earlier in the chapter, also performed at the *Cresta*. June recalls: "Oh – he did drink! Guy was an alcoholic actually, but Billy and I adored him. He was such a wonderful entertainer. He was doing his act – singing – and suddenly a girl just keeled over – fainted. Guy leapt down and undid her blouse. He said: 'Get away everyone!' They were all crowding around. He gave instructions; evidently, he'd been in the medical corps or something like that."

That was his story!

We've reached the summer of '69. During the previous year, our intrepid performer had appeared for a couple of weeks at the *South Shore Casino* in Blackpool, having already been spotted by the producer of the show, Bettina Merson, on that fateful day, at *The St Pancras Reform Club*. Although he hadn't realised it at the time, the two 1968 weeks that she'd booked him for were actually *auditions* for the summer season of the following year – 1969, when Alton performed in the longest running summer show in the UK – thirty-one weeks – at the *South Shore Casino*.

I was on with Rafael Lamas, the Venezuelan singer, a girl singer called Jill Rogers and Jack Freedman, who was a fine concert pianist. He was appearing

Jo and I mime the art of the dance whilst Rafael Lamas checks he's in the frame.

in the cocktail bar, playing the piano, singing his own songs, telling a few jokes – stories, and then doubling as my 'feed' in sketches. It was a typical revue type of show, with five girls in plumes and feathers – tall and very beautiful girls, little sketches and the three acts. Also, in Peter Price's Combo was Pete Lindup, the drummer, who has become a lifelong friend, and now does an act as a comedy instrumentalist, in his own right.

Pete Lindup recalls the occasion: "The first time he came to Blackpool I was actually playing for the *Ice Show* – that was in 1968. He came up to do two separate weeks at the *Horseshoe Bar Casino*. On the strength of that they booked him to do the season, the following year. Again, that was at the *Horseshoe Bar*, at the Pleasure Beach, and he 'headlined' the show that year. I was playing for the show. How I got to know him really was at a party, after the show one night. We found out that both him and me are not really partygoers. We were sitting around and listening to all the pop records, and Alton didn't drink at all – I didn't drink much in those days. So we were nibbling on these things on sticks, in a corner, and he said to me: 'What's that record that they're playing?' I said: 'Well, unless it's *Muggsy Spanier's Ragtimers*, or *Bob Crosby's Bobcats*, I don't really know who it is!' We found out that we had a mutual interest in jazz. We kept chatting and found out that we liked, more-or-less, the same kind of comedy.

"I think we had a handful of LPs between us. I know when he came back two years later, and was booked

Jill Rogers and I really do camp it up.

Honestly, Jack Freedman and I are only acting, Blackpool, 1969.

to do the season again, I said, 'Well, if you've nothing to do during the day, come round and we'll play some records.' We discovered that we like the same kind of humour: we're both keen on Groucho Marx; his autobiography is the funniest book I've ever read in my life."

Alton has a substantial collection of biographies and had already mentioned the book in question. Pete explained: "It's called *Groucho and Me* - the first book I ever read cover to cover – in one go. I found this frock coat, or tailcoat, between shows. I put it on and got some horn-rimmed glasses, painted my upper lip like a moustache. I smoked cigars anyway

Pete Lindup as Groucho Marx and me pretending to booze.

– in those days. I knocked on his dressing room door and I said (Groucho imitation): 'Excuse me, I'm looking for the world's greatest comedian. You don't know where he is, do you?'

"He said: 'We've *got* to put that in the show!' So in the Second Spot he'd say: 'I'm going to do an impression of my favourite Hollywood star - I won't be two minutes. I've just got to go off and change.' So he came off. I went straight on, did a couple of lines, and loped off again. He came instantly back on the stage, took the bows. Then I came back on and said, (still in character): 'Was that alright? Put the cheque in the post!' "

It was very similar to a West End show. If you can imagine the Casino, it had a dance floor that rose up to form the stage. It would finish up almost head height for the audience – seated at tables all round it, and there was a balcony as well. It had an astral stage which, in a blackout, would float out over the audience's heads. The male singer sat there, with just a pin spot on him and sang of couple of songs. That was never me, because with a voice like mine, I didn't qualify for astral stages!

I was ostensibly Top of the Bill, but because there were two singers I suggested to the producer that they sandwiched me between them. We put Jill on first, then I did my act, and let Rafael close the show, purely and simply to give it a good balance. Unfortunately, it went to Raf's head a bit and after about two months, when we lined up for the finale at the end, he started stepping forward to take a bow – all on his own. I asked him not to do it, but he did it again. I said: "We don't have a Top of the Bill in this show, as far as I'm concerned. We have a well-balanced revue show. When you step forward out of the line and take your own bow like that, you're insulting everybody. You're only going on last because you happen, by chance, to be the male singer. If you do it again, I shall kick you so hard, you'll sail across at least three tables!" So he stopped doing it, but he wouldn't speak to me again, for the rest of the season. It didn't prevent it from being a very happy time.

Bettina Merson also produced the *Ice Show* at Blackpool, which Pete referred to. It was one of the most famous ice shows of all. They had a costume made, of a Chinese dragon - if you can imagine a very long dragon - with the girl skaters underneath the costume. As it came out onto the ice, you'd see twenty pairs of legs underneath, skating across. It was a fabulous costume, and as the dragon appeared, it had smoke coming out of its mouth, and its eyes were glowing. As it made this spectacular entrance, Bettina turned to Pete, with enormous pride, saying: "I produced that!"

There were a few antiquated Sunday laws in Blackpool. When performers appeared on stage in the *Casino*, they had to leave the carpeting on the floor, and Alton couldn't even wear the black corduroy cap, which he normally wore when he sang *If I Were A Rich Man*, because the use of any kind of props was forbidden.

I went to see a friend of mine at the Opera House in Blackpool, called Mike Goddard. He was an impressionist in the Danny La Rue Show. He must have mentioned that I was in that afternoon, because halfway through the show, Danny looked down Toni Palmer's cleavage, and she said: "What are you doing?" He said: "I'm looking for Alton Douglas!"

During that summer season, Jo took the train up to Blackpool, most weekends. She recalls one particular Friday journey, which took longer than expected. "I wasn't used to train travel and didn't realise that sometimes the last coaches were hooked off and connected to another train. I was talking to another passenger, when I heard an announcement: 'There won't be another stop for this train until Carlisle.' Oh goodness - I was on my way to Scotland! There were no mobile phones in those days, and consequently no way to tell anyone in the show that I wouldn't be there on time. Me being late – never! To cut a long story short, I reached Carlisle, only to be told that there was no train back to Blackpool. But somehow the station master smuggled me onto a goods train – and I arrived in Blackpool after midnight – six hours late!" Life for Alton, meanwhile, was not exactly problem-free.

I used to park my car in our own car park, at the back of the Casino. Then after about twenty weeks, all of a sudden, the chap on the gate said: "I shall need proof of identity you know." I said: "Hang on – I've been here for four months. You know who I am." But he said: "No, no, I must have proof of identity!" I said: "Oh don't come the little Hitler with me!" He said: "How dare you insult my war wound!"

I had a knock on the door of the flat one morning, at half past five. It was a very well-known artiste in one of the shows in Blackpool. He'd been involved in some sort of nocturnal activity in his car, on the beach. He said: "I'm in terrible trouble – you'll have to come down!" We drove down to the beach and by the time we got there his car had almost completely disappeared. All the rocking had caused it to sink into the sand; you could just about see the top of it! So I looked around and there was a workman at the far end, using one of those diggers. I said: "Go and offer him a fiver!" Money pocketed, the man got the shovel of the digger underneath and pushed the car slowly back up the beach, until he got almost to the wall. Of course, the car was out of the sand by then, but it took us over a week to get the sand out of the car! To this day, whenever I meet this 'very well-known artiste', he always insists on buying me lunch!

Chapter 8 –

DAME FOR A LAUGH

Actually, I wear contact lenses – I'm so religious, on Sundays, I wear stained glass contact lenses.

With the Blackpool season over, Alton was booked for a week, at *Webbington Country Club,* just outside Weston-super-Mare. He was appearing with a group called *The Fourmost,* who were quite famous in the 60s.

We sat down one morning at Webbington Country Club, in front of a roaring fire. The local vicar came in and we swapped stories. Before he left, he said: "I must thank you. When people see this 'dog collar' they always switch off. You have treated me like a normal human being and I've loved it. Before I leave, can I just give you my joke? The three Wise Men were walking along. One of them stumbled and said: 'Jesus Christ!' And the other one said: 'That's funny, I was going to call him Fred!' "

Christmas 1969 was on the horizon and Alton was due to take part in his first pantomime. Arriving at Hastings he discovered to his horror, never having appeared in a pantomime before, that the newspapers referred to 'Robinson Crusoe, starring Alton Douglas.'

Fortunately, after the first read-through, the producer, Audrey Maye, rang Bunny Baron and said: "I think we've found a real dame here." Which is a contradiction in terms, but her motives were good! I played the part as a totally unglamorous, very much masculine-slanted female, but it still led to a misunderstanding:

One afternoon, we had a party of kids in from the East End; they were quite loud and aggressive. When I made my first entrance – (if you can imagine – I'm wearing the latest lime green tights, a bright yellow dress and a ginger 'fright' wig) - as I walked out, a voice shouted: "'ey mum - is that a puff?"

We had a very fine actor in it, George Malpas. He'd been playing one of the leading roles in a television series called

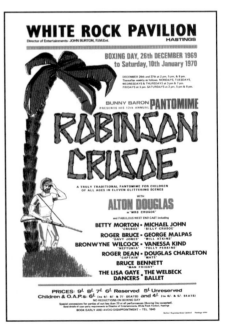

82

'Tom Grattan's War'. I always felt that he should have been Top of the Bill. He was a fine old actor – very, very good.

One day, it was a matinée – and you always try and brighten things up in the afternoon, because sometimes, as you get through the run, it can be quite a sparse audience. I walked onto the stage and thought that I'd try ad-libbing. I said to George (Dame's voice): "Captain Bird's-eye I presume?" He looked at me and without batting an eyelid, or missing a beat, he said: "Madam, the price of pork in China is rising rapidly." I just stood there gaping and I never again tried throwing George. I learned another lesson that day! At the end of the season, when we did the very last performance of all, and flowers appeared for the girls, a box of chocolates came up and it said: 'To Mrs. Crusoe, from one grandmother to another.'

My first entrance, as Mrs Crusoe, even shocks me!

George Malpas points out the error of Mrs Crusoe's ways.

Jo, who apparently had launched a one-woman campaign, to keep British Rail in business, arrived at Hastings Station, taking enough Christmas food to feed her fiancé and herself, over the holiday period. Some of the cast, however, had other ideas! "They came to Christmas Lunch and stayed and stayed," she recalls, "and by Boxing Day, we were eating biscuits and chocolate – but it was great fun!"

Alton's first venue, after the pantomime, was a club in Wolverhampton, called the *Cleveland Court*, which unfortunately, was a bit of a 'dive'. On the first night, a Monday, they absolutely *hated* him. The manager came round to the dressing room. "I'll have to pay you off," he said, "you're obviously not right for our audience. I'm ever so sorry – but that's it."

So I said: "Just let me go on tomorrow night. Little and Large are in pantomime at the 'Grand Theatre', and they're coming to see me. I'd never be able to face them again if I wasn't here! Let me do it and if it doesn't go well, don't bother paying me." I rang Sid and Eddie, and told them about the problem. They turned up the following evening with the entire cast: Frank Ifield, Ken Roberts, and all the dancers; they filled the place! With 'pros' and musicians I always went well, because I did the kind of material that they liked. I went an absolute bomb - and had a standing ovation! The manager came round to the dressing room and said: "I'm ever so sorry. I must have made a mistake. It must have been last night's audience. Please do the rest of the week for me." I said: "Only if you promise me that when the pros are not in, you won't give me the sack." He said: "Oh no, no, no!" Anyway, I died on my feet for the rest of the week!

I never had any trouble making bands laugh, which is often a bad sign for comics. It means you're not suitable for audiences, but you're suitable for 'musos'.

Jo's agency was picking up by then. In addition to dance band bookings, she was starting to get cabaret bookings. We put on little shows and began to book a comedy magician called Mike Gancia.

Mike takes up the story: "One day I had a call from an agent called Jo Ward. I didn't know Jo. She said, 'We're doing this show at the Palace Theatre, Redditch. Would you like to appear?' It was a charity show. I said 'Yeah' - because I was game for everything in those days. I did the show with Alton. I'd seen him compèring at the *Cresta Club*, although I didn't know him at that stage.

"Then they started to get me a few bookings with Alton, and we began to travel around together. It was during that period of time that I realised how professional he was – compared with some of the acts that I worked with. His act appealed to me, because he was methodical in the way he went about it: he had a book of all his gags, and a system whereby he would take out a gag and put another one in its place. He'd mix it up, but they were mainly what you'd call 'one-liners'. All the big American comics like Bob Hope, Jack Benny, Milton Berle, use 'one-liners' – and Alton tended to use them, although he *had* got longer jokes."

Alton's comedic style was quite original, even at this early stage. Mike recalls that Alton didn't remind him of any other comedian, "...because in those days, the club comedians were brash and a bit 'rough-around-the edges' - some of them."

At the dreaded 'Shop Windows' they often had a solitary paid artiste – and on one occasion, they booked Alton. There was a singer who performed Roy Orbison songs: he called himself 'Boy Robison'. During the interval, he came up to Alton and said: "Hi man. I'm very impressed with your act. I think I can probably get you some work; could you give me your card?"

Now bear in mind that I'm the paid act and he's the one doing the free audition. A month later, I'm at Bristol Street Motors, collecting my car after a service. A mechanic's head pops over the counter. "Hello Alton it's me - Boy Robison."

Some of the worst nights that Alton ever had – although he was also doing some reasonably successful shows by this time – were in working mens' clubs. He recalls playing a whole week in the northeast, without once hearing the sound of laughter. It used to be claimed of the clubs in the north that the best a comic could hope for was that the audience would let him live!

In one particular club that I went to, the noise was absolutely earth shattering. They introduced me; the pianist played me on. I walked out. The jukebox was still playing and there was a TV on – by the side of the stage, so that the few people who were facing me were looking across to my right. People were yelling at each other. I swear someone in the corner was boxing a kangaroo! I looked around, pulled a chair over and just sat on it and stared at them! Anywhere else in the world, the noise would have subsided then. But it built and built until this disembodied voice came over the tannoy system: "Give order ladies and gentlemen – the artiste's not working!"

A totally disenchanted Alton came off stage at the *Boilermaker's Club* in Roker Park, to the sound of his own footsteps.

*The concert secretary was standing in the wings, beaming at me. He said (Geordie accent): "You went well tonight!" So I said: "Well? They're supposed to laugh!" He said: "You kept them quiet." I said: "Honestly, I don't get you." He said: "Well, **she** liked you!" And he pointed to a woman, sitting in the front. I said: "How d'you know?" He said: "When you came off she said: 'Well, I've seen wuss!'"*

I played a club in Sheffield once - an area to be avoided by every comic. It gave me more satisfaction than any working mens' club I'd ever appeared at – ever. I made my entrance playing Bir Mir Bist Du Schöen. As I walked on there was a man at the front reading a 'Pink'un' – you know, the local sporting paper – the Argus or whatever. He's reading it after I've been introduced – sitting there - reading the paper! I rammed my trombone through the middle of his paper, pulled it off the end of the trombone and tossed it contemptuously over my shoulder. And I didn't miss a beat!

In Leicester, he was booked to do a *Noon and Neet*, which was a lunchtime show, followed by an evening performance. The audience reaction to the first show was so abysmal that Alton retreated, 'tail-between-legs', to the cinema for the afternoon, absolutely *dreading* the evening show. Needless to say, the second one was just as bad! The concert secretary was waiting for him. "I'm disappointed in you," he said. "After the reception you had at lunchtime, I thought you'd paralyse them tonight!"

That summer, 1970, Bunny Baron, who'd booked Alton for pantomime, also booked him to play the *Knightstone Theatre*, Weston, with Tony Mercer, who'd just completed a very long run with the *Black and White Minstrels*, where he sang with the tenor, John Boulter. Tony had a similar singing voice and style to Bing Crosby.

He was probably their biggest star by this time. He packed the theatre every night, for the whole of the run: it was a huge success. At the very end of his act, he 'blacked-up', on stage. He used to tell them a few gags and put the make-up on – and then go into his last medley.

Tony had a friend who could get **anything***. At that time, small black-and-white portable televisions were a novelty. I ordered one and it was such a novelty that the entire cast went down to the station to pick it up - about sixteen of us! It cost me £70 in 1970. I saw roughly the same set, last week, going for about £45.*

Lawrie Adam, Roy and Yvonne Earl, AD, Tony and Angie Mercer and Jo watch as Tony tries to win our wages for the week, Weston-super-Mare, 1970.

Tony was a lovely man. So much in his life had gone wrong. His son had been killed in a car crash. He got involved in the coach – the vehicle – that took the England Squad around in 1966 – for the World Cup. Unfortunately his business partner had gone 'crook' on him. Tony was actually served a writ on stage, at the 'Victoria Palace' – in the middle of the show!

According to Alton, the other comic in the show, Roy Earl, was *far* better suited to seaside audiences than himself. A journalist in the local press begged to differ:

'The show is strong on comedy, and most of it comes from Alton Douglas, Birmingham-born, but quite capable of telling a variety of gags, in a whole range of accents. He has an engaging style, very much his own, with a penchant for the unexpected, and his clever ad-libbing, when things went just a little awry on the opening night, was a delight.'

Roy was a 'mad magician', and their friendship lasted until Roy died, in 2001.

Tony knew a lot of people who came to the town and did the shows. He knew Terry Scott very well. Terry was appearing at the *Playhouse* for a week. Alton and Jo had supper with him one night.

Terry 'read' Jo's face: he said that her mum and dad were separated, that she'd had a brother who'd died young; she'd been involved in a business that had failed; she'd got a broken marriage behind her. I think every single thing he told her was wrong!

We went to lunch with him one day and my brother Maurice and his wife Gwen joined us. Terry told a story about Patrick Cargill, the actor, appearing for the very first time in a West End play. Patrick Cargill was incredibly nervous, because he had a line that he knew could be a disaster – let's put it that way. The line is: "Don't worry, I'll put Clarrie in the punt!"

Oh God!

He's never been in the West End before, and he's got this awful line; he's incredibly nervous. He hears his cue and he bounces on stage and says: "Don't worry, I'll put Clarrie in the punt - - c*** - - punt!"

For that season, Alton shared the top floor of a house with an actress called Myra Francis, who was appearing at the *Playhouse* with Dickie Henderson. She was married to Peter Egan (who played Paul in *Ever Decreasing Circles*). Jo and Alton had meals with them on many occasions. In fact, Myra was responsible for switching Jo onto green beans – French beans – they were passionate about them.

Brian Close, who was by that time the Somerset cricket captain, brought the entire team to see the show. Tony, being a Yorkshireman and keen on cricket, knew him from Brian's days as Yorkshire's cricket captain. But then, after troubles at Yorkshire, Brian had moved to Somerset.

Tony and I were invited to go and see Somerset play cricket at Taunton the next day. So we go down there and we meet up with Brian. During the course of the

"Oh Lord, you made so many poor people". I grew the beard every night just to sing "If I Were a Rich Man", Knightstone Theatre, Weston-super-Mare, 1970.

morning, Somerset are batting, Brian's out early and we can't find Tony anywhere. (It turns out he's in the bar, having G and T's). We go round looking for him. I get to a little tea bar. I said to the woman there: "Have you seen Tony Mercer?" She said: "What does he look like?" I couldn't resist it – I said: "He's got a little black wig and he blackens his face. He's got a huge white mouth, he's wearing white gloves and he's going round singing 'Mammy'." The woman thought for a moment, and then said: "I'm afraid I haven't seen him - but it's my first day here!"

Later in the season the Kent team came down to play Somerset. They played one game a year at Clarence Park, in Weston itself. Tony and Alton were invited to go along there as well. Alton found himself sitting in the pavilion next to Alan Knott, the Kent and England wicket keeper at that time, and had a wonderful opportunity to talk to him about what it was like playing for England.

Being a cricket 'nut' myself, it was one of the great opportunities of my life. I was just going to ask him when he said: "Oh, we saw the show last night. Tell me about being a comedian." I spent the entire time I was there, talking about the problems of being a comic. I just blew it!

Bunny booked them, not only for the season, but also for Sunday concerts at Hastings and Weymouth. Tony and Alton used to drive down together. Alton recalls a concert at Weymouth. His spot went extremely well. He went into the bar for a drink, in the interval and Bunny was standing there. He said (cockney accent): " 'allo son - bin on yet?"

Mum came down for a week and I put her up at the friendly, family-owned Seaward Hotel, just opposite the jetty that housed our theatre. As a thank you to the owner, Mr. Michaels, I gave him two tickets to the Friday show. At one point during the proceedings, I had to conduct a hula-hula contest for men. Don't snigger, summer seasons were like that then! Mr. Michaels just happened to be one of the five contestants and so, as you would, I engineered a win for him. Just before he left the stage, proudly clutching a stick of Weston rock, I said to him: "To put the audience's mind at rest, you and I have never met before, have we?" He said (Greek accent): "Yes, your mother – she stay at my 'otel!"

On the last but one day, they couldn't think of any way to finish the season, so Jo and Alton decided to get married in Weston-super-Mare. Tony, acting as Best Man, and his wife, Angie, came along to the Registry Office.

Jo interjects: "At last – I can hear people saying! We went to Bristol the day before, to get the wedding ring, and were married on the Saturday morning. Afterwards, we had a hurried meal at the *Webbington Country Club*, just outside Weston. In the evening, (I didn't know anything about it – Angie hadn't said anything), at the end of the show, which was also the end of the season, she said to me: 'Be ready.' She'd got two bottles of champagne and some glasses. Tony moved to the centre of the stage, told the audience what had happened, called me on stage. They poured out glasses of champagne for the cast, and also brought drinks to two or three members of the audience in the front row. They toasted us with the champagne – and that was the end of the season. My parents and Alton's mum didn't know anything about it at all."

They broke the good news on their return home. As they'd been courting for so many years, I wondered how Jo had felt when

Jo and I get a helping hand from Angie and Tony after the deed had been done.

they eventually married. Was she relieved – for example? She replied: "I would have gone on: it didn't matter to me, that much. We were so used to being a couple anyway. So many people had kept on saying: 'It's about time you got married.' I didn't want to *be* the 'little housewife'." The idea of a traditional marriage didn't particularly appeal to her. "I wouldn't say it frightened me, but it was just something that *I* didn't really need to do." Society was, of course, very different at that time. Jo comments: "If it had been today, I suppose I would have got a mortgage and a house – I wouldn't have stayed with my parents that long.

"We went on honeymoon to Spain, but after the first week, not being a couple to laze around in a quiet place, we tried unsuccessfully to get an early 'plane home, to be where the action was. However, on the penultimate day, the tour organiser came to us very apologetically and said there had been a mix-up over the flights – but if we didn't mind flying home a few hours early, they would give us a hefty rebate!"

The only problem now was where would we live? When we did find somewhere, who could ever have guessed that it would be in a community teeming with such a curious amalgam of diverse characters?

Chapter 9 -

ROLL OF HONOUR

Birmingham: the most complex city in the world. They've just pulled down my trouser shop and built a fly-over. They've pulled down the synagogue and built a pass-over. They've even pulled down our Elsie and she's a pushover!

We moved into a flat in Dominic Drive, King's Norton, in 1970, and found ourselves living in the middle of a showbusiness community. Immediately above us was Keith Smart, who became the drummer with 'Wizard'.

TV appearance-wise, 1970 was a particularly good year for Keith. He and Steve Gibbons had a group called *The Uglies*. Keith recalls that two of the best bands he's been in were *Danny King and the Mayfair set*, and also *The Uglies*, because they performed the sort of rock n' roll music that he most enjoyed. Keith joined *Wizard* in 1971. He explains: "I'd come back from Germany, where I'd spent quite a considerable time with another group called *Young Blood*. That's where I met Coletta."

The two couples moved to Dominic Drive at similar times. Alton and Jo moved into flat 26 in Autumn 1970; Keith and Coletta married, then moved in the same month. Keith recalls: "They were in blocks of six: three storeys, with two flats on each level. We were on the first floor, Alton was on the ground floor, to the left of the stairwell, opposite the flat that was underneath us; they were big flats." They lived there for about ten years, except for a brief period of a few months, when Coletta and Keith moved out, but in the event, simply transferred to another flat. "We were looking for another place – and one came up in Dominic Drive again - number 40, I think it was.

"In addition, I was playing in a place called *The Engine House* at the Tardebigge, in a little jazz combo; I like jazz as well." It's an interest that he and Alton have in common, although Keith prefers the more modern variety. Alton's interest started with Dixieland (rather than trad jazz) and moved on to Mainstream /Bebop.

"Alton's solo act was a more sophisticated kind of comedy," observes Keith. "When *The Comedians*, on Granada TV came out, the likes of Bernard Manning, Frank Carson and Stan Boardman came to the forefront. It got a bit earthier – quite mucky. People seemed to like that. It didn't do people like Alton, who were more sedate, much good really. All they seemed to want to hear at the clubs in those days was swearing and dirty jokes."

Alton describes Dominic Drive as "... a buzzing little community." Keith agrees: "Everybody knew everybody else. We had a couple of large barbecues for the whole neighbourhood, on the grassed areas around the flats."

Keith recalls other residents: "Jeff Lucas, road manager for *Black Sabbath* - 'Luke'- we called him. He left *Sabbath* while he was in Dominic Drive and set up his own trucking business. Chuck Botfield, the lead guitarist with the *Rockin' Berries* was there, then he split up with his wife, and his wife stayed on. There was Rob Slater, whose father owned the *Westmead Country Club*. Clive Gillard, whose father was a well-known shopkeeper in Cotteridge: he had a radio and TV shop, and used to put a lot of PA stuff in for different people - all the tannoy equipment." Roy Wood, the lead singer with *Wizard*, used to collect Keith from the flat. " 'Woody' used to come and pick me up, and we'd go to the local pub for a drink. He wasn't a *constant* visitor," explains Keith. "I've never been one for having close relationships outside of the group. I don't believe in living in one another's pockets. It spells disaster, because if you have a little 'fallout', somewhere along the line it causes trouble for the group." He recalls that the similarly named Roy Ward was a more frequent visitor. "He was a drummer with *Black Sabbath.*"

The fact that both couples worked at night precluded any evening 'get-togethers'. However, as Keith explains: "When Alton played locally at the *Cavendish* I'd go over, because Coletta worked there. I saw him at the *Cresta Club*. That was his solo comic act – with his trombone - I never saw him with his group. He was a very good stand-up comedian."

In Keith's opinion, "Alton's a comedian's comedian. Before *The Comedians* type of comedy became popular on TV, people gave more thought to what they said. But later, you only had to add an 'f' word and you'd get an instant laugh. I mean, I can tell you a joke that's totally unfunny, but if I put the 'f' word in, I can get a reaction straight away.

"To me, Bob Monkhouse was the ultimate comedian. I don't think there's anybody, throughout the English-speaking world, who can top him. He's up there with all the 'greats'. But even *he* is a mucky comedian: if Alton did that – he'd be like Bob Monkhouse. But as soon as people got this 'in-your-face' comedy, it didn't do the likes of Alton Douglas and Don Maclean much good.

"Alton would *analyse* things too; he's well read on comedians; he's crazy about Laurel & Hardy and Max Wall – all of the classic comedians." Alton's collection of clowns, of all shapes and sizes, bears testament to his fascination with the different facets of comedy. Other aspects of his personality, such as musician, writer, television presenter, producer of books, researcher and character actor, combine to make this a real 'roller-coaster' of a book!

Much of Alton's material was original, incorporating an idiosyncratic, twisted logic. Keith recalls: "He was always writing – always running gags by me. I'd be coming down the stairs and he'd say, 'I've just written this.'"

A small collection of clowns.

They'd see each other almost every day. "Being in the business, we had common ground for discussion; you'd be out there cleaning your car, or whatever, and we'd talk about what we were doing. I was eight years younger than him, and more of a rock n' roller, rather than into the cabaret scene. But we'd perform at some of the same clubs." As his friend's career developed, Keith watched him in various television roles.

Keith became manager of the *Rockin' Berries* in 1997, a role that he maintains to the present day. Chuck is the only remaining founder member of the group. Alton and Keith eventually moved from Dominic Drive. "We were both house hunting," explains Keith, "but we didn't go into great detail. Then I saw him one day and said: 'I've found a place.' We're still virtually within the same vicinity as each other."

Alton recalls other showbusiness residents, including Jeff Turton, lead singer with the *Berries*, an Italian stripper, and a singer - Barbara Thorpe. During the ten years they were in residence, there was a great *influx* of showbusiness visitors to their flat. The following is a selection – although there were numerous others.

There was Roy Edwards, the singer, from the TV series 'Lunchbox'. Roy sang with the famous wartime Squadronaires and the Geraldo Orchestra. I met him at the Winter Gardens in Weston; he was appearing with the Vernon Adcock Orchestra and we struck up a friendship, straight away. At home, he had the misfortune to fall and break his arm. Expecting his wife, Joyce, to rush out for help, he looked up, in terrible agony, to find her taking his photograph! "Get an ambulance – quick!" he implored. "I will in a minute - it's just that I've never seen a green man before!" Roy had a hairdressing salon in Cotteridge for several years. It's pictured in one of our books, 'Birmingham Shops'.

Alton studiously avoided displaying photographs of celebrities on the walls of his flat.

It was a highly suspicious activity, because when you went to artistes' houses, your picture was always in pole position. But sometimes, around it, would appear a bit of shading, as if the picture underneath it had been larger – or not in the same position! Johnny Singleton, was a compère at the 'Trent Bridge Inn' in Nottingham. Whenever you went round to his house, your picture was always in prime position, over the door.

Harry Bailey, the glorious old Irish comic, arrived at their flat, during a time of political unrest in Bangladesh.

After consuming half a bottle of scotch and mumbling: "You think they'd offer you a drink round here!" he stumbled on a flagstone as he left and dropped to his knees. With not so much as a nanosecond to collect himself, he looked up and said: "There you are Alton – I knew I'd bungle a dash!"

The Scottish comedian, Chic Murray, told me, when he came for supper, that he'd arrived at a working mens' club in Newcastle and the doorman didn't recognise him as the artiste for the night. Being the mild man he was, Chic paid to get in. Just then the concert secretary came round the corner and said (Geordie accent): "Ya canna charge him. That's the turn for tonight!" The doorman was very contrite: "Aw, sorry Mr. Murray – I did'na recognise ya!" Chic said: "Well, ya wouldn't. You see – this week I'm my sister's brother, on my father's side." The doorman was very upset: "Well, I'd never 'ave known!"

Terry Hall, with Lenny Lion on his right arm (catchphrase: "Don't embawass me!") was just about the most famous ventriloquist in the UK, at one time. He was minus the bashful beast, when he visited Alton and Jo.

Chic Murray.

He told me that having been asked to open a school's garden fête, he was invited for a sherry, by the headmaster, before the ceremony and told: (public school accent): "Mr. Hall, we've admired your act for many years, in the theatre and on television. Could you just answer me one question please? How long does it actually take you to get into the skin?"

We thought we could spot a toupée from a mile away, in dense fog, but to our surprise, one particular guest went to bed in a reasonably hirsute condition and then sat down to breakfast, totally bald! Almost equally alarming was the sight of Jack Freedman, standing on his head in the middle of the lounge, at seven o'clock every morning.

We also entertained Tom Mennard – who finished up as Sam Tindall in 'Coronation Street'; Bill Maynard and George Truzzi - a name that will be known to people who loved variety, (he 'fed' a lot of people, in shows). Linda Grant came to our flat for a meal with Dickie Valentine and Junior Jonsen.

Around that time, in early December 1970, Alton had appeared with all three of his dinner guests, at the *Cresta Club*: as one would expect, Dickie Valentine was Top of the Bill.

Junior Jonsen was a Maori singer/entertainer. Maori acts were quite popular in those days: the 'Maori Hakas', the 'Maori Hi-Flys'. Junior also played the guitar – and told the odd joke. Linda Grant was one of the most musical and unusual acts I'd ever worked with. She was a kindred soul in terms of music, humour, and she had a nice sense of irony, as far as showbusiness was concerned.

Linda and Alton had previously performed together on the same bill, for a week, at the *Music Hall Tavern* in Bristol, but she regards the *Cresta Club* in Solihull as the most *significant* show that they appeared in jointly. "I don't think I'm *ever* going to forget what happened on the first night. I was really 'green' – (I'd only done about three weeks in the business). I was also jet-lagged, having just got back from Tokyo. I thought that all you needed to be was musical and clever.

"My act was on before Alton's. There was a moment where I suddenly slipped in a gag that I'd heard him saying. I actually, literally, did one of his gags. Now that is a thing that you *never* do in showbusiness. It's about the biggest sin there is. But I was so stupid and naïve. I'd come out of amateur circles. I picked up an instrument and suddenly a line of Alton's act came out of my mouth. I must have been very tired.

"When I came off stage, it hit me that this was quite serious. I was talking to one of the other acts and I said: "I've got to talk to him. I don't want him going on stage, deliver his line and fail with it." So I confronted him. I wouldn't say that I knew him at that stage; we weren't the friends that we are now. His response – I mean anyone else would have torn me to shreds - probably sued me as well - but he didn't do that. He took me to one side and quietly explained that 'In this business,' – these were his words – 'dog does not eat dog.' He was sincere, and quite calm and collected about it. He said:

'This is actually quite serious, because it means that I've got to adjust a whole section.' It was just half an hour before he was going on. But he didn't fall out with me. I was so grateful to him for not going barmy over it, and thought, 'this must be a really genuine bloke. I must try to emulate his professionalism.' I'll never forget it- it was a turning point."

Contributors to our book are in unanimous agreement that Alton had a sophisticated, intellectual type of act – (the type of act that particularly appeals to Linda). She explains that his gags fell into topics, or 'sections', and quotes the following examples. "He'd say: 'I'm going to sing some Jewish songs for you. I'd like to begin with *Bekosher Mine, Three Cohens in the Fountain* and *Oi Vay Maria*. All of these songs can be heard in the new Jewish discotheque down the road - the *Syna-go-go!*'

"I remember a very funny gag of his about three Italian girls reading a newspaper. It ended with one of them saying, as she read about the new Victoria tube pipeline construction, 'I would like to be Vittoria Pipalini: it says here she was *laid* by 2,000 men'… I saw Alton every night at the *Cresta*. I'd say that I had a drink with him, but I can't honestly remember him *ever* having a drink! Another full week that I remember doing with him was at a lovely place called *La Rèserve* in Sutton Coldfield, right in the middle of the park there - with a lake.

"He helped me to find absolutely fantastic 'pro' digs, in Erdington, although it's not the sort of place I can ever imagine Alton going to (not that he would need to in Birmingham). Because what people do in these digs, is come back from their show, and sit around for about three hours into the night, talking about how badly or how well they did. It's almost like they're never off stage - and he wasn't like that, you see. After a job he'd be talking about something completely different; he hardly ever talked about showbusiness. I was like that as well: I wasn't 'stage-struck' either.

Linda (and the kitchen sink) Grant.

There are some people who live the life, twenty-four hours a day. Even when they're talking to a friend on the phone, if they're a comedian, they probably just tell gags all the time, like they're trying them out!

"Another thing that we had in common was that we had the same 'mind-set' in that you construct the act, and you become so confident about the structure of it that you don't need to continuously prod it over and pick up new ideas, because it works. He was one of the most professional people I ever met in the business. I met people who were actually much 'bigger' than Alton – Frankie Howerd and Bob Monkhouse and people like that. But I have to say that Alton Douglas was an extremely professional guy."

Alton introduced Linda to the idea of making the best use of her time. "He said: 'Well I sit at my desk.' (I thought, 'Blimey! Desk! I haven't got a desk!') 'I get all my contracts out and I have my notepads and my typewriter, and I promote myself as a business. Showbusiness is really two words: show + biz.' I realised - that's a key statement that I haven't quite got yet. I'd been relying on agents, and he seemed to be getting his work out of his own initiatives. I thought, 'I must try to do this.' "

Linda describes herself as 'Alton's Number One Fan.' "I liked his material and his presentation: it was slick and smart. He looked good. The fact that he carried a trombone – whether he used it or not is another matter – but it was there. In one of his publicity photos, the trombone was used as a hat! I just admired him. When you're new in the business there are certain people that you sort of mentally attach yourself to: there's something about them that you admire. I'm sure everyone does this. Alton is such a genuine sort of bloke: the sort of person you'd want to have as a friend. The fact that he lives miles and miles away from here is pretty sad. If he lived anywhere nearer I think I'd be visiting him and Jo quite often."

Linda recalls that Alton introduced his act with a short song, which he'd written himself. "I can't remember the song, but it was one of those catchy 'rooty-tooty' type things." The song in question was *I'm a Bit of a Character*, from *Pickwick*, with Alton's own lyric. "Then he'd stop that," she continues, "and park his trombone. And you'd end up thinking: 'is he ever going to play it?' " (A technique also employed by Jasper Carrott - keeping his guitar on a stand – then using it at the last minute!) However, Alton explains that he *always* played the instrument – "sometimes 'Top 'n Tail' - sometimes at the end."

Dickie Valentine's real name was Richard Bryce. So knowing my real name as well, he'd arrive when the show was halfway through. (I'd be on stage when he got there). But it didn't matter at what point in my act, he'd stick his head through the curtains and say: "Good evening Mr. Price." And I'd say, "Good evening Mr. Bryce," and then I'd carry on as if it hadn't happened.

Mum invited him to tea because she was a fan of his. He had such a nice afternoon, that when he was about to leave he said: "I'm so self-conscious. I haven't brought you a present. I ought to have brought you some flowers." He went to the car *and searched in his glove compartment, but all he could find was a tube of wine gums, which he gave to her. She came to the 'Cresta Club' and he said: "Is there anything you'd like me to sing?" She said: "I'd love you to sing 'My Way'." He hadn't got the arrangement for it, so he sang it for her – with just the piano to accompany him.*

>>> Later, in May 1971, I was in the car and heard on the radio that Dickie Valentine had died in a car accident. I rushed over to tell mum, because I knew that she'd be quite upset. When she died, a couple or so years later, we found, in the drawer at home, that she'd still kept this tube of wine gums – she'd never opened it!

Two weeks after the *Cresta* show, Alton and Jo saw Dickie and Bill Maynard in a Leicester pantomime.

Speaking of Bill Maynard, it's strange really, when I first started as a comic, Bill had been my role model. His type of material and delivery had really appealed to me. He did a routine about 'Buildings of the Future', predicting that they wouldn't go upwards; they'd go further down into the bowels of the earth, so that if anyone died, you could open a window - and throw them out!

Jo and I had seen him in several summer shows over the years. We went backstage to see him, when he was appearing at Bournemouth in 'Lock Up Your Daughters', telling him that I intended to become a comic, as well as congratulating him on his performance. Later, when I was appearing at Bill's local working mens' club, he was in the audience. He invited Jo, myself, and the other artiste, a harmonica player called Johnny Stafford, and his wife, to go back to his house, for supper.

After that we saw quite a lot of him; he came to our flat, we went to see him record a TV sit-com, and he watched my act at Kibworth Lodge. Then he invited us backstage at the London Palladium, where he was appearing with Edward Woodward. Later, he actually booked me for a friend of his, Terry Allen, at the Holiday Inn, in Leicester. The show went very well, and afterwards Bill's wife, Muriel and their daughter, Jane, said how proud they were that I was their friend.

So it was a big disappointment for me when his autobiography, 'The Yo-yo Man', came out and instead of mentioning our friendship, he chose, in my opinion, to make Jo and I sound like a couple of 'Stage-door Johnnies'. He also said in the book that I must have thought that comedy would be easier than band leading! I knew that comedy would be the most difficult thing of all to tackle, but I've always believed that human beings should act out their dreams; it's better to know, than be an 'if only' person.

Whether or not it was inspired by Bill is not for me to speculate, but Alton and Jo began a tradition of entering the names of people who'd offended them, in some way, on a mini loo roll of honour displayed on the wall of their smallest room. As word of it spread any visitors to the flat would rush to check if their name had been added, before taking any refreshment!

At one of Alton's engagements, he and the band would relax around the fireplace of *The New Forest Hotel*, after the cabaret. A television company was also resident there, filming a *Comedy Playhouse*.

One night I overheard the producer, Peter Croft, after a card game, being drunkenly harangued by an actor, Dennis Shaw, with the immortal line: "Den Den wants his bloody sixpence!"

That Christmas 1970, Alton returned to Hastings, to the *White Rock Pavilion*, to appear in pantomime, playing Dame again, for Bunny Baron, taking the role of Queen Wilhemena, in *Puss-in-Boots*. His character was far more Danny La Rue than Clarkson Rose, and Alton wasn't happy about being 'glammed up'.

Strangely enough, I became very self-conscious about my legs. Previously I'd played dame as 'a man in a frock'. I've always had the worst legs in the world. You know the old joke about 'tossed a sparrow for a pair of legs and the sparrow won!'

One matinée, (which, as a reminder, could be more difficult towards the end of the season, if the audience was quite sparse), Sandy Powell, the veteran comic, was in the audience. He obviously thought he'd try and help. Alton was doing the bench gag, where you sit on a bench and a ghost comes out behind you. The only people who don't know, are the people sitting on the bench.

So somebody shouts out: "There's a ghost behind you!" I said (Dame's voice): "Where's the ghost?" Sandy shouted (Lancashire accent): "Behind you." So I did it again. "Where's the ghost?" And again - Sandy Powell's voice – a lot more insistent: "Behind you!" You did it to make the kids shout louder and louder. So again I said: "Where's the ghost?" And Sandy's voice booms out, loud and clear: "Right behind you – you ruddy fool!"

Queen Wilhelmina mixes with the hoi polloi.

99

When the panto finished, Alton went to the *Casino Club* in Port Talbot, boarding with a family, who had a couple of young daughters.

In those days you could play or socialise with children without any problem. I took the two girls from the house, one would be about five, the other seven, into Swansea to buy a pair of trousers – for my stage act. I was measured up for the trousers, in the shop. They had to be altered very slightly, with the intention of going back, before the end of the week, to pick them up. We'd almost got back to Port Talbot, in the car, when the oldest girl turned to me (Welsh accent): "Uncle Alton, that man was just like a lady!" When I thought about it, he had taken rather a long time to measure my inside leg!

I was in bed, on about my third night there, when there was a loud knocking on the door and the landlady calling out (Welsh accent): "Alton, I wonder if you'd like to come into my bedroom?" All the theatrical landlady stories I'd heard over the years came flooding into my head! So, I just paused to gulp down a swig of after-shave, casually sprinted next door, and there was the landlady in her nightie, the woman from next door in her nightie, and five children in their nightclothes. She said: "There's a terrible storm and our husbands are away on nights, so we got together in here. Then we remembered you and we thought you might be frightened, all on your own!"

Alton's showbusiness hours meant that he was out in Port Talbot, during the early hours of the morning, resulting in the same policeman stopping him on three occasions. The third time he said: "Every time I've stopped you, you've said that you're a comedian, but I've never believed you. So I've been down to the club tonight and seen your act - and I *still* don't believe you!"

There were frequent trips to Bristol, appearing at venues, in the city centre and the suburbs: the *Music Hall Tavern*, the *Palm Court Theatre Club*, *Arno's Court, Cadbury Court*, and *The Thirty-nine Steps*. Occasionally, he would do a Sunday night in a working mens' club.

At one venue, I came off and the entertainment secretary said: "Well I can only give you five. I have a points system here – we give you between one and ten; I'm afraid I can only give you five." I did one of those mock-horror sort of things. I said: "For God's sake, surely you can give me more than five? If people get to hear about this, my career will be finished!" There was a long pause, while he thought about it. Eventually he said: "Well you seem a nice bloke. I tell you what I'll do – I'll give you six."

I did a week in London, with Tommy Trinder, for an agent called Johnny Laycock. Tommy had been a massive star. He'd been the comic who'd appeared at the London Palladium more than any other star. We were doing a mixture of clubs and civic halls together. I always remember one joke that he did every night, that made me laugh (gravel-voiced Tommy): "The definition of an alcoholic – a man with a rusty zip and yellow plimsoles!"

Don Maclean remembers working with Tommy Trinder too, on a Sunday night, at the New Theatre, Cardiff. "It was a good audience, and everything was going well. I went on and had a good time doing a short spot. Tommy

Trinder went on and died the most awful death. I thought: 'Well this man was a *giant* of comedy, and should have packed up.' I'm still getting laughs at the moment; when I stop getting laughs I shall pack up."

The same thing happened to Harold Berens: he went down to earning fifteen pounds a night, after being one of the highest paid comics, in the country, in the 40s.

I did a week at 'La Resèrve', with Ivor Emmanuel, the Welsh singer, who'd been such a big hit in the film 'Zulu'. And again, our dear friend, Linda Grant. I remember saying to Linda: "You can't think much of my act: you haven't pinched any of my jokes!"

I'm still amazed that anyone ever booked me!

Chapter 10 –

NIP ALONG TO THE BOOKING OFFICE

It's lovely to be in such a salubrious town, where the Fountain of Youth springs eternal and ladies of eighty take the pill!

They re-booked Alton for a second season in Blackpool, two years later, in May 1971. With him, on the bill were pop singer Garrie Spencer, Gerrie Raymond, the girl singer, and Jack Freedman again as his straight man. Alton and Pete Lindup, the drummer, were back in each other's company, for thirty-odd weeks.

It was a much happier show – no temperamental Latin acts involved. We used to go and eat late at night, at a restaurant called 'The Blue Parrot'. They had a resident pianist playing there, who came up to me one night and said: "I'm so flattered that somebody like Jack Freedman would come in here. He listens, and every time he'll give me a little smile and a wave. When he leaves, he shakes hands and compliments me on my piano playing. Jack is such a fine musician that I consider it the ultimate compliment." What he didn't realise was that Jack sat through the entire meal with earplugs in!

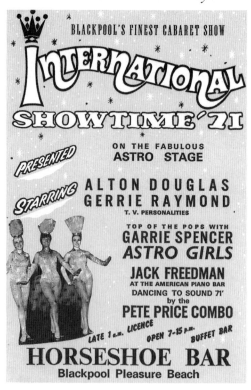

The *Central Pier* at Blackpool had a turbulent season. American singer, Dick Haymes, was topping the bill. Unfortunately, he had a drink problem and was consequently sacked during the run.

I was talking to Jim Couton, a Liverpudlian comic on the bill. He had a dog named Rex. They used to announce "Jim Couton" and Rex

AD and Jack Freedman try to ignore Gerrie Raymond's offer of a free handbag.

would run on first; the whole audience would laugh at a dog running on. He said: "About tea-time, I get me telescope out. I lean out of the bedroom window, and if me name's on the poster, I go to werk!"

Bettina Merson, the producer of our show's great friend was Hilda Baker. She was appearing in a show at the 'Grand Theatre' and she had a penchant for young men. Before the season ended, her chauffeur actually ran off with her furs, jewellery – all sorts of things. I can remember quite vividly, sitting in 'The Lemon Tree' restaurant with Hilda Baker, with her right hand at the top of my left thigh, and her left hand on the right thigh of Freddie Garrity, of 'Freddie and the Dreamers'.

When the season finished Alton toured a club circuit for three weeks with the Canadian singer, Edmund Hockridge. Their agent was Dougie Douglas. Unfortunately, Alton then recommended Edmund to a friend of his, who was just starting up as an agent and was financially inexperienced.

Edmund Hockridge was consequently never paid in full. Sadly, although we'd become quite good friends during our tour together, he wouldn't speak to me again after that. I feel he was totally wrong. If you recommend somebody, you recommend them in good faith. Once the other person makes the decision, the responsibility becomes theirs.

Alton then visited Paul Elliot, in London, who staged pantomimes. He would have preferred the role of principal comic, but the only part Paul had to offer was principal boy; at the time they had begun to break with tradition by hiring men.

He asked me if I could sword-fence – that was the first essential. I said: "Of course I can!" Never having held a sword in my entire life. I've still got the scars on my knuckles to prove it!

In the event, Alton was booked to play principal boy, opposite Helen Shapiro, in a pantomime at the *Forum Theatre*, Billingham, with a first-rate cast. Tom Mennard was the principal comic. Macdonald Hobley, former BBC Television continuity announcer, in its early days, was also on the bill. Alton's mum liked him, because, appearance-wise, he reminded her of Sidney, so she was doubly keen to see the show. There was a brilliant Dame called Sandy Lane, who had previously appeared in the summer show, at the *Derbyshire Miners' Holiday Camp.*

The pantomime was 'Goody Two-Shoes' and I'm playing the straight man. It's been emphasized to me beforehand that I must remember that I'm playing the straight role. But they don't tell me that MacDonald Hobley has broken his ankle during the day. So they pushed him on in a wheelchair. I have to say: "Take him down to the village green and throw him into the duck pond." They push him on, and I said: "Take him down to the village green, throw him in the duck pond – and don't get his wheels rusty!" I was reprimanded for that one.

I played rather a romantic part. I'd grown my hair quite long, and was bombarded with phone calls and gifts by a fan; unfortunately it was a man! There was a show-stopping moment, when we did a schoolroom scene, and I was due to play my trombone. We'd got a trombone in the pit and we'd discovered that MacDonald Hobley and Tom Mennard had both played trombones. So we hired two instruments from a music shop, and we stopped the show, every single night, by four trombones suddenly belting out 'When The Saints Go Marching In' – which had never been heard of before, or since, in a pantomime. And every night we got yells of "More!" You can't imagine the sound of a trombone choir, filling the theatre: it was glorious!

During the course of the show, Alton and Helen sang a duet. A reviewer from the local paper said that it must be the only time in the history of pantomime, when the principal girl had a deeper voice than the principal boy!

Helen Shapiro and the singing eunuch, "Goody Two-Shoes", Forum Theatre, Billingham, 1971.

At the opening week of the 'Talk of the Midlands', in Derby, when we arrived for our band call on the Sunday afternoon, they were still painting the place. Frankie Vaughan was the bill-topper. At the end of the week he said: "I don't seem to have had much chance to talk to you, but I have been very impressed with your act. I think maybe I can put some work your way." Well, maybe next week …?

One of the most bizarre episodes occurred in the early part of 1972. Alton had been booked to appear at a post office social club.

Being nocturnal creatures ourselves, we took it in our stride when a man rang at eleven o'clock at night, to book me. His next call, on some slight pretext the following day, was at midnight. Again, fortunately, I'd just come in from work and he explained that he worked nights as well. But his third call was a week later at 2am. in the morning. It was a night when I'd gone to bed about three hours before. I told him that this was all getting a bit strange and I really didn't have to decide there and then where I wanted the microphone stand placing! That released a torrent of abuse. I snapped and told him to forget the whole thing.

During the next week he wrote to the BBC and told them that I was also working for ATV and vice versa, and then to the tax authorities to say that I was not declaring the majority of my earnings. Coupled with that, we had more abusive telephone calls. I contacted the police, filled in a statement. Although officially at that stage they could do nothing, they did go round to his house to lean on him a bit. Their arrival at his home caused him to rush upstairs, barricade himself in, and throw furniture out of the windows at them. As a consequence, he finished up in Rubery Mental Hospital, with electrodes clamped to his head. As a friend said: "It's best not to 'mix it' with Alton!"

He then spent a week in Leeds, with a comic he didn't get on well with at all - Lennie Bennett.

In fact, I moved out of the digs after about four days, because we just didn't hit it off – he seemed to be continually trying to goad me into arguments. But he did give me a line, which helped me later, when I decided to give up comedy. He said: "There's nothing more undignified than a forty-five-year-old comic who hasn't made it." Fortunately, I was only thirty-two at the time!

It was around now that Alton met Don Maclean. He went to his house in Selly Oak and Don visited the flat. Don recalls: "I went up there a number of times, and we talked about comedy. With the type of material he was doing, he needed to be working a certain audience. He would probably have fitted in better now – where people go and work universities. Although I must admit, that would frighten me to death – to attempt to work for the younger generation!

"We started at the same time. There were several young 'comics' in Birmingham. Dave Ismay, who is now my agent, was one of them; Malcolm

Stent and Jasper Carrott came that much later, although we're all 'much-of-a-muchness' age-wise. But people were talking about me and Alton, at the same time. Clubs, of course, were enormous, at that time. Then there were the older, established comics in Birmingham, Bob Hatch, Dick Lawler and people like that. You could become – not that I ever wanted to be – but you *could* become a club star, so that they'd put your name up outside the club, and people would say: 'Oh I want to go and see him.' "

Don is of the 'sock-it-to-them' school of comedy, whereas Alton's act had a more 'throw-away' or 'laid-back' air about it: if you laugh that's great, but if you don't – I can take it – (probably the opposite to what he was really thinking!)

I don't think Don liked working the clubs any more than I did, but, with hindsight, he was a little better suited. He did something extremely generous. He said: "The one thing you're lacking is good publicity," and he recommended me to his own press relations man, George Bartram. Now when you think about it, it was an act of extreme generosity, because I could have been taking away work from him, particularly locally, as another Birmingham comic. I joined George Bartram for the next fifteen years, and he and his right-hand man, Robert Holmes, were responsible for much of the attention and good work that I got. Over the years, they'd represented people as diverse as Alan Ladd the film-star, Tony Bennett, Morecambe and Wise, Dickie Henderson, Vince Hill, Little and Large, Joe Loss – a great many big names.

Don comments: "Alton was always very much a thinker, wasn't he? He was also a man who was never that satisfied with his performance – even when it went well. I talked to you earlier about consistency. I think anybody starting out in any profession has this problem: one day you'll be good, another day you'll be incredibly bad. I died some horrendous 'deaths', in all sorts of places, for various reasons. But I got some good advice. Bob Monkhouse once said to me: 'There's no such thing as a bad audience, there's only a bad performance.' He added: 'Now that's not true, but that's what you must believe if you're going to progress.' But I think maybe Alton took that a stage further, and blamed *himself* too much. He was very intellectual: he used to do some great gags - that his audiences weren't quite ready for."

Mike Gancia, the comedy magician, explained that sometimes Alton's jokes went 'over the top' of the audience's head, a view that Don confirms: "*Often*, but I remember seeing him with all professional blokes. The material that he was doing was 'thinking man's' material, and he went really well. But I seem to remember he came off *then*, and wasn't that happy; if there'd been more of an opportunity to work better 'gigs' he'd probably have been quite a star.

"I wouldn't want to go back to working mens' clubs now. But that's what we were doing, because that's where the work was, in those days. You were working to people who didn't bother to read a newspaper, so if you went on and did something topical – something that had happened in the news that day – they'd all look at you, because they wouldn't have a clue what you were talking about!"

Frequently such audiences might be chatting amongst themselves, or waiting for a particular act to appear. Don comments: "I used to make 'em have it you see: I was loud and brash, but I think Alton was much gentler than me - 'cause he's a gentler sort of person. I always thought he'd become a comedy writer." Alton eventually branched out in precisely that way and wrote for over thirty TV programmes, although it was never his sole occupation.

On the subject of nervousness among comedians, Alton recalls a conversation between himself and Don, when they were both appearing at the *Cresta*. Don made the comment that he'd never been nervous in his life, to which Alton replied: "Haven't you? If I'd got to go on there now, I'd be in a state of absolute terror!"

Don explains: "If I was, I'd have given it up. Relatively early on in my career, I knew both Roy Hudd and Mike Yarwood. Now Roy Hudd was incredibly nervous before he went on, and started smoking because of that; he smokes ever such a lot of cigarettes and wishes that he didn't."

Mike Gancia revealed that in the early days of his career, Jim Davidson was, allegedly, very nervous. Don comments: "Was he? I don't know that he is now. Mike Yarwood's life, of course, was completely ruined because of his nervousness. He used to be physically sick, just before he was going on, particularly for television performances. He'd be in the loo - in the most terrible state. And of course that's what started him drinking, and everything else.

"So I made up my mind that it wasn't worth it. Also, I think you've got to divorce the two sides of your life really: your performing side and the rest of it. Even now, I sometimes have a bad night, but there are two factors that keep me on the straight and narrow: if I go there tonight and die the most *terrible* death, it's not going to make a pound's difference to the income that I end up with at the end of the year, is it really? It's going to make no difference at all. Secondly, when I come back here, the wife and kids are going to love me just as much as they did when I walked out of the door!"

Don differentiates between the two types of comedian: those who are naturally funny and those who 'do' funny. "I suppose the best way is to give you some examples. Tommy Cooper used to walk on stage and everybody would fall about laughing. Les Dawson used to pull a funny face, and everybody laughed. Frank Carson is just jumping up and down all the while and saying (mimics) 'Ha-ha, ha-ha-ha, it's the way I tell them!' Ken Dodd is a *very* funny man: he walks on stage: 'How tickled I ham!' and everybody... So those are funny people.

"I don't think I ever looked like a comedian, neither did Alton. But I don't think that made things more difficult. I used to try to be funny with everything I'd got. In other words, when I was telling a joke, hopefully the joke itself, or the material I was using was funny. But then, I was illustrating it: by vocal dexterity, accents, facial expressions, and by body movements. I was 'of my time' - and Alton was of the *same* time.

"As Alton observed, I was Jerry Lewis for a long time - that was something that came through from my school days. But then I became influenced by Ken Dodd, I think, Bob Monkhouse, Bruce Forsyth. Although Bruce Forsyth never had a style of his own - Bruce was always somebody else. I reckon it took me seven years to achieve a style, and then I hit on a style that was me - it was my Evolutionary Period!

"I think Alton has definitely found his niche now, in what he's doing. Had he continued with the comedy – there were a lot of people interested in him you know - local television, and that sort of thing. If he'd have continued he would probably have progressed, and maybe he'd still have been doing some kind of comedy, or presentation work.

"Comedy is *generational*. The people I would entertain best are a roomful of people between – say – fifty-five and sixty-five - that's a generation surrounding the age that I am now - all of whom went to school in Birmingham! You know what I mean? People will only laugh at things that are within their experience. So if my experience and your experience are exactly the same, then we're going to have the same sense of humour!

"Alton has always been very generous towards his contemporaries. There's nothing worse than a comic of a 'certain age', forever saying: 'Look at these young comics, they're doing this and they're doing that.' We've had our go, particularly as far as the media are concerned; let them have *theirs*. If, because of what we learned twenty years ago, we're still able to turn that into financial reward – then what more do we want? The last thing I want to do is be on some stand-up show late at night on Channel Four; I can't imagine anything worse!"

One of the things I liked about Don, (apart from thinking that he was an excellent comic), was that when he broke through in the business, and played the 'Palladium', he put an advert on the front of 'The Club Herald', thanking all the working mens' club secretaries who'd endured his many 'deaths' through the years, and enabled him to reach that level. I thought that was lovely –' cocking a snook'!

We've reached the summer of 1972. Dougie Douglas, (no relation) who'd previously used Alton for *The Edmund Hockridge Show*, now booked him for a summer season with *The Temperance Seven*, at the *Pier Theatre*, Shanklin.

Pete Lindup, the drummer from Blackpool, hadn't got a season, so I managed to fix him the summer, with me. We shared a large flat with the organist with the show, John Garr. He was a delightful Scotsman, and would turn up every so often wearing his kilt. At one matinée, to try and liven up a fairly dead audience, I said: "Go on then John, give us a twirl!" So he climbed on to the organ stool and he twirled. Now unfortunately, that day, he'd decided to be an authentic Scot! And a horrified crowd saw more of the Isle of Wight that they would have wished!

Being nosy, Pete and I opened a drawer in John's desk, while he was out, and there were hundreds of photographs. We realised that every time he stepped out onto the seafront, instead of explaining to the seaside photographers, who were waiting to snap people, that he was a resident, he posed for a picture.

John had an excellent command of the English language and was always pulling me up about mispronunciations. I did a joke about a tortoise, and he reminded me, of course, that it was pronounced 'tortus'. I could feel his gimlet eyes boring into me, if I made a mistake of any sort. So I thought at one point I ought to sing: 'Fish-eye Were A Rich Man'!

After the season ended, we heard that John was standing as a Liberal candidate for the Isle of Wight. Sadly for democracy in general – and the House of Commons in particular – he didn't make it. I think the House would have benefited from a healthy dose of eccentricity, and his general anarchic sense of fun. I've always been drawn to eccentrics. I particularly like Whitney Balliet's definition of the word, when he was describing the jazz instrumentalist, Pee Wee Russell, he said: "Eccentricity – the kindest form of defiance."

The cast of The Temperance Seven Show (minus Vivian Stanshall). I'm in the centre next to Pete Lindup. John Garr is the white-haired gent.

Speaking of eccentrics, the lead singer with the show, the famous man with the white suit, had left *The Temperance Seven* and been replaced by Vivian Stanshall, a well-known figure in the pop world. He was an ex-member of the *Bonzo Dog Doo-Da Band*.

I had one of the most exquisite thirty minutes of my life, one afternoon, in the theatre. A party of deaf and dumb children came in. Vivian abandoned the spot he was going to do and did half an hour of pure, exquisite mime. I'd never ever been so entranced in my life.

I said to him afterwards: "You are a supreme clown." And he said: "That's the highest compliment that anyone's ever paid me." I was very sad to find out what a tragic end Vivian came to - descending into a drug-induced haze and an early death, in a fire. It was all so sad, because I honestly believe that Vivian was the only real genius I've ever met.

Pete Lindup explains that, because business was so bad, in order to encourage customers, he and Alton used to do what was called 'spiel' - at the end of the pier. "That's sitting in the ticket office with a microphone saying: '7.15 tonight at the *Pier Theatre, The Temperance Seven Show*.' I did it for about an hour-and-a-half in the morning, then Alton took over. We did the same in the afternoon. We got rather good at this, because we could actually 'pinpoint' somebody going by; they couldn't see you, but you could see them. If we saw an elderly couple going by, we'd say: 'Half-price for senior citizens tonight. (Raising voice) Half-price tickets! Turn right at the pier gates, you can't miss it!' Or children going by – 'Half-price tickets for children!'

"Alton was waiting to take over from me one afternoon. We were just watching people coming through the turnstile. I was saying: 'Tickets still available – come along to the booking office.' A girl went through the turnstile, and it was the time when girls were burning their bras. I don't know if you remember that? Well this girl had burnt hers!

"The wind lifted the top of her blouse and exposed... Alton said: 'Nipple,' - and I said: 'Nipple?' – (through the microphone). 'Erm, erm – Nip along to the booking office for tickets for tonight's show!' She giggled. Apparently, about six months later, he was doing a cabaret somewhere, and a girl came up to him and said: 'You don't remember me, do you?' He said: 'No - I'm sorry.' She said: 'They were *my* nipples!' "

Every Thursday night Alton performed late night at the *Metropole Hotel*, Ventnor, for the proprietor, Mildred Mastern. It was just a cabaret spot – nothing extraordinary about it. But after about the fifth or sixth week, a very irate Mildred complained to him: "You've lost me two customers!"

I racked my brain. There'd been children in that night, which was very unusual. I'd tried to think of a childrens' joke. The only one I could think of was:

'Two gingerbread men met in the street. One said: "How are you?" And the other one said: "I mustn't crumble!"

*She said: "That was the joke. These two men were very offended by that – and they booked out." I said: "Hang on a minute. Were the two gentlemen sharing a room?" She said: "Well, yes." I said: "Were they slightly effeminate?" She said: "Yes." I said: "Well the only thing I can think of is that they must have mis-heard me, because 'ginger beer' is cockney rhyming slang for 'queer'. I was telling a joke about ginger**bread** men." To this day, that's the only explanation I can think of!*

During the course of the season, on several occasions, a fellow called Reuben Martin came backstage and complimented me on my act. He was part of an act called 'The De Milles', a strongman act, and he also choreographed fight sequences for films and West End shows. Rueben was very keen on my act. He and his wife, Beryl, went out with me on two or three occasions after the show. I said to him one day: "Look, you're so complimentary about my act, but tell me what's wrong with what I do?" He said: "I don't want to, because it might destroy you." I said: "Well I want you to tell me." He said: "I love your comedy, I love your timing, but you want to work even prouder than you do. Comics these days have no presence." (This was in the era of 'The Comedians'). "They shuffle on and they hold the mike-stand. You're tall and you're straight-backed. Work from the waist, like a ballet dancer: work proud. Height controls an audience. Swivel from the hips, wear built-up shoes: make yourself even taller. Cut out all the duff bookings and remember, every act has to find its level."

Alton took his advice and by the end of the season had decided not to do any more working mens' clubs, fired by the realisation - 'I hate them - and in most cases they don't like me anyway.' So he rang his various contacts, saying: "That's it!"

It's funny how you get the inspiration - that gives you the strength to do these things.

'The Temperance Seven' didn't prove to be any draw at all during that season, and they left the show about a month early. We re-named the show 'Ship Ahoy' and put a little variety show on. We packed the theatre most nights, for the rest of the season.

Among Alton's unique clown collection, there is one (looking rather like Max Wall) that stands in splendid isolation, on his study windowsill. It's of the large, heavy, black-and- white variety, and - as his co-writer suspected - thereby hangs a tale...

By the time the season came to an end, the cornetist- bandleader, Cephas Howard, had bought a pottery on the island. On the last night, he gave me a model of a tramp clown and then he broke the mould, to make it unique. Which reminds me of other celebrity items we've temporarily acquired. One was an excellent painting of a clown, by Vince Hill, which he loaned to me for six months. He always mentioned that it was not a self-portrait, but I don't agree. Probably the most priceless item was George Formby's scrapbook, compiled by George and his wife Beryl. By this time it was actually the property of Alan Randall, and what a fascinating glimpse it gave into a comic's career. (Going into Formby mode): "Turned out nice again. Eeh – can't catch me - he-he!"

The Temperance Seven was suing Dougie Douglas, after the season ended, because they were still owed several weeks' money. Alton was also owed for three or four weeks, so his accountant advised him to seek advice from a Commissioner of Oaths.

I sat in the commissioner's office and said: "Is there any point in my going on with this?" He said: "Well, I'm afraid I can't give you any advice of any sort at all. But would you like to go and sit behind me?" So I sat behind him, facing the wall, back-to-back. He said: "I'm afraid the man has no money at all – it's absolutely pointless. Right – you can come back now!" I went and sat back on the other side of the desk, facing him again. He said: "That will be a pound please. I have a drawer here. My grandchildren come and visit me at the weekend and I give them some pocket money." So he dropped the pound into the drawer, and that was the end of that!

Motoring through Oxfordshire, en route to a 'one-nighter', Alton spotted a beautifully painted sign at the side of the road. It said: 'Woodstock needs a bypass.' Underneath it was a little tiny sign, badly written, with the paint dripping off the side, ostensibly put together by a numbskull - except that it said: 'And Snoopy wants one too!'

Another of my favourites was an official council notice, (in the middle of Balsall Heath, Birmingham's notorious red-light district), which read: 'No ball games allowed.'

I worked with Roy Hudd on several occasions. He was the only 'name' who ever asked comics for their photographs, no matter where they were on the bill, because he collects them. So there he was, asking me, a support act, for a photograph. The stage crew said to me: "We've taken a lot of trouble over making this lit-up sign for Roy. It will be behind him during his act. It says his name. Can you do a little 'fill-in- spot', immediately prior to his act, so that we can lower the sign behind you? Then it will be ready for him." Well, I forgot all about this, introduced him and on he walked. And there was this great cranking noise behind him. (Mimics excruciating sound). Of course he made a few gags about it. He never let me forget it

Roy recalls those days, in his own, inimitable style:

"As I write these few words, I'm gazing at a photograph Alton signed for me when we first met. How attractive those sepia prints look these days! How well I remember that meeting. I, of course, was a child star, while he was headlining in *Veterans of Variety*. (He was Dan Leno's toy boy). I like to think that my introducing him to, what at the time was a technological marvel, had quite an influence on his subsequent career. Until I showed him just what a microphone was, he had *shouted* his jokes and his songs. He had even shouted his books, until I put a pen in his hand!"

Geoffrey Thompson, millionaire owner of the *Blackpool Pleasure Beach* and the *Casino*, offered Alton a third season for the following year in Blackpool. But he declined the offer, preferring to advance his career, rather than return to old ground.

I was asked to judge a talent contest at the 'Hunter's Moon' in Castle Bromwich. My fondest memory of that night is the sight of my fellow judge, the comedian Dave Ismay, being pinned against the wall afterwards, by the father of one of the losing acts.

Meanwhile, back at Dominic Drive, a harsher existence lurked, just on the periphery, of the ephemeral world of showbusiness...

We had our own illegal immigrant. Actually, he was a tramp that we discovered, sleeping in the bushes, outside the flats. He turned out to be completely harmless and was known to everybody as 'The Bottle Man': he was interested in collecting them, rather than their contents. What touched me most was the alarm clock by the side of his sleeping bag! At Christmas, I'd caught Jo sneaking out to leave some turkey and some mince pies for him. Some weeks later, in the road outside, there was a screech of brakes and the sound of shattering glass – and that was the end of another chapter.

Sadly, that was to be the first of two deaths, in a short period of time – but the second one would hit me in a far more personal way.

Chapter 11 -

THE GOLDEN SLOT

On the way home I was stopped by a policeman. It's most unfair – I blew into his bag, but he wouldn't pull my cracker.

I was getting quite a lot of my best work at that time from the agent Billy Lowndes. He rang me to say that Dave Ismay had decided that he no longer wanted to do the studio warm-ups for 'The Golden Shot'. They were stuck at the last minute. Could I go along?

They'd already tried out another comic, who'd had a few drinks in the bar beforehand, because warm-ups can be quite nerve-wracking - particularly if you're new to it. He'd walked out onto the floor and fallen flat on his face! So they needed somebody who would prove to be more reliable. Of course, I didn't realise that it would lead to almost a thousand.

June Lowndes explains: "He wasn't signed solely to us, so some bookings would be personal engagements that he arranged himself. Our connection with him was mainly via *The Golden Shot* and bookings at the *Cresta*. However, doing warm-ups for *The Golden Shot* would have helped him a lot, to secure other work; they'd know that he must be up to a certain standard, because you get a mixed bag in the audience, and you've got to go among them. You've got to go up and down the aisles and still be talking – and go back to the stage again. It's not an easy job at all, because they're all nattering and they've come to see Bob Monkhouse – or whoever the big star is."

According to Linda Grant: "Bob Monkhouse is not popular with everyone. Some people don't understand what a nice person he is. You try to explain to them, but it's quite difficult, if they're biased. He has a great similarity with Alton, I think: a sharp intellect and a mind like a computer – that can pull a gag out of nowhere. One of the things that Bob did was to challenge the audience to pick out a subject, and he would tell a gag on that subject. I believe that Alton would be very good at that, because he must have a huge 'comedic brain'."

Alton has a collection of albums containing newspaper cuttings and other memorabilia relating to his career, beginning during this *Golden Shot* period, in the early 1970s, and continuing into this day. Don Maclean recalls: "Alton started doing a tremendous amount of television warm-ups. He was very good at it, because that was more than comedy: it was being a host, it was cajoling people, it was encouraging people – telling them what they'd got to do, et cetera."

"He did hundreds," recalls June. "That particular show went on for years. He'd go out and people would be trying to find their seats - messing about. The cameramen would be lining up the different marks for people to stand on. There'd be people walking about behind him – and all over the place. He had to just stand there and do it. You see, he gave it a nice friendly atmosphere. You can't go on: 'Oh, look who I am!' You've got to be: 'Oh look who you are – you're a nice lot!' You've got to warm to them first– they haven't got to warm to you, and then you've got to *get* them to warm to you.

"He was extremely smart; we'd talk about wardrobe to him while he was waiting to go on. He'd tell us what a bargain he'd got from *Rackhams* or somewhere like that! He could buy something at a really reasonable price, because he'd got the time in the day to go mooching around the town. He'd wear things that other people couldn't – because of his height. Because it was for the stage, he'd just get away with it, and look extremely smart in it. His presentation was *very* good indeed."

In addition to warming-up 'The Golden Shot', I also appeared on the show several times. The first time, supposedly caught doing a warm-up: it was deliberate; they were showing what went on before the show, and I knew all about it in advance, but it wasn't supposed to look like that. As a consequence of that, I got a letter from a scriptwriter called Gordon Stretch.

According to Alton, the gist of the letter was: "I like your timing, but your material's not very good." Gordon recalls: "He responded by telephone and invited me over to see him. I started writing for him regularly." Gordon would write about twenty jokes, and Alton selected the most suitable ones. "He'd tell me what context he wanted the various jokes for, and the differing subjects. Sometimes it was for general things, but mostly it was 'I want a joke to go in here, or there,' to fit in with a particular theme. These were for his act, which he was constantly updating.

"He used to particularise," explains Gordon. "He'd say, 'I want something to lead from one particular joke to another.' We'd discuss them on the phone. I'd tell him what I'd got and then he would give his reaction. If it wasn't quite what he wanted, we'd both work on it separately, then revise our ideas again on the phone and work them out between us. With some of them it would be a joint effort - not all of them by any means. I would get back to him with my suggestions for revised versions, in the light of his comments.

"Most of the jokes had to be at least of a specified nature. But some (fortunately a minority) had to serve as a natural lead from one topic that Alton had been following, to another topic. This was always a hard nut to crack, bearing in mind that the gag had to be strong." Gordon wrote for Alton's cabaret act from 1973 to March 1986.

After that initial appearance on the show, I was driving down the motorway and I stopped at a restaurant. The girl behind the counter did a 'double-take' and she said to me: *"You're him, aren't you?"* I could hardly deny it: *"Yes, I am."* And she said, with enormous sympathy, *"Aah."*

The show was live, so we'd got to time it exactly: in and out and off, not only the opening, but in the commercial breaks too. You had to be careful, warming up, that you didn't use material that was too strong - that killed the show to follow. Bear in mind that the warm-up comic could use tried and tested material, but the show would be working gags that had never been tried before and that may, or may not work. So you'd got to underplay. What most of us did was to write little routines that would work purely for warm-ups – and that would be it.

In one respect it represented us badly, because when big stars came with a retinue of people – London agents, managers, people like that, if they weren't too imaginative – and some of the bigger people exhibited the imagination of a coat-hanger, they thought that was all you could do! So they found the material quite weak and didn't realise that we were being 'special' for that job.

One or two of the more enlightened people spotted exactly what we were doing. When I warmed-up 'New Faces', Arthur Askey came to me after the show, absolutely delighted with what I did – and said so – in no uncertain terms. I wrote to him the next day and thanked him. That started a correspondence that lasted, right up until his death.

ARTHUR ASKEY

11 Abbots House
St. Mary Abbots Terrace
London, W.14

8.4.74.

Dear Alton

     Many thanks for your letter - much appreciated.   And may I say how impressed I was with your "warm-up". Where do you get your gags?   I had only heard one of them before - and that's a record.

     Am just off on a Cruise, so won't see you for a few weeks.   Try and help the poor sod who has to take my place!

          All the bestest.
           Yours aye.

Arthur

Alton Douglas. Esq.

The terrible irony about Arthur Askey was that he'd often finish his letters by saying: 'Remember, it's the legs that go first!' Tragically, he finished up having both of his legs amputated.

One of the guests at 'The Golden Shot' was Granada Television producer, Johnny Hamp, who offered me the chance, after seeing me work, to appear on 'The Comedians'. Bob's scriptwriter, Wally Malston, overheard this conversation and said that he would happily write some material for me – free – if, once I became a regular, I would employ him as a scriptwriter. But I turned down the chance, because I felt I would be completely lost in this welter of northern aggression, with my quiet sort of throwaway humour.

When I did the Val Doonican series, in Borehamwood, I was warming-up lots of other shows by this time. Peter Dulay, who was the originator of 'Candid Camera', watched me and said afterwards: "I'm quite sure that I can get you quite a lot of television work." Sadly, the very week that I was due to go and see him, he had a heart attack, so that didn't materialise.

I used to warm-up 'The Golden Shot' at the ATV studios in Birmingham, then Jo would drive like stink down to Borehamwood. She honestly never went over the speed limit. The greatest ad-lib of my entire life came out of Borehamwood – and I was not responsible for it. As we came out after the show, we got to the barrier, and it was one of those where a man leans on the end and a bar lifts up. As we reached it, a fox shot from the bushes, straight under the barrier. Now this fellow, as a pure reflex action, dives like a goalkeeper; he's obviously been told to keep everything and everyone out of the studio. So he dives full-length. Of course he misses, stands up, brushes the dirt from his trousers and says: "What the —- was that?" And Jo, as quick as a flash said: "I think it was Basil Brush's warm-up comic!"

Alton did the warm-ups for *New Faces* at the *ATV* studios, and sat in on one or two of the auditions that they held, at places like *La Dolce Vita*.

During one of these, the comic John Paul Jones told the audience that he'd managed to get there from Bristol, despite the road blocks set up by Alton Douglas! But the funniest line came from an elderly comic, whose name I never knew. He weaved his way onto the stage, through all these amplifiers and guitars and loudspeakers. He got to the front and he said: "Don't take any notice of me. They've just sent me out here while the group clear up their debt!"

Incidentally, after two series of 'New Faces' I gave up the show because I couldn't stand the sight of people being 'shredded' in public. I moved to 'Lunchtime with Wogan' and appeared on the programme several times. Terry Wogan was particularly generous. If it said 'Tex' or whatever my name was supposed to be, in a sketch or whatever, he'd always use my real name, to give me maximum exposure. After every show he would knock on the dressing room door and thank me for the warm-ups. In fact, one of Maurice and Gwen's fondest memories was having lunch at ATV. Terry sat with us, despite the fact that some of the 'big-wigs' wanted him to go and have lunch with them.

Alton was often asked to go out and find contestants to appear on the programme. One particular week, he went to the Registry Office, at the top of Bridge Street, and selected a suitable couple. Terry announced them. In walked, sight unseen, a husband with four children in tow, and a heavily pregnant wife. Terry said (tongue-in-cheek) "If you ever do that again, I'll have you straight out – but I'll do it on the show!"

Maurice says: "I went to that particular show, and they kept putting the camera on me. I didn't know this. One of the fellows who worked with me was sitting at home watching, and having his lunch. When we returned to work he said: "You've been watching me all morning, at work, and now you're sitting there watching me on the ruddy television!"

One programme would go out live and we'd record another for the following week. One time we were talking in the Green Room, in between the programmes, about writing gags. There was an American scriptwriter, Jimmy Coghill, who looked and sounded like Edward G. Robinson. He claimed that he could write a joke about any subject – instantly: you give him the subject – he'd write the gag. So I said to him: "Right – helicopter!" In less time than it takes to move from a comma to the rest of the sentence, he said:"How is it that when a man gets out of a helicopter, he always walks like Groucho Marx?" Then the other writer on the show, Charles Hart said: "Go on then – try me!" So I said: "Trombone!" And he said: "I always carry a trombone around with me – you never know when you're going to meet a parade!"

Terry Wogan explains: "Warm-up is the toughest job in television. The audience is more interested in the equipment and the cameras than they are with what the man in front is talking about. Warm-up is the most under-rated of the arts and Alton Douglas is one of its greatest practitioners."

"I was sat in *The Golden Shot* audience one day," recalls June, "and suddenly a man got up from the audience and started to go down the stairs towards Bob Monkhouse. Bob never moved a muscle and two security men threw themselves at this man's ankles, brought him down before he came into view of the camera, and dragged him off. But Bob didn't move. He could have had a knife, acid or anything, because you get some peculiar people in this world don't you?"

Terry Wogan.

Alton wrote some jokes for Don Maclean when he was on *The Golden Shot*. "It was while I was still living in Selly Oak," explains Don. "It was a live show, so if anybody dropped out, I was the first person that they used to ring up! Alton and I worked out some 'cross-over' gags. Bob was on, talking, and I walked across behind him, two or three times – literally crossing over behind him, from one side of Camera Left to Camera Right. Bob's talking to the camera, and I walk behind him, doing something. So then Bob would turn round and say: 'so-and-so, so-and-so, so-and-so.' We had the old gag, you know – the cabbage on a lead! I walked behind. He said: 'What are you doing?' I said: 'I'm taking this dog for a walk.' He said: 'That's not a dog, it's a cabbage.' And I said: 'Oh, my mistake, I thought it was a Collie!' "

Bernard Manning also appeared on 'The Golden Shot'. I said: "Would you like to come on in the warm-up and just say hello to the people?" He said: "Sod off!" He got a little way down the corridor and then turned around and said: "Were you trying to help me?" I said: "Yes, I thought if you came on in the warm-up you'd then be three-dimensional, an old friend, instead of someone they'd just seen on the screen." He said: "Oh, I'm ever so sorry. I thought you were trying to undermine me. I'm so used to working with 'The Comedians', where everybody's at each other's throats. Will you come over and see me at 'La Dolce Vita' this week? Be my guest. There'll be a bottle of champagne for you and two tickets at the door."

I went along that week to see his show and took my friend Andy Wade. We had a front table; there was a bottle of champagne for us. Halfway through the act Bernard said: "There's a comedian here who I'd like you to meet – a local comic, who was very kind to me. Please give a big hand for Alton Douglas." As I sat down he said, "He and George Roper are about as funny as a burning hospital!"

Fortunately, there's a 'rider' to this story. A couple of years later, Alton was walking down Broad Street, in Birmingham.

A 'limo' pulled up alongside me, and Bernard Manning's head popped out of the back window. (Imitates him): " 'allo, where are you going?" "I've just come out of George Bartram's office." (Bernard): "We're going to Pebble Mill Studios – I'm singing with the Radio Orchestra. Can you give us directions?" Well, I tried to explain, but it turned out that they were running late, and the route was a bit complex. So, after a promise that he'd pay my return taxi fare (forgiving soul that I am), I jumped into the car and took them to the BBC. Now, this is where the petty-minded side of my nature comes into play, because with Bernard's ten pound note stuffed into my back pocket, I walked the three miles back to my car - saying every few yards - "Touché, Bernard!"

Neville King the ventriloquist was a guest, with his old man dummy. Alton tapped on his dressing room door because he'd never met him before, so he wanted to introduce himself.

He opened the door and launched into: "It's only a lump of wood with a few bits of cloth around it; it's not a real person you know! I never think of it as a person – it's just a dummy!" I said: "Hello – I'm Alton Douglas!"

At the time, they were having a lot of bomb scares. "I think they were people playing 'stupid idiots'," recalls June Lowndes, "because we had to keep coming out of the studios and standing on the side of the road. Anita Harris was on the show one day, wearing a very flimsy dress – beautifully dressed as always – and it was a very cold day. We all had to run out. Everyone thought it was someone with a grievance: possibly someone who'd been sacked from there. They had to go through the studios with a fine

Geoff and June.

tooth-comb before we could go back in. It was a bit frightening because you didn't know whether a bomb really *would* go off; we started to laugh about it in the end, because it happened so many times."

Another June, June Hooley, was formerly one half of a duo, with her singing partner, Geoff Farnall. The couple worked on *The Golden Shot* for seven years, fulfilling a range of functions, such as standing in for contestants and adjudicating scores. She provides another tale: "Stephane Grappelli (the jazz violinist) and Sacha Distel were guests on the show. We received a warning call and as usual, the studio was evacuated to the road outside, in Bridge Street. All our audience, of around 250 people, stood along the pavement, and these two superstars, with their precious instruments, (Sacha was an award-winning jazz guitarist, long before he was a singer), went along the line of audience and technicians 'busking' and entertaining everyone."

We had about six hoaxes altogether. By a strange coincidence there was a bomb scare the second time that Stephane appeared on 'The Golden Shot'. In some of my flights-of-fancy moments, I've often wondered if it was just coincidence that it was twice with Stephane Grappelli. During the Second World War, when it was first announced that Stephane Grappelli and Django Reinhardt had recorded 'The Marseillaise', in London, there was an outcry: the French thought it sacrilegious that there should be a 'swing' version of their national anthem. But, when it was released, there was so much 'joie de vivre' and obvious patriotism about it, it became an enormous hit and a great morale booster. I just wondered if the bomb incidents were connected with someone who had a grudge! It's an interesting 'off-the-wall' theory of mine; it probably had nothing to do with it at all!

Anyway, everybody was out in the street. I looked around; just a small group of us had remained inside the building: Stephane, Len Skeet his bass player, Denny

Wright and Diz Disley - the guitarists - and me. I said: "Well, if I'm going to be blown up I'm going to be in very exalted company, aren't I? With some of my favourite jazz musicians of all time!" He said, (imitates Stephane's voice): "Do you want us to play a tune for you?" I said: "Oh, yes please!" He said: "Gentlemen, Crazy Rhythm!" And they played 'Crazy Rhythm' just there – four crazy rhythm musicians and me! In an empty studio, that's going up at any minute. I thought, 'This is as near to Paradise as I'm ever going to get!'

Speaking of coincidences, how about this? Les Cocks – the producer of the show, Dickie Leeman – the director, and Alton, all shared the same birthday --January 22nd.

Speaking of Aquarians, the actor, John Taylor, who was Peter Sellers' understudy in the Pink Panther films, rang me once to say: "I know I'm supposed to meet you at one o'clock, but I may be two minutes late." Only someone with our birth-sign would be as precise as that.

Still on the subject of bomb scares, during the rehearsals for *New Faces*, someone spotted an odd-looking case propped against the wall.

They sent for the Security Man and he backed us all against the opposite wall. He's standing there with his arms outstretched, keeping us all back. He's talking on his two-way radio: "I don't know Charlie, there's a suspicious-looking case here. We'll have to get the studio clear." And right in the middle of it, the piano tuner, Ron Barrows, walked round the corner, picked up his case, said, "Cheerio everybody," – and walked off!

Ron told Alton a couple of tales, from his days at the *Birmingham Hippodrome*. He was tuning the piano, when the Danish pianist-humorist Victor Borge, famous for his 'phonetic punctuation', walked in.

He could sense that he was being closely watched, as he cranked the wires and clinked the keys. Then Victor Borge suddenly asked the manager: "Vhat is this man doing?" He said: "He's tuning the piano for your act tonight, Mr. Borge." "No he's not – he's doing my act!"

Later, the maestro said to him: "How old is this piano?" Impishly, Ron replied: "A hundred years old today guv'nor." Victor Borge, without a moment's hesitation, walked over to the keyboard and played: "Happy birthday to you, happy birthday to you, happy birthday dear piano…"

Speaking of theatres, Derek Salberg told Alton that when he owned the *Alexandra Theatre*, he booked Marlene Dietrich for a week.

Before the rehearsal, she called him to her dressing room and demanded that the hook on the back of the door be lowered six inches. She said that he was to send someone out to her car when the job had been completed, then she'd come back and finish her band call. It was – and she did. The next morning, when he arrived at the theatre, he found her on her hands and knees, scrubbing the stage. As soon as that was completed, she got a pair of stepladders and moved the lighting to her satisfaction. He realised then the ploy: having established exactly who was in charge, she immediately set to and made everything perfect for her show. For the rest of the week, there wasn't the slightest sign of temperament.

Derek was a shy, diffident character, who somehow always seemed to handle things well. When I mentioned his book, 'My Love Affair with the Theatre', on a radio programme, 'Pete Murray's Open House', he rang and profusely thanked me. At the launch of my uncle, Victor J. Price's new book, 'Birmingham Theatres, Concert and Music Halls', Derek came to the house and charmed everyone. As a consequence, I was able to recommend him to my publisher, who then published his book on cricket – another of Derek's great love affairs.

In May of 1973, I was voted the most promising comedian in the Midlands. Unfortunately, I failed to fulfill that promise. We were presented with the prizes at the 'Cresta Club'. It was about the eighth time that I'd appeared there for a week.

They asked Norman Vaughan, who had now begun to compère *The Golden Shot*, to come along and present the prizes. He sat at the table – Jo sat opposite him. Afterwards, when they got home, she said: "Look at my shins!" They'd been kicked black and blue; poor old Norman had got so nervous at the idea of having to get up on the stage.

On page 269 of Bob Monkhouse's book, 'Crying With Laughter', he pays me a very nice compliment, but sadly, tells a story that didn't actually involve him at all, because by this time, he was no longer fronting 'The Golden Shot'. So, for the record, I'll tell you the real story behind it. In June of that year, I was appearing at Ashton Court - again in Bristol. I was woken up at seven on the Friday morning, 15 June, by a call to the digs and a voice that said: "This is the 'News of the World' here. I understand that you're compèring 'The Golden Shot' on Sunday." I said: "Look – I don't know who you are, but I didn't get to bed 'til four o'clock." And I slammed the phone down.

That afternoon, I went to the pictures with comedienne, Ruth Saxon. There was an announcement over the system: "Would Alton Douglas please

Norman Vaughan.

go to the manager's office?" It was 'The Golden Shot' office, to say that Norman Vaughan had been taken ill; he'd lost his voice completely and I'd got to compère the show. There'd been all sorts of names suggested – Dickie Henderson, Leslie Crowther. Dickie Leeman said: "Look, Alton's here every single week. He knows the show inside out. He's the only person that we ought to get." So the whole team came down that afternoon.

After watching his cabaret act that night, Les Cocks suggested that they cancel the programme altogether!

The next day, as my warm-up comic I chose a very good artiste called Pete Conway, who did a fine job. Pete's wife was pregnant at that time. The child turned out to be a boy, the boy – in turn – turned out to be Robbie Williams.

On Sunday 17 June 1973, I compèred 'The Golden Shot'.

Keith Smart was watching the show, at Dominic Drive, in the flat immediately above the new presenter's. "I know that Alton did it better than the guy who was doing it regularly. I couldn't believe that they brought Charlie Williams in afterwards, when they'd found someone who'd proved himself, by taking over at short notice and doing a better job than Norman Vaughan. Norman was like a 'fish-out-of-water' and Charlie Williams was an absolute nightmare! Alton seemed to have done his homework on the contestants: he could chat to them and make gags about things. With Charlie Williams, it seemed the first time he met them was live on camera and he hadn't got a clue what to say." Several people whom the co-writer has discussed the show with, have compared Alton favourably with Bob Monkhouse, saying that they're alike in the sense that both are sharp-witted and have good memories.

GREETINGS TELEGRAM ✳

ALLPURPOSE

1143   AP8   4.45   KINGSTON T 20

ALTON DOUGLAS GOLDEN SHOT ATV STUDIOS EHAM=

DEAR ALTON WISHING YOU THE VERY BEST OF
LUCK SINCERELY
= NORMAN VAUGHAN+

Despite my having been rude to them and slamming the phone down, a very complimentary article appeared in the 'News of the World, the following week. Bob Monkhouse, in his book, actually did get the last bit right. Although I'd put in a successful performance, as I came off the set I said: "If that's what it takes to be a star, I quit!"

The show had gone extremely well, and Francis Essex, ATV's Head of Light Entertainment, rang to say: "That's exactly how I wanted the show presented – exactly! You've done yourself a lot of good this afternoon." All the papers were enthusiastic.

AND FROM THAT DAY ONWARDS, MY CAREER STARTED TO SLIDE BACKWARDS.

Proof that our hero did make it to the screen, compèring "The Golden Shot".

Chapter 12 -

FLAWED BY SUCCESS

AD: Doctor - you'll have to help me - I'm leading a dog's life.
D: A dog's life? Get on the couch.
AD: I'm not allowed on the couch.
D: Alright – sit.
AD: Only for a biscuit.
D: Your trouble is you're indecisive. Take one of these tablets a day.
AD: Which one?
D: Your trouble is you're idle.
AD: I'm idle? I'M idle! I've got a friend who's so idle, if it wasn't for me, he wouldn't be getting the Family Allowance!

The problem was that after the brouhaha of 'The Golden Shot' and the very good reviews, agents were afraid that I still wouldn't be well known enough to top the bill and too expensive to be a support act. So I fell into a kind of 'No-man's Land'.

Interviewed by a local newspaper, soon afterwards Alton admitted to being "still a little shattered about the week's events," adding, "I think you had better call me the Golden Shock!" After his debut as the show's host, he received a flood of letters, telegrams and phone calls, from John O'Groats to Land's End. Although it was only his fourth TV appearance during a five-year career as a comic, such is the power of television, he became instantly recognisable; people would stop him in the streets, to ask him for his autograph. It was also reported that the ATV phone lines were jammed solidly, for two or three hours after the show, congratulating him on his performance. Letters appeared in the press. The following example, from a woman viewer was typical of many:

'What a terrific difference he made to my viewing and that of all my friends. He was calm, cool and totally relaxed. And above all, his laughs didn't come at the expense of contestants.'

Dickie Leeman and Les Cocks had given him his big chance, only weeks after Alton had been named as the Midlands most promising comedian. When French bacteriologist, Louis Pasteur commented, in 1854, that "...chance favours only the prepared mind", he was referring to scientific observation. The same maxim however, could be similarly applied, to Alton's situation, on three separate counts: not only had he earned the coveted Midlands title, and done his homework before hosting the show, but also his diligence and past experience had prepared him for such an eventuality.

In *Derbyshire Diary*, columnist Johnnie Singleton suggested that a programme should be specially designed, to showcase Alton's personality and 'sheer professionalism'. Alton was quoted as saying:

'My thoughts are now firmly on the future and I will be working in an all out effort to realise my own ambitions. Firstly, I would like to appear in a pantomime season in Birmingham, and from there move on to the London Palladium and possibly 'The Talk of the Town.' Ultimately of course, I would dearly love my own TV series.' I had no way of knowing that two of these targets would eventually be hit.

He received offers from various people. Ian McGlynn, of *Midland Management*, who handled *Little and Large* and *Paper Lace*, rang him, offering him a deal - and several London agents too.

I was particularly nervous after my year with Astor Productions, and was determined to be in control of my own destiny – as much as a human being could be. So I turned them all down. A lot of people have said that that was probably one of my major mistakes, that I'd trodden on my own stumps, because if I had been prepared to go along that road, a manager would have built a career for me. But I wanted to be me - to paddle my own canoe.

Afterwards he 'jetted-off' to Guernsey for three nights – we won't mention the hotel – we'll spare their blushes. Because on the first night, the waiter managed to pour hot coffee straight into his lap!

With the result that I was in hospital, having my injured parts – which were not so private by this time – being bathed and tended by nurses. Which, under any other circumstances, could have been quite pleasant; but 'raw' was not the word! The hotel, after that, couldn't do too much for me. As part of their desire to pacify me, they sent a masseur up to my room. But you've got to bear in mind, that there's a red-faced comic sitting there – wearing what looked like a nappy.

Let's face it ... we're not exactly talking 'James Bond Scenario' here...

The masseur had hysterics when he saw me! What made it worse was that he was Egyptian, and my attempts to explain things to him only made it worse. The more indignant and pompous I became, the more he laughed. The net result was that we both finished up rolling around the floor. I howled so much it was a good job I was wearing a nappy.

One night Alton appeared in cabaret at the *Miramar Hotel*, a Chinese-owned establishment, specialising in oriental cuisine.

After the show I was invited to join orchestra leader Robert Farnon, who lived on the island, and the film star, Dennis Price, for a meal. The latter had travelled over from his home on the island of Sark. He was terribly crippled with rheumatics by this time, and wore carpet slippers, with his very smart lounge suit.

>>> Several years later, I auditioned for Robert Farnon's brother, Dennis, for a BBC musical play, but mention of his sibling didn't get me the job (nothing to do with being a lousy trombonist, you understand).

Whilst I was on the island, I also had tea at the hotel owned by Ronnie Ronalde, and was able to tell the siffleur (whistler) that his recording of 'In a Monastery Garden' had been one of my prized possessions, as a young boy. (I've never been sure whether comments like that are much valued. I suppose it's a bit on a par with: "My Granny used to love your singing.") >>> In 2003, at the age of eighty, Ronnie has undertaken a performing tour of the British Isles.

Returning to our story, three weeks later he was appearing at the *Theatre Royal* in Norwich, for the week, with Anita Harris. The opening night was 9 July 1973.

A newspaper review gave Alton full credit for using his expertise to warm up an erstwhile chilly audience for Anita's second spot, after the interval. As the show's compère, it was reported, he reeled off a fast line in gags, and didn't take long to find the funny bone of his audience. Surprisingly, the reviewer described Alton's jokes as 'a little near the knuckle' - an expression one wouldn't normally associate with him. But his initial success turned out to be 'the calm before the storm'.

I received a totally unexpected telephone call, telling me that mum had been taken ill – and rushed into hospital. They thought that she had days rather than weeks to live, and was very poorly.

Dorothy had been a constant support to her son, and a tower of strength, throughout her life, particularly after Sidney's early death, in August 1948. As those of us who have lost parents know only too well, it's all too easy to cling to the fond hope that they will simply 'go on for ever'.

At that time I still believed in the showbiz adage that 'the show must go on'. So I stayed an extra day, while they found a replacement,

Anita Harris.

which turned out to be a tap-dancer called Joe
Chisholm. When Anita heard that my mother was
ill, she rushed out and bought a rose. She left it
in my dressing room, with a little note on a bit of
writing pad – which I found so moving, I still
have it as a keep-sake.

I arrived at the hospital in the early hours.
Mum just managed to hang on until I got there
– then she slipped away. I can't believe how upset
I get – even now. I'm a sentimental old clot! It
was a huge blow. I mean, mum had looked after
me, on her own, for twenty-five years. She'd
supported everything I did: virtually every First
Night she'd be there in the audience. At
Blackpool, the dancers used to say: " We know
when your mother's in, because when you're on,
there's a little pink glow coming from the balcony,
where she's sitting."

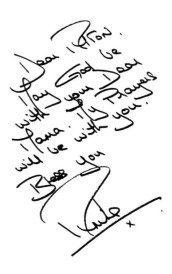

The note from Anita.

I think the word 'feisty' would have described her, although it wasn't in current
use in those days. She was a woman with a lot of fight, and it was terrible losing her.

Dorothy had been born at the turn of the century, and was just seventy-
two years old when she died; five months away from her forthcoming
birthday, in December.

She died of cancer. Two days later, I'm going to warm-up 'The Golden Shot'. As
I'm getting ready to go on, I start to shake from head to toe with the shock of it all –
this terrible loss. Les Cocks said: 'Are you ready to go on then?' I said: 'I don't think
I can do the warm-up.' He said, 'Oh God – it's not the warm-up. Haven't they told
you? It's to go on and do a spot!' The comedian, Johnny Hackett, hadn't arrived and
they wanted me to be the Golden Partner. I had to put an act together and not only
do the warm-up but do a 'spot', in the middle of the show.

With no more than twenty minutes notice, Alton grabbed an idiot board
and scribbled a few hasty notes on it.

Ray Seaton, a reporter for the 'Express and Star' got hold of this story - that I'd
gone on in a terrible state and managed to get through it. He wanted to do a piece
about the 'Broken-hearted Clown'. I begged him not to, and to his eternal credit,
although he'd got a scoop, he didn't write one word about it. I really appreciated that.

Two days after appearing on 'The Golden Shot', I'm back on screen again,
performing a sketch in Terry's 'Lunchtime With Wogan' show. Again, he insisted
on calling me by my Christian name, to help me – give me a plug – which is a
thing he always did. The very same night, Ivor Jay gave me a glowing write-up
in the 'Birmingham Mail', advocating that I should be given 'The Golden Shot'
job permanently.

Shortly afterwards, however, it was announced that Charlie Williams was taking over in September. Subsequently, Alton had the distinct impression that Charlie felt he was 'breathing down his neck'.

So we never got close at all; he would never have very much to do with me. I don't know whether you want a Charlie Williams story? It might appear bitter, coming from me. It's said that he used to read every word from idiot boards - every single word. (Yorkshire accent): "Good afternoon me old flower. How are you?" Not just 'key' words, for example 'train'- and then you'd talk about a train for a minute or two. Every word. One day, the poor devil holding this plethora of boards, developed a double hernia and dropped them on the floor. Before anyone could stop Charlie, he'd read two Exit signs!

Alton recalls that *some* of the agents he was working for took advantage of the extra publicity he was getting, and started inflating his fees unfortunately, without giving him a percentage of the increase. Each time he complained, there would be a big bust-up, and another contact would be lost. Consequently, he didn't net the amount of work one would have expected.

In October 1973, Alton made his acting debut, with a small part in ATV's *Crossroads*, as a lorry driver who demolishes Mrs. Bullock's cottage. Graham Cooper, joint proprietor of *Cooper's Road Services*, helped to put Alton through his lorry driving paces, to lend authenticity. The two men were already acquainted through Graham's role as chairman of the *Staffordshire Society for Brain Damaged Children*. According to a local newspaper (which included a photo of a puzzled Alton, emerging from a crashed-up lorry) Graham's father, Reg, was heard to comment: "As a lorry driver, Alton is obviously an excellent comic!"

I pressed what?

Another article about the role, pointed out that, in addition to his success on the small screen, Alton "has played in practically every nightclub in the British Isles and is rapidly establishing himself as one of the brightest comedy newcomers of the 1970s."

I was walking along the corridors at ATV, wearing my overalls, dressed for 'Crossroads', covered from head to toe in dirt, and I saw 'The Golden Shot's' producer Les Cocks, in front of me. I tapped him on the shoulder, he turned round, saw this apparition, and without hesitation he said: "There you are Alton, I told you I'd make you a star!" I told Noele Gordon that story. She thought it was so good, she contacted Clifford Davis, who was writing her biography, 'My Life At Crossroads', and they included it in the book.

Noele Gordon, at the Crossroads' Motel, being as kind as ever to a poor jobbing actor.

I also compèred the 'Express and Star Personality Girl Contest', at the 'Park Hall Hotel' in Wolverhampton.

Two months later I appeared again on 'Crossroads': a guest appearance, as a drunk, on Vera's barge – with Larry Grayson.

Early in 1974, our 'man-of-many-parts' began to record 'voice-overs', for the about-to-be-launched BRMB radio station.

They soon realised that a lot of 'actors' only had a limited range of voices and dialects, but a 'turn', such as myself, could offer a very wide range of sounds. So, in a short while, I conquered a small segment of the local market. Independent companies were being set up at this time, to cater for the demand. I worked a great deal during the daytime, being everything from a Korean advertising ginseng, to an owl sitting on a branch, or a tiddly reindeer.

......and I was a worthy winner.

On one occasion, the actor, John Le Mesurier, (who was Sergeant Wilson in 'Dad's Army'), arrived so drunk that an impressionist was called in to cover his lines. I don't know, to this day, if the company realised that they'd got me and a 'double'! I also did voices for several soft toys, including Uncle Bulgaria and Orinoco, of 'The Wombles' – and even Winnie the Pooh. I remember spending an entire soft toy day, getting the lines exactly right and delivering them in a big sort of pseudo-Santa voice: "I love you!" "Hold my hand." "Give us a kiss!" At the end of the session – a whole afternoon – I could hardly croak "Good-bye" to the engineers.

Then six months go by and I see this Womble, Uncle Bulgaria, in Woolworth's. So I go over and pull the drawstring at the back – keeping in mind this awful afternoon I'd had, croaking away. I pull the drawstring and I hear: "Aargh! Grumf! Muffyump!"

At this stage, *George Bartram Press Relations* had been handling Alton's publicity for almost two years. They continued to maintain a successful partnership with Alton for many years, until 1987.

George was very conscious of his Birmingham accent. So he enrolled for a course of elocution lessons. The morning after his very first session, the phone rang and with perfect elocution George said: "Good Morning!" And the reporter, from the 'Daily Mirror', said: "Blimey George, what's the matter with you? Gone all bleedin' big-time?"

Warm-ups were still occupying many of Alton's evenings. He was booked for *The Max Bygraves Show*, at Elstree. Unlike other shows, he wasn't required to work on the studio floor, with the cameras, technicians and all the usual distractions.

Instead, you were on a raised stage, with a spotlight: two things that are an enormous help to an artiste. That afternoon, my friend Anne Beverley, who'd been doing a photo shoot for 'Tit-Bits', was in the audience and she said she'd never seen me go so well. The next morning, I got the sack! Alec Fyne, the head-booker at ATV, was so unhappy with the situation, that although I hadn't got a written contract, just a verbal agreement, he insisted on paying me for the whole series.

On the last day of March 1974, *The Golden Shot* came to an end, so everyone piled onto the screen, for a 'Farewell'. Alton was then free to embark on a series of theatre tours, via *George Bartram Enterprises*, for the *Stanley Sher Organisation*.

Jo and I had been adopted, by now, by a marvellous Old English Sheepdog puppy -called Groucho Max – after Marx and Wall. When I mentioned this to Max Wall he told me that it was the best compliment he'd ever had in his life – having a dog named after him.

Max also regaled Alton with one of his favourite stories, about a Jewish lady - sitting on the beach, with her young son:

Suddenly a large wave engulfs him and washes him out to sea. "Oh Lord, please give me back my son. I'd do anything to get my boy back." Whoosh! Another wave deposits him back by the side of her. "Oh thank you Lord. You've answered my prayers, what can I say? I'm forever in your ——————————— where's his cap?"

Groucho accompanied us everywhere. At the 'White Rock Pavilion' in Hastings, he was sitting onstage, when Vince Hill's drummer, Paul Shepherd, gave a test roll on the drums. Groucho was so startled, he jumped over the orchestra pit and chased straight down the central aisle. By the time we retrieved him, Vince had laughed so much, that he promised his son Athol, he could have an Old English Sheepdog.

>>> Today, the Hill's are now on their fourth Old English Sheepdog, called Teddy.

Alton also toured with Windsor Davies and Don Estelle for a while. They'd had a big hit with the TV series *It Ain't Half Hot Mum!* As Sergeant Major Williams and Gunner (Lofty) Sugden, they had also recorded a single, *Whispering Grass*, which became a Top Twenty entry.

>>> *Eleven years on, Don Estelle was singing in the Bull Ring, in Birmingham. It was to commemorate the fortieth anniversary of VE Day, and he was standing there singing war songs. A friend of mine overheard two women talking. One of them said (broad Birmingham accent):"Shall we goo down there, to see what's gooing on?" The other said: "Nah – I wouldn't bother. It's only Vera Lynn, tryin' to sell her records."*

Moving on to 23 June 1974, Alton was booked for a Sunday concert at the *London Palladium*. He was on a very strong bill, which included his old friend, Max Wall, Matt Monro, Tommy Trinder,

AD and Anne Beverley make it to the London Palladium.

Dailey and Wayne, and the pianist, Bill McGuffie, who told him some lovely stories about working with Benny Goodman's orchestra, in America.

My friend Anne Beverley, the singer from Netherton, was on the bill too. The only thing that came from it was that there was a television producer in the audience, called Peter Whitmore, and he booked me for warm-ups for 'The Dana Show', but I had achieved one of my major ambitions, and made it to the 'Palladium'.

I also did a week at 'The Commodore Club' in Nottingham, with Bruce Forsyth. After going extremely well on the first night, I was demoted for the rest of the week, to a spot before the dancers, which must be a 'first' in showbiz terms, to actually go on with the soup.

The other side of the coin was a 'one-nighter' at the Civic Hall, in Grays, Essex, with 'The Dick Emery Show'. Being one of those multi-purpose buildings, it had folding partitions, to separate the dressing rooms. I was talking to Johnny Clamp, the other comedian on the bill. At that time, neither of us was getting much work. Dick Emery overheard us and called me into the corridor. He said: "If ever you find you're short of work, contact me and I'll be more than happy to help you out. I've got so much confidence in your act that I know it will only be a temporary setback, and you can repay me at your leisure."

> > > Five years later, he was appearing at 'La Dolce Vita' in Birmingham. I went backstage, not expecting to even be recognised. I walked into the dressing room and he said: "Hello Alton. So things turned out alright for you then, didn't they?"

It was about this time that Alton took on two additional roles. After Eric Morecambe had his first heart attack, he and Ernie Wise decided to give up some of their peripheral activities. For several years, they'd been presidents of the *British Beermat Collectors' Society* – 'tegestologists' - to you.

Number One phoney beer-mat collector, 1974.

*To my surprise, the boys proposed **me** to be the President, and to my even greater surprise, bearing in mind what great stars **they** were, the Society accepted. I was just a figurehead originally, but as I went around the country, people would appear at the stage door – usually men – bearing beermats, which they obviously expected me to swap. I quickly collected a set, and a game of 'pass-the-parcel' began.*

Alton was also asked to become a patron of *The Birmingham Tapes for the Handicapped* (and remains so, to this day) – an excellent organisation, chiefly run by two local characters, Derek Hunt and Richard Harmer.

It involved recording messages, information about help available, toilets where Radar keys could be used – that sort of thing. The tapes then circulated in a 'round robin' fashion, all over the country. One of the other patrons was my old friend Max Wall. Each Christmas we would chat to each other on tape, as part of our Christmas Message to the members. (Imitating Max): "Well, I've heard it, you'll have young Freddie Starr after you. 'They've broken all the windows in our house, so that they can hear me better!' I'll have you for nicking my gags!"

Max recommended Alton for a part as his manservant in the film *Jabberwocky*. He went to London to meet the producer, Terry Gillam, of *Monty Python* fame, but unfortunately, nothing came of it. Max, for some reason, took to Alton. Probably because he'd been hurt so much in his life, he had a very guarded approach to friendship, but somehow they just clicked.

Also around that time, I was asked to audition for a part in 'Billy-the-Kid and the Green Baize Vampire', but I think they thought I wasn't Paul Newman material. Max

LAURENCE MYERS
AND
GTO FILMS

HAVE GREAT PLEASURE IN
INVITING YOU TO AN
EVENING WITH

THE
INIMITABLE
MAX

★ ★ ★ ★ ★

THE RICHMOND
THEATRE
The Theatre On The Green
Richmond Green
Surrey

Sunday 15th September
1974

THE EVENING WILL BE FILMED AND
INCLUDED IN A GTO PRODUCTION

Max Wall.

subsequently invited Jo and I to see the filming of his one-man television programme at the Richmond Theatre, in Surrey: that's one of our most treasured memories.

George Bartram and Robert Holmes (the person who looked after Alton's publicity) came up with the brilliant idea that Alton should make a record. They'd been sent a song by one of Ken Dodd's scriptwriters, Maurice Bird, *The Ballad of Big D*, which he'd written specifically for Alton.

We thought that would make a very good starting point for the record, so I went to Zella Records in Edgbaston, and we put together an EP called 'Alton Douglas Sings?' It consisted of 'The Ballad of Big D', my impression of Topol singing 'If I Were A Rich Man', a ballad called 'I'm Confessin' That I Love You', and 'The Saints', with me dubbing three trombones.

Alton's co-writer has spent several sleepless nights listening to the disc in question, and can honestly say – 'hand-on-heart'- that I swear by it!

I asked Les Dawson if he'd supply the sleeve notes and his contribution (as follows) still makes me laugh to this day:

'You must be joking!' …. Sez Les

'Alton Douglas and I have been pals since we attended a mother-in-law swapping party several years ago. I have no doubt that this recording will be a phenomenal success in Outer Mongolia, or failing that, it could be sold as a job-lot for the manufacture of chapatis and other Indian delicacies in such far away places as Bradford. Like the singer, the songs on this EP are designed to grate on the nerves, but since playing my copy to the mother-in-law, I have to admit to a certain liking for the melodious twang of the Douglas voice. The first few bars sent her scurrying to the air-raid shelter in the belief that war had broken out. By the time the record was in full swing she was convinced that Manchester was under seige by an army of drunken musicians and a choir of strangled felines. In short, this plastic con-trick is marvellous as a mother-in-law repellent and as such gets the Dawson seal of approval.'

I think it was a very good record – as long as you don't play it! It was at Zella that I first met Jasper Carrott. He was arranging to record his folk club act, at the same time.

On the day that the record came out, I was so excited, I forgot to put any money into a parking meter, and I was duly fined. So George and Robert had the bright idea that I should pay the fine with a copy of the record. They expected that I'd get a letter back, telling me not to be so stupid, but instead, I got a receipt. Somebody in the Engineer's Department had decided to pay the fine, which was 50 pence in those days.

The 'Birmingham Mail' got hold of the story, and it started a whole tranche of correspondence, because people complained it was illegal, to pay a fine on someone's behalf, which of course it wasn't. The publicity generated was quite considerable and didn't do me any harm. In fact, it stretched nationwide – it got into the Nationals.

It's amazing how stories can suddenly mushroom. In 'the blink-of-an-eye', Alton found himself on Eamon Andrews' London-based television programme *Today*, with Dougie Brown, Warren Mitchell, Freddie 'Parrot-face' Davies and reunited with Arthur Askey, which prompted Alton's quip: "Arthur's so short, he's never heard thunder!"

I'd also been spotted at 'The Spinning Wheel', in Westerham (one of those venues where they kept booking me for three or four days on the trot) by Hugh Charles, the songwriter, who'd written, 'There'll Always Be An England' and 'We'll Meet Again'. He and his wife, Joan Mann, were putting on the 'Fol de Rols' at the De La Warr Pavilion in Bexhill, that summer. They thought I'd be ideal as principal comic. Unfortunately, I wasn't.

Arthur Askey.

Chapter 13 -

THE ODD COUPLE

There was an outcry in Bexhill today. Somebody thought they'd seen a visitor. It turned out to be a resident who'd forgotten his baseball cap!

It's so quiet here, the hotels get the dustman to sign the visitors' book. Even the tide won't go out after eight o'clock. For excitement, the locals go down to the promenade and watch the traffic lights changing.

Actually, the season itself wasn't that bad. All the papers gave us excellent reviews. But I felt that the role I was in would have been much better suited to Jack Tripp, who was topping the bill at Hastings. He'd been principal comic with 'The Fol de Rols' before, and I thought I'd have been better suited to his role really, which was a more modern show.

Every Sunday we made an eight-hour round trip to Bournemouth, to appear at the Pavilion. By one of those strange coincidences that seem to pepper my life, I was allocated the very dressing room that my friend, Don Maclean, used during the summer season. With the change of programme at Bexhill, it meant learning three completely different shows. I lost a stone in weight, just during the rehearsal period. George Bartram also managed to get Pete Lindup booked as the drummer with the show – and we shared a luxury flat on the seafront.

The 'Fols' originated in 1911 and some of the sketches seemed to date back to that time!

Joan Mann topped the bill with Alton, as his versatile leading lady. Her husband, impresario Hugh Charles, in his capacity as the show's producer, resisted all of Alton's attempts to modernise the material; the dialogue and songs, he recalls, had to be treated as if they were 'holy writ' - the antithesis to Alton's usual approach. Undaunted, he and Pete set about producing a whole stream of gags about Bexhill.

*I used to put those in every chance I got –
to try to bring it up-to-date. The cast as a
whole got on extremely well and it was a
happy season. Frankie Murray, the other
comic in the show, was a real throwback to an
earlier age. He did pratfalls, comedy walks
and a side-splitting routine about a man
trying to open a deckchair.*

The *Fols* had last played in Sussex, at
an Eastbourne venue, in 1968. The new
season opened at the *De La Warr Pavilion*
on 30 June 1975 and ran for eleven
weeks, until 13 September. Despite
Alton's preference for a more modern
show, he had high hopes for his role as
the show's principal comic. This is clear
from a press interview that he gave,
before the show's opening night, in
which he explained that he considered
the season to be one of his most
important summer dates, since he
became a professional comedian in 1968:

*We three, outside the De La Warr
Pavilion, Bexhill-on-Sea, 1975.*

*'The Fols is one of the best known summer shows in the country, and it has helped
many top comics on their way, including Leslie Crowther and Arthur Askey, who have
both given me plenty of good advice in the past.'*

He referred to the success of the previous year's one-nighter, at the same
theatre, when he appeared with The Bachelors. Judging by audience
responses on that occasion, he considered that the *Fols* were in for a great
new season in Bexhill. The same article referred to the fact that Alton had
risen to national prominence in 1973, when he hosted The *Golden Shot*, and
that his work as a warm-up comedian had 'done much to enhance his
professional standing.'

The Bexhill-on-Sea Observer invited Alton to write a weekly column, for the
show's duration. In the opening paragraph of his introductory article he wrote:

*'Though I have been in Bexhill for almost two weeks, I haven't really had a chance
to look at the local scenery. This is because 'The Fol de Rols' company has been
rehearsing extremely hard, in readiness for our opening night (always a traumatic
occasion). The first night of any long-running show is always a rather nervy occasion.
Things have a tendency to go wrong and the unexpected frequently happens.'*

He refers to the fact that Vera Lynn had recently been made a Dame in
the Queen's Birthday Honours, and mentions several of his fellow artistes in
the show including,

'*...drummer Pete Lindup who doubles very effectively as my co-scriptwriter. Pete lives in Blackpool and has given up his usual season at the 'Tower Ballroom'. I am delighted that I have him 'captive' for eleven weeks – it should result in some marvellous material for my act.*'

Pete recalls the season clearly: "The rest of the cast dubbed us *The Odd Couple*. There was a TV series of that name, starring Tony Randall as 'Felix' and Jack Klugman as 'Oscar'. It's amazing how like them we were! Of course, me being the slob, I was Oscar. I'd come up with cigar ash and he'd flick a duster, or bring a dustpan-and-brush! The flat was semi-luxurious, with a very well appointed kitchen. Alton didn't want to mess it up, so we ate out all the time! How the hell we managed to share a flat, without coming to blows, I don't know!

"Bexhill-on-Sea has one of the main importers for jazz records in the country, so we were down at the record shop, *Flyright Records* every day. At the warehouse nearby we used to haggle over who was going to buy which record, which was ridiculous, because it didn't matter who owned them - we both listened to them anyway! Alton owned a portable 'music centre' record/cassette unit, which really earned its keep."

It's obvious, simply from glancing at Pete's e-mails, that's he's a 'natural' comedian. On asking him to pinpoint the start of his comedic career, the co-

writer half-expected him to say "From birth!" "Well I don't think I can go back any further than that!" he quips. "I did a comedy-mime act as a youngster. I used to write gags with Alton, you see. He encouraged me. He said: 'You should be doing your own act; you're wasted, playing the drums.' I said: 'Well, that's funny, most of the people I worked with said I was wasted. You know – 'It's a waste of time having you here!' "

Even the best of friendships don't always run smoothly. Jo recalls: "They had some sharp words over something that they disagreed with. Pete went off to Brighton for the day. I can remember Alton ringing me back, some time at night, before the show. He said, 'Jo, I'm ever so worried. He hasn't come back yet!' He was *really* concerned about him, because he'd gone off in a huff. That was his sensitive attitude coming out. Pete would probably never have known, and he wouldn't have realised that Alton was worried about him."

Alton has often been described as a very literate comedian, who shows great professionalism in whatever he undertakes. Pete elaborates: "He'd always set great store by his material: his material had to be right *first*. He called himself 'the original comedian'. I said: 'Well you're not that old!' He said: 'No, no, no - the stuff I do is original.' "

On one occasion, Jo was driving down to visit Alton at the *Fols*, when her car broke down. She was obliged to walk the country lanes accompanied by the ever-faithful Groucho, in search of a phone. "We came to a country pub. The publican gave us something to eat and 'phoned the local garage, to

The bloke in the middle of the Fol de Rols looks as if he wishes he wasn't.

come and look at my car; it was petrol-pump trouble. The mechanic got us going and in return I arranged for theatre tickets for the publican's family, in Bexhill, the following week - to repay him."

From an article headed 'Groucho Is Bexhill Draw', one discovers that Alton's ten-month-old, Old English Sheepdog was proving a great attraction to people in the area who were arranging fetes and summer shows, during the *Fols* season. The journalist suggested that Alton might be persuaded to accompany his celebrity dog as an optional extra!

Press cuttings confirm Alton's recollection, that the show had excellent reviews. One columnist wrote of him 'It cannot be long before his showbiz career takes off in a big way.'

As soon as the Bexhill season ended, I was awarded the first 'Bob Hatch Memorial Trophy', given in memory of one of Birmingham's greatest comics. Tragically, some years before, comedian Bob had been injured in a car accident, the night before he was due to appear at the 'Windmill Theatre', London. This had blighted the rest of his career, but he was a really great comic.

Pete and I went to 'Severn Manor Hotel' in Stourport, to see him. Bob was about twenty years older than me. By this time he'd got a very serious drinking problem. He'd been told by his doctor that he'd got to cut down. Pete, not knowing this, and being bowled over by his off-beat style, insisted on buying him a drink. So Bob quietly replied: "Thanks, I'll have a scotch." The barman handed it to him. He looked at it lovingly, for a second or two, then poured it into the water jug and drank the entire contents!

1976 started with, amongst other things, a TV documentary, all about a revolutionary new building process. The producer asked Alton to find a straight man to 'feed' him his lines. He enlisted the help of Mike Gancia.

We filmed on a freezing cold day in February. The first scene involved a conical container, filled with liquid cement. Mike managed to get into a tangle with it. The cement went straight down his front, and in the cold temperature it set immediately. For the rest of the day, he walked around like a man with a plank down each trouser leg.

Without my realising it, the cameraman on the shoot had found my contribution to the filming very funny. He put one of my brochures on the desk of John Clarke, who phoned me and asked to see me work. He chose 'The Fellows Club', which was in the grounds of Dudley Zoo, on a night when the artistes outnumbered the audience.

In the 1970s and 80s, John Clarke was a Regional TV producer in the BBC's Midland Unit. John explains: "There were three of us, and my colleagues and I were required to originate about sixty programmes a year between us, covering different aspects of life in the Midlands, which in those days stretched from the Welsh border to the Fens. My interests lay in the direction of Light Entertainment, and I was constantly looking for ways of presenting entertainment of a Midland regional flavour. We were somewhat limited on this because L.E. is a high budget area of TV and our budgets were about a tenth of the Network equivalent shows. Add to this the fact that the editorial chain of command above us were all journalists and thought that we should be doing current affairs programmes all the time, and you can see that the job was tricky.

"I was looking for comedians to present some factual programmes, because I believe that the comedian's art is to present life in an entertaining way. I had done a series with Don Maclean and he had impressed me with his abilities in that direction. It was about this time (mid-seventies) that I heard about Alton and went to see him at the *Fellows Club* at Dudley Zoo. This was a small but interesting venue, with the tables set in a semi-circle. Alton did his act, (or 'turn', as he delights in calling it), and the tiny audience was warm but rather quiet." All that is, except for one man in the audience, who endorsed Alton's act every so often, with the comment: 'I like him. I like him.' Despite the limited size of the audience, Alton's performance, combined with the man's reaction, was enough to convince John: "He struck me as a highly literate comic, whose strength was in linguistic humour, not belly laughs. This was the kind of comedian I was looking for, so we got together in several projects after then."

John was in my life for the next seven or eight years. The first thing he booked me for was a cricket programme called 'The Gentleman's Game'. Gordon Stretch and I wrote a spot which had me in 'whites' and pads, bemoaning the fact that there's a tear-away fast-bowler playing. The punchline, of course, is that he turns out to be on my side! It gave me a chance to be reunited with Roly Jenkins, the cricketer who'd walked around the Worcestershire ground looking for my mack.

I then embarked on a series of theatre tours with Vince Hill. One of the shows was a Sunday concert at the 'Alhambra Theatre' in Bradford. After the bandcall I nipped over to a tiny sweetshop, just across from the theatre. There were two very large ladies in front of me and the one said (northern accent): "Eeh John, you'll have to get a bigger shop." And I said: "Or smaller customers!" Then I sidled out of the shop, without being served!

One of the nicest dates I ever did was a couple of days at 'Heatherton Grange', near Taunton. I was interviewed for Hospital Radio, by a character called Ken Windsor.

Alton and Ken have remained firm friends for over a quarter of a century. Ken explains: "I was one of the founder members of the Taunton Hospital Radio Service. I used to do celebrity interviews. The job took me to London a lot, when I was doing my full-time job, so I found I was in the right position to do them. When I heard that the local hotel, *Heatherton Grange*, was putting on cabaret nights, I approached the manager and said: 'Well look, we'd like to do some interviews with some of the stars out there.' He said: 'Great, it will give us publicity as well.' One of the stars who came out there was Alton. So that's the first time I met him – doing a radio interview."

Heatherton Grange was situated between Taunton and Wellington. Ken lived in Wellington, so the venue was very handy for him. The interview was about Alton's beginnings in showbusiness. Ken recalls: "He explained at length about his favourite comics - how he liked comedians like Tony Hancock – and his love of jazz as well. That's really how we started to 'gel' together – because we both had a love of jazz. We both like the music of the 1950s-60s West Coast America, which is Stan Getz, Chet Baker etc. One of the things that we both cringe about, is when people come up to us and say: 'Oh we know you like jazz. We thought you'd like this LP that we've found.' And it's something like Kenny Ball or *Mrs. Mills Plays Dave Brubeck*."

Ken interviewed a wide range of celebrities for Hospital Radio: "Norman Wisdom, Morecambe & Wise, Tony Bennett, Howard Keel – the whole spectrum basically. My most memorable interview was Harry H. Corbett, at his home in St. John's Wood. It was a wonderful morning.

"I arrived one night at *Heatherton Grange*," he continues, "to do an interview with Billy Fury. The owner-manager came up to me. He said: 'I'm in a terrible state: I've just sacked my compère, I've got no one to do the show. Will you do it?' Of course, I didn't know what to say really. I said, 'Well look, if Billy Fury's happy – I'll have a chat with him – then I'll do it.' I was the compère for eight years after that. Alan Davey, the owner, would re-book artistes about every six months; he'd bring back the acts he liked, all the time. I think I introduced Alton three times, while I was there; he used to do a comic spot of about forty minutes."

Ken played host as well as compère, so it's difficult for him to recall any of the details of Alton's act. "I used to go on and introduce the acts, then take them off, I was usually having to socialise with a lot of people as well. So I'd only see about half an act."

As Ken has said, we worked together several times, until eventually he became an agent. Realising that we were never going to get away from each other, we formed a friendship based on a mutual love of jazz, cricket and showbusiness, that survives to this day, and it's one of the greatest joys of my life. I talk to him three times a week. He's a lovely man.

Speaking of jazz, in October 1976 I compèred a radio broadcast of 'The Norman Dovey Big Band,' at the BBC studios at Pebble Mill, which was most enjoyable. It was based, to some extent, on the programmes that the 'Northern Variety Orchestra' used to do, with Roger Moffatt. It was big band music, with bits of fun in between.

In the same month, Alton began warming-up the Terry Scott-June Whitfield series, *Happy Ever After*, at Shepherds Bush.

After the first programme, there was a tap on the dressing room door and it was Terry Scott. He said: "Would you come up to the bar please and have a drink? I want to have a chat with you." I thought: 'Oh dear, he's not happy with the material.' So with a quaking heart I followed him. He said: "I watched your warm-up, and I've never been so excited by a young comic before!" (Remember that at this point I'm thirty-eight)! He said: "What I'm prepared to do, if you can find a scriptwriter who can put together a half-hour radio sit-com, I'd be prepared to act as your straight man. I've set my heart on seeing you become a star." I told him that after my experiences with 'The Golden Shot', I didn't have too many ambitions in that direction. He said: "Nonsense, every act wants to be a star. Do as I said, and we'll give your career a jolt."

So Alton contacted Les Lilley who was one of *The Golden Shot* writers, and in no time at all, he put together a script that was very funny.

Terry and I were brothers. One of us was running a Health Farm, the other running a tuck-shop around the corner. We arranged to see Terry in the West End, at 'The Duke of York Theatre', where he was appearing in 'A Bedful Of Foreigners', with June Whitfield.

He looked at the script, stared at us as if we were mad, and said: "What's this? You've got me reading all the straight lines! Alton's got all the laughs – you'd expect me to get all the laughs! You'd better go away and re-write this completely, or at the very least, reverse the roles." So we left, tails between our legs. Sorry Les – all that hard work.

The next week, as part of the Bromsgrove Festival, I was compèring a variety show. The programme read: ' 7.30 Alton Douglas, 7.45 – Show opens.'

To Alton's great delight, John Clarke booked him for a local BBC television programme called *The Knockers*, in which a team were given the opportunity to 'knock' anything they didn't like. He chose the working mens' clubs.

I opened with, 'The audience was dreadful. They cheered the acrobat when he stood on his head. So he said: "Well you can come up and do it." So they all came up and stood on his head! The top-of-the-bill was a singer who, unfortunately, had one too many: it made her dress look ridiculous!'

One of the stories I didn't tell on the programme involved a comic, who was performing a cabaret spot at a dance. He was standing on the floor, as a middle-aged lady walked past. Of course, he trotted out a typical comic's comment. She walked over to him, grabbed his elasticated dickey-bow and let it go with an almighty twang! As he staggered back, gasping for breath, she said: "And next time it will be your bollocks!"

Or the story of Squire Ronnie Hayward, the rural comedian, who was on a show with me. He got fed up with people walking past him during his act – up and down - one chap passed him for the umpteenth time, with a tray of drinks. Ronnie raised his prop-gun, containing blanks, and fired it at the ceiling. This fellow was terrified and dropped to his knees, without spilling a drop – cue thunderous applause!

Alton had a tremendously varied list of engagements, at this stage. For example, taking one particular week, he was at a Civic Hall one day, performing on a barge, with singer Ora Pasco the next day, and the following day, attending a charity event at an old age pensioners' club, with two other old friends, the singing duo, Geoff and June, (previously mentioned in connection with *The Golden Shot*).

Somewhere, deep in the heart of Norfolk. The audience look as if they can't even understand my trombone playing.

By the strangest coincidence, Ora used to be a friend of Alton's co-writer. She was a Jewish vocalist, with a powerful delivery, in the Shirley Bassey tradition. She and her husband Cyril lived in the flat above us, in Vicarage Road, Edgbaston. We accompanied her to cabaret venues, on several occasions. Cyril doubled as her manager. Just a couple of years before his co-writer first met her, Alton would call at Ora's flat, to take her to their evening engagements. Cyril was in the jewellery trade – he even made the co-writer's engagement ring!

When I did the charity event with Geoff and June, I opened with: "One of the senior members streaked in here last week- took off his clothes and walked stark naked across the floor, wearing nothing except a Sainsbury's bag over his head! A lady shouted out: "That's absolutely disgraceful!" Her friend said: "And he's not even a full member!"

Alton performed a 'one-nighter', at a Students' Ball. As he walked on, something hit him squarely on the head. In his most pompous voice he said: "Someone has hit me with a bread roll!" And a voice came back: "Waste of good food!"

Going through my diaries, I found that I warmed-up a programme that I have no recollection of! I don't know what it was about, or who was in it. All I know is that it sounds like some sort of sexual perversion. It was called 'Mother Muffin'.

145

Chapter 14 -

THE SPICE OF LIFE

Thank you ladies and gentlemen for that welcome. I walked in tonight and the manager took my case from me. He said that if I get a lot of laughs I'll get it back. So you wouldn't want me to lose my case, would you?

We're into 1977 now. Rod Hull, (accompanied by his emu), I found to be a thoroughly objectionable character. Just before a Sunday concert at the 'Congress Theatre' in Eastbourne, we met for the first time - on stage. He talked to the sound impressionist, Mike Carter, as if I were invisible. "If the compère cracks any dirty jokes before he introduces me, I shan't go on." I turned to Mike and said: "Will you tell the Top of the Bill that first of all, the compère doesn't use 'blue' jokes, and secondly, if he comes anywhere near me with that emu, I'll break his arm!" That night, I walked out, and a girl threw a rose onto the stage. Shades of 'The Best Cellar', almost ten years before. Brickbats and bouquets – all on the same night!

The same week, I experienced another example of the lack of fraternal feeling that sometimes exists between comics. At a hotel in Gloucestershire, the owner told me that Dave Butler, one of 'The Comedians', a comic I'd never even met, had come up to him and said (West Country accent): "I see you've got Alton Douglas here next week. I don't know why you've booked him. I'm a better comedian than he is!" "Sorry Dave," he replied, "with my audiences you're not!"

I should mention that, on the whole, unpleasantness and spite are the exception, rather than the rule, as most acts find a way of 'rubbing along' together.

During the day Alton was fully occupied, recording commercials. For one of them, the instruction was to "Make it Robert Preston, in *The Music Man*."

So I studied his song (impersonates him). "You got trouble brother, right here in River City!" The advertising man said: "What we could do with is a bit more Sammy Davis Junior." I said: "I could black up!" He looked puzzled and said: "Sorry?" (I knew we were in trouble). After a couple of hours of trying to be Preston crossed with Davis, he said: "I'm not getting enough of you." I said: "Well, let me try it just once, the way I would have done it, without your instructions." We got it in one.

In March 1977, the TV producer, Derek Smith, asked Alton if he would record three, one-minute sketches, for a new series to be called *Top Gear*. His trade union, Equity, were contacted. They demanded that he be paid three separate fees, instead of the one all-inclusive fee that the BBC was offering, for a day's work.

Derek decided that instead of going to all that expense, which in any case was out of the question because of the budget, he would write a slightly longer script for Angela Rippon and Tom Coyne. The show ran very successfully for over twenty-five years without me.

Back to more shows for Stanley Sher, including several with Mike and Bernie Winters. We always got on very well because we shared a great love for Duke Ellington. When you looked inside their car, they'd got a pile of Ellington tapes on the back seat. Also, Bernie played drums and Mike played the clarinet, so we shared the problems of playing a musical instrument as well.

During the first months of the year, we were nursing Jo's mother, who bravely and very uncomplainingly fought cancer. At one point I was jokingly insisting that she took her medicine, or we'd have a row. Despite being in a terribly drugged state, she looked up and said: "We'll have a contretemps – c-o-n-t-r-e-t-e-m-p-s." She passed away shortly afterwards, and our lives became irrevocably poorer.

A cutting in one of Alton's albums, taken from *The Messenger*, 15 April 1977, announced that he was to star in his own television comedy show, *The Original Alton Douglas*. The show was scheduled for screening on Friday 27 May at 10.15 pm.

John Clarke came up with this 'one-off' television programme, which had me 'gagging', performing sketches, and singing with the marvellous Tommy Burton Quartet. Tommy couldn't read a note of music, but after a brief chat, he played my music to perfection. Also in the show was Anne Beverley, with whom I'd appeared at the London Palladium. As ever, the scripts were written by myself and Gordon Stretch.

It was a thirty-minute, Midlands-based show. In an article for the *Sunday People*, Alton showed a healthy scepticism: "I've been discovered more often

Bernie Winters, AD, Mike Massey (Managing Director) and Mike Winters, Jollees Nightclub, Longton.

Get Switched on to
**"THE ORIGINAL
ALTON DOUGLAS"**
Starring Comedian ALTON DOUGLAS
Produced by JOHN CLARKE
Directed by DESMOND O'LEARY
BBC1 - TV (MIDLANDS)
27th May, 1977
10.15 p.m. - 10.45 p.m.
Enquiries to:
021-458 5599 — 021-472 1079
or
GEORGE BARTRAM: 021-643 9346

Captions on a postcard please.

than a cure for baldness." Also taking part in the show was Peter Brookes from Harborne. (He was playing Vince, the postman, in *Crossroads*, at the time). Anne Beverley was described as 'a glamorous blonde singer, from Brierley Hill.' This venture into comedy, was a new departure for her.

Elsewhere, Alton described the show as his "second big chance, (after *The Golden Shot*)." It incorporated his patter act, sketches, the trombone, and one or two surprises. The accent, as the title suggests, was on originality. Although they were hopeful that the programme might be networked, as things turned out, it only appeared in the Midlands.

Don Maclean was certainly a 'guest-with-a-difference' on the show, because he never actually walked on to the set! The gag was that they kept announcing that he was to appear, and they'd got to get out of the studio before he did. He eventually appeared, but remained standing in the doorway (toothy grin etc.)! BLACKOUT.

In July 1977, Alton and Groucho appeared together on the front page of the *Birmingham Evening Mail*. They had staged a 'one man and his dog' protest about dogs being banned from Rowheath Playing Fields, where Groucho used to enjoy a daily romp. Despite local support, the 'demo' was to no avail. When they re-opened the *Lido*, in the park, they booked a team of performing police dogs!

Anita Harris and Alton were reunited in August 1977, for a three-week season at the *Kings Theatre* in Glasgow, in a show entitled, *Meetanita*. It was rather ironical that on the previous occasion that they performed together, Alton lost his mother, Dorothy, and on this second occasion it was Jo's mother who had departed, just weeks before.

It was a revue-type show: just about my favourite vehicle. On the opening night, I inadvertently referred to a late-comer incorrectly, by saying: "Let's have a round of applause for the Lady Mayoress!" It should have been the 'Lady Provost'. The local paper, after giving me a good 'write-up', said: '...and his act will be well-nigh perfect, when he gets the nomenclature right.' It was the word 'nomenclature' that got me!

In one scene we had to enter, riding bikes, and dressed in shorts. The stage manager said (Scottish accent): " Are those your legs?" "I'm afraid they are!" "You're not going on that stage with those legs!"

I loved Glasgow, and the audiences seemed to reciprocate, but I wasn't always 'at one' with the shopkeepers. I went into a shop in Sauchiehall Street, to buy a copy of the 'Jewish Chronicle', because they'd given us a good review. I asked for a copy and the assistant said: "I'm sorry, we don't sell foreign newspapers." In another shop I asked for some pasteurised milk, but was told, "We haven't got any – we only sell it in bottles!"

Our enterprising comedian was interviewed for a local television programme, *Watch This Space*, along with cockney actor, Arthur Mullard.

> > > *Twenty years later, I bumped into Jon Pertwee ('Doctor Who') in New Street, Birmingham. He reminded me that after we'd both worked on 'Celebrity Squares', we'd been sitting in the Green Room afterwards, enjoying a buffet, when Henry Cooper quipped: "Whatever you do, don't put your hand on the table, otherwise Arthur will eat it!"*

I stayed with a very 'twee' Glaswegian, Mrs. Skilling, who informed me that the last time she'd had theatricals there, "I caught them in the bath, Mr. Douglas – they were doing it!" I said: "Well, it's better than fighting!"

Without realising it, the sight of my trombone had sent the local musical society into a frenzy. (Scottish accent): "Come along to our musical soireé on Sunday Mr. Douglas, and bring a friend."

Foolishly, Alton invited Jack O'Reilly, the Canadian ventriloquist. BUT – remember his vocation! Jack, was also appearing in Anita's show. Without doubt, he was one of the finest exponents of 'throwing the voice' in the world. He had actually written, possibly the definitive book on the subject – *The Belly Speakers* – the original name for ventriloquists, as people thought at the outset that the voice came from the stomach.

The Society were an extremely friendly crowd, and we were led through a packed hall, onto the platform, where we were seated as honoured guests, behind the musicians. The quartet had an unusual line-up, consisting of a lady on the grand piano, a French Horn, Cello and a Double Bass. Picture this, there we were, in full view of the audience, and I'm sitting next to a ventriloquist.

The music, though not to my taste by a long stretch of the imagination, was melodious enough, and the first ten minutes passed very pleasantly. Then I heard an ominous creaking, coming from the piano – bear in mind that I'm the only one who can hear this. A few moments later, from the bell of the French Horn, Maurice

Chevalier whispered: "Oh, mais oui, Alton mon cher." I could just about cope with that, but when Dick Emery chimed in, in a very camp voice, from the middle of the Cello with: "Hello there, Honky Tonk," I'd almost had it. I struggled to keep my composure, and my giggles under control, but the final blow was yet to fall. All of a sudden, the Double Bass let out an almighty fart. Tears coursed down my face and dripped off the end of my chin! I was wracked with a coughing fit and Jack O'Reilly, (totally non-plussed by all of this, of course) had to hold me by my heaving shoulders and guide me through the musicians, off the platform, through the audience and out through the swing doors. The moral of the story? 'It's OK to invite the comic, but I should pass on his friend!'

Back to Shepherds Bush, to replace Barry Cryer and warm-up a series of *The Generation Game*. Alton's usual practice was to approach the show's star, to see if there were any specific requests or instructions. So he asked Bruce Forsyth: "Is there anything special that you want me to do?" He snapped: "You'd better not be blue," turned on his heel and that was that!

My spot went well, but as I handed over to him, instead of thanking me, which was the normal procedure, he just totally ignored me. On the way home I thought about how nice the atmosphere had been with Bob Monkhouse and Norman Vaughan. How Terry Wogan had knocked on the dressing room door after every show and thanked me. How Lance Percival had been so appreciative with 'Up The Workers'; Derek Hobson, with 'New Faces', Michael Crawford, with 'Some Mothers Do 'Ave Them'; how Val Doonican had invited Jo and I to his dressing room after every programme, for a drink, and I decided I didn't want to be involved with this one. The next morning I phoned the producer, Robin Nash, and asked to be released from the series.

However, I had committed another one of my awful faux pas during the preparations for 'The Generation Game'. I'm stripped to my underpants, standing in the dressing room, telling the other occupant that I'd belonged to a gym for the last few months. If you can picture this: I'm standing there, just in my underpants, hardly a trace of muscle definition, and my fellow occupant strips off and I thought: 'My God!' So I crept out and said to one of the crew: "Who's that bloke in there?" He said: "That's Dave Prowse. He's playing the part of Darth Vader in 'Star Wars'."

By the way, one of the fellows at my gym was telling me that he drank fifteen pints at the weekend. I said: "What sort of time does your wife have?" He said: "How the bloody hell d'you think I'd know?"

More Stanley Sher shows followed. In April 1978, Alton was on the bill again with Windsor Davies and Don Estelle - this time at the *Civic Centre*, Aylesbury, followed by more warm-ups for *Citizen Smith*, with Robert Lindsay.

Ken Windsor had been running a small theatrical agency for five years – *Kew Entertainments*. The licensing fees and running costs had, sadly, become too prohibitive. In a letter to *The Stage* newspaper, Ken described the problems facing small agencies. His business was to close, the following January, but he took the opportunity to thank Alton and Ronnie Hayward for their advice to a 'green' agent.

Also in April, Alton compèred the *Tom O'Connor Show*, at Malvern, and did a comedy spot. Tom, a young Liverpudlian schoolmaster, taught his pupils by day and entertained his audience by night, before he became successful. Like Alton, his material was 'clean'. He rose quickly to fame through TV series such as *Wednesday At Eight* and as quizmaster of the popular programme, *Name That Tune*.

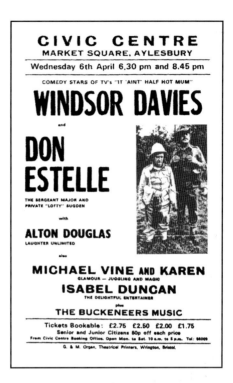

Tom would look for my trombone and suit, and take it and me into the Number One dressing room with him, and Paul Daniels, who also liked to share a dressing room, rather than being on his own, used to do the same thing.

In Lowestoft, we picked Paul up on the seafront and Groucho, who thought that Paul was the 'bee-knees', immediately leapt upon him in the back seat. I've got this lovely image of the two of them, snogging, all the way down to a little tearoom, where Paul treated us to tea.

From 18 May 1978, Alton appeared once again, with Vince Hill, at the *Princess Theatre*, Torquay. Ken Windsor kept him company: "I went down to Torquay to actually see the show. Alton was down there on his own - Jo wasn't there that time. I spent Saturday afternoon and evening with him, and we went out for a meal."

Vince took the show on tour to most of Britain's premier resorts, including, amongst others, Bournemouth, Weymouth, Hastings and Eastbourne. A press article refers to several of Alton's prestigious theatre tours that year, with Tom, Vince, Roy Castle and Paul Daniels.

In a recent letter, Vince recalls:

' I well remember working with Alton in Torquay for the week. There was a female singer on, Joanne Aspey, and Bruce Thompson - a one-man-band. Also Paul and Barry Harman, who went on to become *The Chuckle Brothers*, and a favourite, with their BBC TV Kids' Show. The band was in the 'pit' for the first half, and on stage with me for the second.

When Alton was on, he introduced the orchestra and they took bows by noisily erecting stepladders – climbing up and waving to the stalls, over the pit rail; sometimes in crash helmets and goggles, woolly hats, wigs; mop heads thrust upwards; all to great laughs, I must say. But did it faze Alton? Not a bit! He took it all in good part – as they say.

After one evening's show, we all went to an hotel, off the front somewhere, because we thought we could get a late drink; we were refused entry, by a burly doorman. Alton said to him, "Now look, we are not going to give you any trouble. Just let us in. If you don't I'll do my act. I'm warning you!" The doorman gave way!'

Vince Hill.

I remember Roy Castle and I, literally hanging on hysterically to each other in the wings, the first time we saw Paul and Barry Harman, at the 'Thameside Theatre', Ashton-under-Lyme. I toured with 'The Bachelors', and they would greet me at every bandcall with: "How's yous today?" I'd reply "Fine." The query would be inverted. Then in a dozen meetings, we never ever exchanged another single word!

I did a one-nighter with the singing duo 'Peters and Lee'. Despite Lennie Peters being blind, he was a great lover of practical jokes. When it came to the second house, I blew into the trombone, only to find that he'd inserted a piece of paper, between the water key and the end of the instrument. Result? A glorified raspberry. The problem with pranks like that, is that they only amuse the perpetrator – the unfortunate comic is left with no finish to his act, the band are embarrassed and the audience are totally mystified.

Gordon and I were then asked to write the script for a BBC TV programme, 'Hits and Mrs', featuring bandleader Eddie Gray and singer Patti Somers. The guests were Carl Wayne, (who's now the lead singer with 'The Hollies'), Eileen Cameron and Billy Howard.

At the end of July 1978, I played, of all things, a scriptwriter, Paul Witzisky, in an ATV sit-com, 'A Soft Touch', starring Maureen Lipman. During a break in rehearsals, she came out with one of the most perceptive lines I've ever heard, when I referred to my affection for eccentrics. She said, "I've never met a human being who wasn't eccentric" - absolutely one hundred per cent true!

In a recent broadcast Alton heard her quip: "I think I'm suffering from Jewish Alzheimer's - I've forgotten everything – except how to bear a grudge!"

Moira Anderson and Vera Lynn were two other stars whom Alton appeared with that year. Jo has fond memories of one particular show, when

Would you buy a used joke from this bunch? AD, Ken Morley, Paul McDowall and Johnny Dennis in "A Soft Touch", ATV 31 July 1978. Paul was the original "man in the white suit" with The Temperance Seven.

Alton was on the bill with Dame Vera. "I've never seen any performer work an audience like she did. I don't think there was anyone, anywhere in the theatre, she wasn't singing to! Some artistes will probably just turn, and if they're right-handed, work predominantly to the right-hand side of the audience, but she was *so* professional. She looked into everyone's eyes (or so it seemed)." Rather than being seated in the audience, Jo was standing at the back, so she had an ideal vantage point from which to observe the singer's technique.

Jo had a chance to appear on celluloid, in the late 70s, (she wasn't exactly desperate to do so!) "I was asked by another agent to provide an actress for a small part in a promotional film, *The Rise and Fall of Papa Rossi*, with Anthony Morton ('Carlos' from *Crossroads*). I couldn't find anyone available at short notice, so I thought, 'Well, I'll have a go' (never having acted before). It went well."

Time and again I played the 'Cresta Club'. One of the most memorable was with another bunch of old friends – 'Freddie and the Dreamers'. I was doubling as compère, and Freddie wanted an off-stage introduction. You know the sort of thing? There's a roll on the drums and a voice from the Gods says: "Ladies and gentlemen, the 'Cresta Club' is proud to present…" If only the audience could have seen me, because behind the curtains, as I'm trying to introduce Freddie, he's 'goosing' me and I'm leaping around, in a fond imitation of him – trying to get away!

It's not the sort of introduction you'd normally associate with him…

No, well I realised he only wanted to do it that way so that he could goose me!

I also started writing a newspaper column for my local paper, 'The Northfield Messenger', just covering artistes living within the area covered by the paper. Someone predicted that it wouldn't last a month, but it lasted for just over three years.

By another strange coincidence, Pat Roach, the biographical subject of one of the co-writer's books, was interviewed twice for Alton's column in the *Messenger*, as he lived in the vicinity. The interviews were about Pat's Health Club and his showbiz career. Looking through a selection of articles that Alton wrote for the paper, it's surprising how many interesting celebrities were to be found, within the Northfield area alone.

My friend, Ronnie Hayward and I, wrote a TV script for the ventriloquist, Roger de Courcey and Nooky the Bear. Then by coincidence, I went back to Glasgow, to appear with Roger at the 'King's Theatre' again, in October 1978. Having past memories of the theatre, I felt 'simpatico'. I've never been one for practical jokes, but Roger and I got on so well, I couldn't resist it. As he came out on stage, he saw a man sitting up in a box, reading a newspaper, with cigar smoke coming over the top of the newspaper. I thought I'd got away with it - until the last night.

I used to finish my act, at that time, by singing a song, taking a bow and almost exiting. Without looking, I'd stretch out my arm into the wings, they'd hand me the trombone and I'd take it – and appear to be startled, to find a trombone in my hand. It doesn't sound funny, but it always got a laugh. On the last night, I reached out, without looking, and came back on stage, carrying a lamp-stand, complete with a frilly shade!

Pete Murray invited Alton to talk about the problems of the warm-up comic, on his BBC radio show, *Open House*, from London. Pete explained that when Wilfrid Brambell (Dad Steptoe) appeared on the show, he put his hands flat on the table. He was so nervous, that when he lifted them up, there was a pool of water under each hand! Readers may recall Ken Windsor's comments, that the other half of the comedy-duo, Harry H. Corbett (Steptoe's son), had provided his most memorable radio interview.

>>> The full interview is currently included on the scriptwriters, Galton and Simpson's website.

*I told Pete: "It's a strange thing about comedy. You can have an entire room laughing **helplessly**, on their backs, arms and legs waving in the air, and the one man at the front, who isn't laughing, bugs you." Harold Berens said to me: "Forget him – he's Polish!"*

This is the real trombone.

There's an annual event that takes place at most RAF camps, where the officers play the sergeants in all sorts of games, up and down the corridors of the Mess. I was at RAF Scampton, on the day of this event, which coincided with the new station commander arriving. His very first duty was to kick off the five-a-side-football, in the corridor. So the referee blew the whistle, he stepped forward, kicked the ball, and was tackled by a sergeant, who broke his leg. He had to be carried out of the camp!

Towards the end of the 70s, corporate entertainment was starting to take over. Quite frequently, comics were being booked as after dinner speakers.

I found that this type of entertainment really suited me. Generally speaking, the audiences were more attentive. Also, you were on earlier, before they got too drunk! At one dinner, the comedy impressionist, Audrey Jeans, sat next to me. I loved the one story she told, about shopping in the West End. She stopped in a shop doorway, just to look at the gowns. She heard a voice saying (Jewish saleswoman): "Good morning madam, have I got a dress for you!" She said: "Well, I'm only looking." "Madam, do me a favour please – try the dress on." Being a compliant type, she said: "Oh, alright," went in and tried the dress on. Came out of the cubicle: "Oh Madam, that dress suits you to a 'T'!" But Audrey was trying to explain that she was only window-shopping. "Madam, we'll get a second opinion – my partner Becky. Becky - madam's

Two constestants for the Miss Sunday Mercury Competition. Groucho was disqualified and, looking at Jo, we wuz robbed.

dress!" "Madame, it's so you!" *Audrey's panicking a bit by this time, thinking: 'How do I get out of this?' So she goes back to the door, ostensibly just to look at the colour of the dress, in the natural light. She turns round, to walk back into the shop, and a voice says: "Good morning madam - have I got a dress for you!"*

One of the agents Alton worked for wore the most atrocious, ill-fitting toupeé, but nobody, under any circumstances, ever mentioned it. They came out of *Llanidloes Community Centre* one night, and got into his car, which was badly misted up. Without saying a word, he snatched his wig off, polished the windscreen with it, placed it back on his head, and *still* nobody referred to it!

Another agent, Sheila Tozer, also ran a dancing school. She'd frequently contribute lines such as: "I can't speak to you now Alton, I've got all the girls up on their points!"

On the earnings front, things had been going very well for several years, but unfortunately our accountants had not had the same good fortune. One finished up in a mental hospital, another nursed a parent who developed cancer of the throat, and a third developed skin cancer.

The net result was that Alton's accounts were neglected, and left in a terrible state. He was summoned, with some trepidation, to the offices of the Inland Revenue.

By a stroke of luck, a financial advisor had put me in touch with another accountant, Colin Beale, and we teamed up, with just half an hour to go before the meeting. Once inside, this seemingly quiet and inoffensive man demonstrated that he was actually made of steel. In a calm, but very firm manner, he put my case so well, that with the co-operation of the tax officials, it was sorted out in short order. In a matter of weeks, I paid a substantial amount in back-tax, but then received a whacking refund that completely wiped out the payment. > > > Almost a quarter of a century later, we are still with Harrison, Beale of Coventry.

Although Jo and Alton had loved being part of the showbusiness community in Dominic Drive, for almost ten years, they made a decision, prompted by their new accountant, to buy their own house.

In May we moved further out, towards the Lickey Hills. On the day we moved, another friend, John Spragg, was helping us carry bits and pieces in, when he spotted that the house was then called 'The Pines'. "What a shame Alton," he said, "you've got the vowels in the wrong order!"

The house heralded a new era for us, especially when John Clarke, at the Pebble Mill studios, came up with something that completely suited me. I was just about to step into a new role that would take me headlong into a different direction - something lasting, enjoyable and very rewarding.

Chapter 15 –

NO – YOUR PLACE

Question 1: Where would I find the quotation: And Adam saith to Eve, in the Garden of Eden, "After I've eaten this apple, you want me to WHAT?"
Question 2: Who wrote the score of the Jewish musical 'Morrie Poppins'?
Question 3: Who attended a school that was so poor, the games master had a black belt in ludo?

In February 1979, Alton dropped into *Rackhams*; seated at a table in their café, he realised that the assistants were sniggering at him.

I turned round, and there behind me was a veritable barrage of me's. The 'Warwickshire West Midlands Star' magazine had put me on their front cover and I was sitting against a backdrop of about thirty copies!

John Clarke came up with the idea of an inter-town quiz, in the summer of that year. It had long been acknowledged that, if they had nothing else going for them, at least comics could think quickly on their feet. This is why they used Bruce Forsyth, Jimmy Tarbuck, Ted Rogers, Bob Monkhouse and Des O'Connor. Alton came up with the title *Know Your Place*.

John, taking his career in his hands, asked me to 'front' the new quiz series. I suggested that Gordon and I should set the questions and write the scripts, but John, quite rightly, wasn't totally convinced that our background as comedic writers was the right one for this. We therefore wrote him a sample script, which was tested in the sombre atmosphere of the BBC boardroom. Despite the forbidding surroundings, it worked.

John explains: "*Know Your Place* was a knockout tournament, with four quarter finals, two semis and a final. Seven shows in all and eight towns to be researched. Four of the towns would have to yield material for at least two programmes, because obviously we couldn't ask the same questions on the second round. The nightmare was if a town with hardly any historical interest or local interest fielded a good team. This could mean them going through to the final (i.e. three programmes) with a sparse research file to find questions in. However, the nightmare never came true, fortunately. As it happened, most towns had a degree of interest, if you looked deeply under the surface."

Being hyperactive, I volunteered to accompany John to each town, helping to interview the would-be contestants, eliminating the least likely and finishing up, hopefully, with a well-contrasted trio, (plus a substitute, in case of injuries).

John elaborates: "Alton presented three series of this Midlands' local knowledge quiz, and I was delighted that he expected to take on a lot of the work in preparing the script and the material himself. We both felt that the internal chemistry of the teams needed to be right, because the answers were intended to be discussion points rather than mere facts."

The research involved personal visits to every competing town and long sessions in local libraries. There were also discussions with museum curators and visits to newspaper offices. Their diligence was frequently rewarded with surprising questions and answers, thereby enhancing the show's audience appeal.

"Alton told me that whenever the programmes went out he was so nervous," recalls John, "that he always watched them sitting on his stairs at home: he would see the television through the struts in the staircase. Of *course* he was nervous. If he hadn't been, *I* would have been nervous. I was always happier working with a presenter who was on edge to get things right. The ones who didn't care usually resulted in retakes, goofy grins, and remarks like: 'The viewers love it when things go wrong.' That may have been the case, but the producers don't love it, I can assure you. We had limited studio and editing time, and over-runs in either place were frowned upon."

The September 1979 issue of the *Warwickshire West Midlands Star* ran a full-page article about the show, describing John as '… one of the most prolific and imaginative producers at BBC's Pebble Mill headquarters.' A later paragraph referred to the series as ' a triumph of co-operation between John Clarke and Alton Douglas.'

The aforementioned duo, arriving in Burton early one morning, with time to kill, went into the only place showing any signs of life, which happened to be an Indian restaurant.

We explained to the owner that we were there representing the BBC. It's amazing how those three initials could open all sorts of doors. We just wanted coffee, but as he walked back up the restaurant I heard him say (Asian accent, very akin to Peter Sellers, in *The Millionairess*): *'Two coffees:* **two coffees** *– oh dear – declare a dividend!'*

If your idea of a television studio is a vast, hangar-like place, with a large demonstrative audience, I should tell you that we recorded our performance in the News Studio (at Pebble Mill) with just an audience of twenty-five people, twelve for each team, and a bodyguard for the quizmaster!

An article in the *Birmingham Mail* informed readers that Alton had been occupied for several weeks, researching the series. He elaborated:

'We have tried to get some real local characters, folks with something to say, to take part. We will have lots of trick questions – like well-known buildings photographed from strange angles, as well as some more complicated ones. It should be a lot of fun.'

> > > Some months later, a bright spark at the BBC decided to call a radio sit-com, starring Roy Dotrice, *Know Your Place*. Alton's first series was between teams from Hereford, Warwick, Stamford, Loughborough, Shrewsbury, Dudley, Burton and Hinckley. It commenced its seven-week run on 11 September 1979.

A favourite image stays with me. In Stamford's opening round, I asked Stephen Walker a question about the Buzzard Song. Without a second's hesitation, he stuck a finger in his ear, tuned himself up, and sang it with enormous gusto!

Jo gave valuable assistance by typing out all the scripts. Whilst recalling the show, she was reminded of another occasion, "... when Alton was doing an interview slot for *ATV Today*. I was interested to see how the programme went out on air, so the producer Ted Trimmer took me into the control room and I watched the whole broadcast. I love the practical side. It wasn't until afterwards that I realised that Ted's sister was the film-star Deborah Kerr."

Our programme was an immediate success, and in no time at all, attracted a huge audience, for a region that covers about a twelfth of the UK – a very big audience - it was confirmed in 'The Stage' newspaper. It said: 'What was wrong with national television programmes, when local programmes like Know Your Place could attract 2½ million people?'

One of the local newspapers criticised me for over-using the phrase 'in fact'. So we re-ran the first programme and found that, in fact, I'd only used 'in fact' twice.

A contestant from Loughborough told me that he'd gone home and proudly announced that he'd been selected to appear. His daughter wasn't quite so sure: "Are you going to be on television daddy? Oh, how embarrassing!"

We had one complete round where no one got a single question right. Panic! When the programme was timed it was four minutes over. Solution? Take the whole round out. Perfect!

Gordon Stretch recalls his role as Alton's fellow researcher: "I was employed by the BBC, and went to some of the towns featured in the series, finding people who had local knowledge. I remember going to Burton and a few other places. Much of the research was done over the telephone, for example, contacting local historians; their names and addresses could usually be provided by the town's library."

When Alton's present co-writer referred to his considerable skills as a wordsmith, and also the originality of his comedy, his brother, Maurice, who has watched these talents blossom, over the years, commented: "I think Gordon Stretch brought a lot of that out in him. If you work with people, things rub off on you, don't they? I always say to people: 'Don't copy; pick out the good points and use them.' "

Once Alton and Gordon had gathered the information, generously assisted by a variety of people, the next step was devising the questions. "There'd be teams from two towns competing in each programme," explains Gordon. "These were mainly about their own town. There was an odd extra – when the towns in the contest had reached the second or third round, they were asked questions about the others. Alton and I would work independently at first, and then co-operate together. The interesting thing for me was the trick questions, because you could have a bit of fun with those!"

The trick round involved asking simple questions in as difficult a fashion as our crafty minds would allow. The show painted a vivid picture of the West Midlands towns involved. I'm no fuddy-duddy, but reading books and visiting museums has always been of great importance to me. The intention was to rekindle some of that interest and get people back into their local museums and libraries, which are such a great source of knowledge and enjoyment.

In 1980, as John and Alton began plans for a second series of *Know Your Place*, the BBC suddenly announced its intention to cut regional budgets. In the concluding paragraph of a *Sunday Mercury* article, dated 6 April 1980, Alton took a philosophical view:

'Everyone has to suffer cuts to help curb inflation. There's no reason why I should not be affected like everyone else. Anyway, I find that invariably out of something bad, something good will turn up.'

A minor outcry developed in the Midlands' papers and the show was hurriedly put back into the schedules. However, the delay meant that the second series couldn't be broadcast until the beginning of the following year.

Meanwhile, Alton continued with a variety of cabaret bookings, and warm-ups for *'The Grace Kennedy and Lena Zavaroni Shows'* at Shepherds Bush. His records from that period show that he received a princely repeat fee for an edition of *Citizen Smith* 'for videos at sea' - £1-55 - (he'd originally thought it was £155, but the point had been put in the wrong place!) More theatre shows followed, with, amongst others, Walter Landau, Joe Brown and the Bruvvers, John Boulter, The Brotherhood of Man, Keith Harris and Orville.

In October 1980, they started recording *Know Your Place* again and transmission of the second series began on Tuesday 6 January 1981. The show ran for seven weeks, culminating in the grand final on 17 February.

*Modelling for a
knitwear company
(or was it a plug for
a tree surgeon?)*

Bookings were coming in at a far greater rate than in previous years. Alton's career was going 'from strength to strength'. On 27 January 1981, viewers were able to watch him in two different programmes, during the *same* evening: shortly before his appearance in *Seconds Out*, starring Robert Lindsay, Alton was on screen, hosting his popular quiz programme.

Ray Butt, the producer of 'Citizen Smith', not only asked me to warm-up this new series, 'Seconds Out', but also to appear in one episode, as a dozy headwaiter, who is constantly getting in the way, during a fight in a sporting club. He gets a custard pie in his face!

After rehearsals for *Citizen Smith*, on Wednesday of that week, Alton hurtled along the motorway, in order to arrive on time for a booking as guest speaker, at the annual dinner of the *Burial and Cremation Authorities*, in the *Winter Gardens*, Weston.

They turned out to be one of the jolliest crowds I'd ever entertained, even if they did sit me next to a man who spent most of the evening describing in detail, how to embalm a corpse – just in case – you understand? I think what helped in my speech, was that I came up with a 'final' story that no one had heard before, because obviously, they'd heard almost every 'death' tale in the world:

An old lady, living way up in the Highlands, was on her deathbed. Her son said (broad Scottish accent): "Mother, is there any last wish ya have?" She said: "I've never heard the bagpipes." He said: "But mother, ya must have heard them a thousand times!" She said: "No, living up here in the hills, I've never actually heard them in the flesh." So he booked a piper and the man played everything, from strathspeys to reels, to laments to jigs. His mother was absolutely appalled at the sound, and sank further back into her pillows. Her son saw her reaction and was horrified. He said: "Mother, are ya alright?" She said: "Och aye - but thank God there's nae smell!"

During the quiz show heats, Alton was cornered by an irate woman, who was firmly convinced that he'd been biased against her town.

She proceeded to give me the 'dressing-down' of my life. I've often wondered how she would have reacted if her team had lost! One of the towns featured was Wolverhampton, and we chose as our panel, Tom Bennett, Dennis Moore (little did we know that this was the first step in another lengthy road for both of us), and Rachel Heyhoe-Flint.

Dennis Moore recalls: "Alton and John Clarke came to a hotel in Wolverhampton. They had previously mentioned the programme in the newspaper. I hadn't seen it, but my children suggested that I ought to have a go at this. John and Alton were in company with Rachel Heyhoe-Flint; also present were Tom Bennett – (who was a local lecturer at one of our large schools or colleges) – and myself. We were not exactly *grilled*, but we had a nice little meal and chatted about it. That's how the team came into being."

Rachel was perhaps not the most knowledgeable person we ever featured, but she was certainly the most fun. Due to her background as the ex-captain of the England Women's' Cricket Team, we both discussed our favourite sport at some length. She told me that whereas men wore a box, to protect their nether regions, the ladies' protection was known as a 'manhole cover'! At the end of the series, which, incidentally, Wolverhampton won, she presented me with a miniature cricket bat, bearing the legend: 'To Alton, love Rachel, Know Your Place Dunce'.

Dennis comments: "We *did* win the trophy, and were presented with a magnificent piece of plastic, by the BBC, which was a sort of 'zigzag', with one or two local places on it. We therefore said that we ought to give it to the Mayor of Wolverhampton. So we went along and met the mayor and gave him this trophy, to put with the mayoral silver. It wasn't silver, of course; it was the cheapest plastic you could imagine! I've been into the Town Hall on many occasions now, and I've never seen it on display. It must be tucked away somewhere.

"We got lots of publicity out of it, and really, what I enjoyed so much was the 'street-cred' it gave me, as a result of being on the television, doing radio broadcasts, meeting an author and eventually becoming an author. It's been absolutely wonderful! In fact, it's been almost wall-to-wall humour and goodwill with Alton.

"We played three rounds," continues Dennis – "Cheltenham, Leicester, and then we got to the final." Cuttings show that the first round, between Wolverhampton and Cheltenham, (the third of seven programmes) was played on 20 January.

John Clarke recalls: "Cheltenham, with its long tradition of respectability and genteel veneer, yielded some eyebrow-raising moments. In the museum we found a flattish disk made from brass and mahogany, with a small glass lens in its middle. This turned out to be a concealed camera for private detectives, to be worn under the starched dickey shirt front, in full evening dress. The idea was that the detective could take photographs of ladies dancing with their boyfriends and provide evidence in divorce cases. I don't believe the team got that one."

We discovered a turn-of-the century wicker ball with a bell in it. After a great deal of agonising it turned out to be a ball for blind children to play with!

Although the programme had been a public and critical success, not everyone was of the same opinion.

A man stopped me in the street with, (broad Birmingham accent) " Ay yo - yo do that programme on the telly, don't yer?" I said: "Know Your Place?" He said: "Ah – that's it – yeah!" I said: "Yes." He said: "It's crap!"

In March 1981, Alton found himself warming-up the most prestigious show he'd ever done - *The Peggy Lee Show.*

She's always been my favourite singer, and despite being very poorly, she was absolutely magnificent. Because of a technical breakdown, she had to sing 'The Folks Who Live On The Hill' three times; it just got better and better. Afterwards, I sat next to her in the Green Room and collected a signed photograph – one of only a handful I've ever requested. Although I'd been asked to do my usual job, for shows featuring Vic Damone and Ann-Margaret, I decided that night that I couldn't possibly top that one. So after hundreds of shows, I decided to make 'The Peggy Lee Show' my warm-up swan song.

From 14 - 18 April 1981, Alton appeared in a comedy thriller by Raymond Dyer, performed at Birmingham's *Old Rep*, and directed by Norman Painting (Phil, of The Archers). This was the inaugural performance of a new company of theatrical performers, entitled the *Media Players*. As their title suggests, the company members were all successful radio and television performers, who also happened to love the theatre. Other cast members included Jonathan Owen of BBC'S *Triangle*, Stella Monsell of *Grange Hill*, Ralph Lawton – *Crossroads*; also, Kay Styles of *Z Cars* and musical actress, Sandra Carrier.

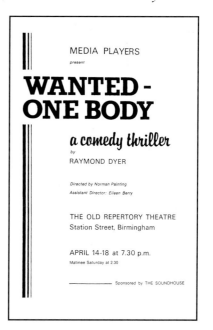

MEDIA PLAYERS

present

WANTED - ONE BODY

a comedy thriller

by

RAYMOND DYER

Directed by Norman Painting
Assistant Director: Eileen Berry

THE OLD REPERTORY THEATRE
Station Street, Birmingham

APRIL 14-18 at 7.30 p.m.
Matinee Saturday at 2.30

———— Sponsored by THE SOUNDHOUSE

I was cast as the murderer, Dr. Brown, in a whodunnit called 'Wanted – One Body'. To age and disguise me, I had to wear a white wig, which one cast member insisted on calling my 'ski hat'.

As with all creative projects, it's inevitable that some are more successful than others. Fred Norris, writing for the *Birmingham Mail*, was initially very enthusiastic about the company's venture, but less so, after the performance. In his opinion, the play's direction was insufficiently sharp, and was 'allowed to ramble.' He comments: ' I would have thought that a new company of such experienced players would have decided on something more theatrically rewarding – both for themselves and the audience.' However, Gordon Stretch recalls Alton's performance, and commented recently: "I can honestly say that I thought his acting was brilliant." Dyer, meanwhile, had changed his Christian name to Charles, and had become one of Britain's leading playwrights, his most famous play being *Rattle of a Simple Man*.

On 19 April 1981, the day after the final performance of *Wanted – One Body*, Alton appeared at the *Pavilion Theatre* in Torquay, with Alan Randall, (famous for his impersonation of George Formby). Once again, Vince Hill, Alton's friend and fellow performer, topped the bill. An article about the show referred to a new programme, which Alton was due to record later that year. Producer, Marek Kanievska, it announced, was putting together a drama series called *City* (later changed to *Muck and Brass*).

In tandem, Alton continued to appear in cabaret. One of these engagements was a booking at the *Savoy Hotel* in Blackpool, entertaining delegates from the Labour Party Conference.

I got into the lift, wearing a dress suit and carrying my trombone. The only other occupant, Dennis Healey, greeted me with: 'My God – this is a first!" The other artiste that night was Roy Rivers, who performed his act on a unicycle. The audience did their utmost to trip him up. I've often wondered if Roy's fellow trade unionists would have been prepared to recompense him, if he'd broken a limb. I think brotherly love took a bit of a backseat that night!

At the *Mount Hotel* in Tettenhall, during a firm's dinner, Alton performed most of his act to almost complete silence, except for the top table, who laughed in all the right places.

Afterwards, the M.D. came over to me, pumped my hand, and gave me the biggest monetary tip I'd ever received. I asked him why – considering the mixed reaction? He said: "Last year we had a comedian who was 'filthy'. The workforce loved him, and my bank manager walked out. This year, he stayed for your act – sod the workforce!"

As a souvenir of a very strange evening, Jo and I used the extra money to buy a set of four Anton Pieck illustrations.

Back to 'Weymouth Pavilion' for a Sunday Concert - this time with The Wurzels. After the show, a woman came to the stage door and asked for my autograph: "I remember you some years ago, when you came here with Tony Mercer. At one point you came on dressed as Bernie Winters, with a bowler hat, a long overcoat, your trousers hitched up, and big boots on. How on earth did you manage to balance on those little white stilts?" MADAME, THOSE WERE THE FAMOUS LEGS!

Chapter 16 –

AIRING MY PARTS

Our producer wanted to be a do-it-yourself merchant – but unfortunately, he couldn't reach it.

Around August 1979, I made friends with a man who lived next-door-but-one to me, Dave Jones (stage name, Dave Mitty):

Dave started out as a musician in the late 50s, pursuing that professionally for about ten years, then became a singer/vocalist with his own band, followed by a three- year spell at Edgbaston School of Speech and Dramatic Art.

He explains: "With Alton's help, I did a lot of different, 'extra' work on TV. Then I got parts in a couple of TV plays, and did a lot of radio plays. After that I went solo as a comedy impressionist. Previously I'd had a residency at two or three clubs, as a musician – when Alton came to see us. I was doing comedy impressions with my own band at *The Engine House*, in Tardebigge.

"I'd seen him on *The Golden Shot*, and in Cotteridge, going into the bank. I thought: 'I know that bloke!' His wife was a very good agent - I did a couple of jobs for her. We hadn't met, but I just used to ring up and she'd send us to places. Then one day, my neighbour here, came round and said, 'Ooh – there's somebody moving in next door. Have you heard of him? His name's Alton Douglas – he's a comedian.' I said: 'That's right, he's been on TV.' She said: 'He's moving in next week!'

"My son was playing in the front garden one day. I think Alton's wife said something to him, and I had a chat with them then. A couple of days after, I was trying to get into *Equity*, but I didn't know what you had to do. I took the 'bull by the horns', and knocked on Alton's door, one Sunday morning. He opened the door in his dressing gown – a funny place for a door!

"He invited me in and from then on we became good friends. He gave me so much help and advice. It doesn't matter whether you're a painter and decorator, musician, comedian, or street cleaner - he'll do anything to help you on in your career – almost to the point of *bullying* you into it! 'Come on – do it!' But he means very, very well.

"Alton and I sat in a coffee house one day, in town, wondering what I should call myself. He said: 'You'll have to get a good name. What about Dave Norton?' So I put that one down. Dave this and Dave that – and I thought of a few.

"It was Alton who came up with 'Mitty'. He'd been to see my act, and one of the props was a large wicker basket, with lots of clothes in it. I used to step into it and come out as someone else. So he said: 'The Make-believe World of Dave Mitty' – like the Danny Kaye film.

"I joined the Birmingham branch of *Equity*, with his help. He told me how many contracts you have to have, and so on. I was quite qualified to join. Then you have to have a professional person to come and see you, and recommend you; he arranged all of that for me." Alton taught Dave a range of aspects, concerning the technical and business side of showbusiness.

Like me, Dave was just starting to break through and get a few acting jobs. So when I was asked to record a play for the Derbyshire Education Authority, and knowing that they needed another voice, I thought of Dave.

Dave recalls: "I went to a few shows that Alton was on. One day he came round; he was always passing work on to me - do this and that - introducing me to agents. He said: 'Do you fancy a ride to Derby?' I said: 'Yeah.' He said: 'I'm recording an educational tape: it's a play.' I said: 'Oh that will be interesting.' We stopped halfway to Derby, to have a cup of tea, because of course, everywhere he goes he's got to have a cup of tea. He knows all the teashops and coffee places, where to get a nice cake - in Birmingham – and in the surrounding areas.

"He said: 'By the way, when you get there, tell them that you've done this sort of thing before.' I said: 'Done what before?' He said: 'Been in a play.' I said: 'What do you mean?' He said: 'Well - you're in it!' I said: 'Pardon?' What he'd done, he'd 'sold' me to *The Jack Denman Agency*, in Nottingham, knowing they were looking for another character. So he sold the idea of me to them – and I didn't know about it!

"I said: 'Well I'll have a go!' We got there and they gave us a script, and this bloke who was in charge, the producer, said: 'Who can do a Geordie accent?' Well I turned round – and at that moment there wasn't a soul in the room except me! I managed to get through it – they were all very pleased. I've still got the tape here somewhere. But I sound like a Scotsman – with a Welsh accent!

The scripts had been co-written by Clive Hardy, a great bear-like character, with an enormous zest for life; someone who was about to take me down another avenue. His partner, Cyril Sprenger, turned out to be a jazz pianist of repute, so we were bound to hit it off. Eventually I dragooned Cyril into being a member of the Derby team, in 'Know Your Place'.

Clive recognised me from the quiz series and asked if I'd ever thought of putting together a book? I told him that I'd approached BBC Publications with the idea of a quiz book, but because it was only a regional programme, they weren't in the slightest bit interested. Clive said: "I'll publish it." It transpired that he was a partner in Thomas Aleksandr Publishing (the Russian spelling; the title derives from the names of his lads). He was as good as his word, and our first book was about to appear.

Dave Mitty continues: "Alton and I did a lot more work for those people after that, including some educational programmes for Spanish television; they really liked us. For the one job, they wanted a Russian. I couldn't do it, Alton got it straight off: did a beautiful Russian accent.

"Another day he said: Do you fancy a ride to Cambridgeshire? I'm appearing at *The Barking Fox*, at Market Needham.' So I went to a country club with him – one of the last of the nice places, before the discos took over. We got there about five o'clock. We had the bandcall. Then a couple of coaches pulled up – and they were all ladies. I thought: 'How's he going to cope with this?' Because normally, when all these women come down – all giggling and laughing – they'd be the ideal audience for a male stripper, or a 'blue' comedian.

"Well, Alton came on. He had them in the palm of his hand; he never swore once – he never told one blue joke. They loved him: I think he did two encores! I thought: 'How lovely to be able to do that, with a roomful of women, who you'd expect to be entertained by a stripper or a blue comedian.' But he did it with his *own* sense of humour, his original jokes. I think he walked around the room at the end, playing his trombone!"

Alton confirms that he'd had no advance notice about all-female audience; as on so many occasions in his career, he had to make a rapid adjustment.

Here I am as the slightly self-conscious guest speaker at the South Staffs Townswomen's Guild Dinner, Masonic Hall, Aldridge, 13 February 1981.

They used to book me to appear at 'The Barking Fox', each year, to coincide with a Test Match, so that as I commuted every day I could listen to it, on the radio.

Dave confirms: "He never did the *easy* thing, by turning himself into a working mens' club act. He was sophisticated: he never swore, he never told a dirty joke – and they absolutely *loved* him! I thought: 'That's fantastic.' I was really proud to be with him!

"Alton brought John Clarke up to *The Engine House*, once again, to try to get me into television. He introduced me – and I was doing my act – comedy impressions and a bit of singing. They had dinner, while they sat there, watching me, and the band. I saw John laughing. He enjoyed it, but I don't think I was the sort of thing he was looking for. But I appreciated what Alton had done. He was fantastic."

John decided to go with 'Nights at the Swan' instead – (nothing personal Dave).

John asked Alton to compère a trio of programmes, under that collective title. The first of these was broadcast on 21 August 1981. They were recorded at the *Swan Theatre* in Worcester, and consisted of a *Black Country Night Out*, a magic show and an evening of jazz, featuring the *Jenny Miller Band*, fronted by Harborne-based husband and wife team, Jenny Miller and Eddie Matthews. Mike Gancia was among the four Midland magicians featured in the final show.

"They were outside broadcasts," explains John, "and challenged the internal system of the BBC, because they were done much more cheaply than network shows. One evening I was wearing a very brightly coloured sweatshirt, because when I'm working I don't expect to be in the public eye. However, circumstances required me to go out on stage and talk to the musicians, during a break in recording. Alton, keeping the audience warmed up, explained to them that the producer was the man in the rainbow shirt, trying to look inconspicuous."

In November 1981, the third series of 'Know Your Place' was recorded. There had been quite a degree of opposition at the BBC, strangely enough, because the show had been such a smash hit. A kind of snobbery existed among some older members of the corporation, that associated success and large viewing figures, more with commercial television, than with the 'Beeb'. Initially, they said no, to another set of programmes, but they had reckoned without yours truly!

Dennis Moore observes: "It beat a lot of records, and *was* really popular, but if you know your BBC very well, and I've come to know them, they will always take a programme off, when it's right at its peak. They will never let it go off-scale. They took it off at its peak – and that was it."

Gordon Stretch explains: "Alton, using positive thinking, said: 'No, it's not going to be the end of the series.' To put it simply, if you say you're going to achieve something by such-and-such a time, and you really believe it, your subconscious takes that on board. So all the time afterwards it's looking out for any opportunities to guide you in the right direction, to achieve what you set out to do. As Alton once put it: 'It puts out antennae, picking up anything.'"

Alton explained this approach to his co-author, during one of our early meetings, when we were first becoming acquainted, adding that it's often a two-way process. (I drew comfort from reassuring myself that I'd been following a similar approach for years!)

"He put me on to a book called *The Magic of Believing*," continues Gordon. "It hadn't come home to me that that was the organised way of doing things. But when I read it, I became excited, because I could see then how it works. A number of authors have written books on the subject, all very inspiring. There's nothing complicated about it – it's so simple. Just believe that you are going to achieve such a thing or have some certain thing come your way, within a certain time. The subconscious mind immediately begins to work and continues to work. Instead of vaguely believing, you repeat mantras of your own to reinforce your EXPECTATION, which is necessary to the achievement of the goal."

I should explain that some time earlier I read an article by Liberace, in which he said that he'd asked Phyllis Diller how it was that she'd become the only successful patter comedienne in the States. She said it was after reading a book, 'The Magic Of Believing', by Professor Claude M. Bristol, and it had changed her life. He bought a copy and it changed his, so I went out and bought a copy and it changed mine. So if you want to buy a copy... The concept of this can be summed up in one sentence: "Believe that you have it - and you have it."

One of the key concepts behind positive thinking is that the mind cannot hold a positive thought and a negative thought at the same time – so why not think positively?

So I devised a system whereby, just before I went on stage, I would form a circle with my thumb and index finger, representing the hole that the positive thought would fit into. After doing this a few times, I started experiencing a minor electric jolt, going up my arm – and I knew it was working! It doesn't matter whether anything physical happens or not, only that you believe that it works – for you.

I would always have new lines to try out and I would click my fingers to embed them into my mind. I don't know now if I was conscious of it or not, but so many people asked me why I was muttering to myself, and clicking my fingers, in the 'wings', that I don't know which came first. One of the offshoots of positive thinking is that you also learn to compartmentalise the different sections of your world, so that even if terrible things are happening in your private life, you can shut them off for a while and get on with the business of getting laughs. (If you're a comic, that is!)

In November 1981, our modest first book was published, and 'Know Your Place – The Quiz Book' was the first link in a chain, which stretches on to this day, and hopefully, on into eternity.

A London-based agent, Alan Foenander, rang Alton, offering him an audition for a Tesco's commercial.

Dave Mitty, on reading the brief, suggested that I went along in an anorak, a university scarf, and carrying a pipe. I walked in for the interview, and, miracle-of-miracles, there on the storyboard was a figure, looking exactly like me. The advertising agent took one look and said: "Christ – you're him," and sent all the other actors home! It turned out to be the most lucrative job I'd ever had. For a one-day shoot, with repeat fees, I earned over two thousand pounds. Yes – I did buy Dave a drink.

This was also a significant time for Alton, because of two major television programmes. The first of these, the new series *Muck and Brass*, ('telegraphed' in our previous chapter), hit ITV screens at 9pm, on Tuesday 19 January.

In the belief that comics could portray sincerity as well as any actor, producer Marek Kanievska had cast several of us – Mel Smith, Tony Kent, Les Wilson, Jim Bowen and myself - in straight parts.

Johnny Allan was featured in the local press, with his own variation on this theme - namely that "The best actors in the world are wrestlers." As 'Farmer Jim Allan' he had been a successful wrestler, winning both the British and European middleweight championships, at the peak of his career. Having acted in several other popular TV series, he was offered the role of John Roman, a builder, in *Muck and Brass*.

Lindsay Duncan, AD and Martin Oldfield try to look intelligent while Mel Smith reads us the Riot Act, "Muck and Brass".

As some of us were playing councillors, we went to the Council House to do research and get the 'flavour' of the place. Sir Stanley Yapp, seeing several comics in the balcony, came running up, fearing I'm sure, that we were going to 'take the mickey' out of council life. If only he'd known – it was worse!

'Muck and Brass' was about corruption in high office. I played a sixty-year-old character called John Rutland, the owner of a sweetshop. (ATV rented a real shop, chosen because it was quite grotty, and found out, the day before shooting, that the owner was painting the outside, to improve its appearance!)

For a fortnight we travelled from ATV each day, to various locations. Every night, Mel Smith would insist that I had a lift back, in his chauffeur-driven car. We got on famously, and at the end of the two weeks he presented me with a badge that read: 'You are a boring old fart!'

Alton's role was that of a man twenty years older, so once again, as with the *Old Rep* play, he had to be aged. Every morning, for ninety minutes, his face would be sprayed with liquid rubber latex, and in anticipation of his own ageing process, lines would be pushed into place. Ironically, a photograph in the *Evening Mail*, showing the end result of the process, is captioned: 'Make-up shows what Alton Douglas will look like in 2002'. However, we are co-writing this book, in 2003, and readers can be assured that his present appearance is more youthful, and far less doleful, than predicted!

My hair was thinned and I had to develop a slight stoop. I walked up to a crowd of 'extras' the first day and spotted an old friend, the comedian, Dick Pleasant. I re-introduced myself to a startled Dick. As we were talking, he kept giving me strange looks. After about five minutes, I couldn't stand it any longer: "Have you noticed anything Dick?" A shade too quickly, he said, "No mate, nothing." "Are you sure Dick?" "No, honestly mate, nothing at all." "Dick, they've aged me twenty years!" He said: "Blimey, I thought you looked old!"

Gordon explains: "Alton was hoping to be a villain, but he couldn't be a villain. He wasn't supposed to be a 'JR', but I think he had aspirations to

The four faces of Alton, 1979. (1) Aged to play John Rutland. (2) Sick at the result. (3) Your friendly "Know Your Place" chairman. (4) Back to normal? All the photographs were taken the same week.

leave comedy behind for a while, and play serious roles. He was interviewed by the chappie on the *Mail* - Fred Norris: the heading was: *The JR of the Midlands*. That was Alton's opinion of himself, you see - not Fred Norris' opinion! I mean to say, can you imagine J.R. handing a bag of sweets, or something similar, over a counter and saying: "That'll be 25p please!"

We discussed the sardonic nature of the Birmingham sense of humour, which invariably takes the form of an *ostensibly* serious comment, about a subject that can't possibly be taken seriously! "Alton had to dance", recalled Gordon, – "and Alton can't dance – any more than I can." Did he, perhaps, have two left feet? "Three, I think! He had to glide through in a dance scene," recalls Gordon. "They didn't show his feet – just the top half!

There was an Asian actor, who was a member of our little group, Darien Angadi, who did a really superb job as Mel's 'side-kick'. Sadly, before the series was transmitted, he died in very tragic circumstances. The programme did provide me with one wonderful legacy. I met a very fine actor, Raymond Mason, who gave me so much encouragement and advice and even an 'intro' to his agent, John Cadell. It's always amazed me how generous artistes can be, sharing contacts, even if it meant that you could be poaching some of their work. Raymond and I are friends to this day.

Raymond has made over a thousand television appearances – "...some good, some bad and some I don't even care to think about," he comments. "I'm one of those actors to whom people say, 'Yes, we know who you are, but what's your name?'

"Alton and I have been mates for over two decades. In the course of his long and varied career – broadcaster, comedian, author, raconteur et al, Alton has proved himself to be a splendid character actor. But there's no surprise there! I've worked with him twice, in the series *Muck and Brass* and in *Boon*. I remember his 'bent' councillor in *Muck and Brass* with much affection. Of course, almost all the councillors in the series were bent (I certainly was!), but Alton's councillor was of a much more subtle bent than most!"

A congratulatory card, sent to Alton, from 'Raymond, Jill and the boys', reads as follows:

'Saw episodes 1 and 2 last night – you've given a super performance – should do you a lot of good – thought it all worked very well, and should be a great success. Marvellous camera-work, and utterly different from anything I've seen before! Hope you and yours have a super and prosperous '82.'

The second of Alton's January '82 television programmes was the third, (and as

Raymond Mason.

it transpired, the final) series of *Know Your Place*. Taking part were teams from Derby, Walsall, Birmingham, Melton Mowbray, Coventry, Ludlow, Gloucester and Bromsgrove.

Katie Wright had directed the opening series; the director for the second and third series was David Nelson. Following transmission, Alton was sitting in a coffee bar, opposite an elderly tramp, who stared, then stared again. Suddenly he shouted: "Alton Donald – *Know Your Towns!*"

I stopped a lady in Lichfield and asked for directions. She said, in one breath, "Go down to the bottom of the road turn left first left again I know who you are you're that Alton bloke on the telly and it's the second on the right." Another time, I was travelling on a train and the man next to me kept doing 'double-takes'. I thought: 'Any minute now, he's going to either mix up my name, ask me for an autograph, or insult me.' He peered again, reconsidered, and then decided: "Hey mate - hasn't this been a long week?"

At times I was accused of all sorts of mayhem, from downright cheating, to making one town's questions easier than their opponents (no, I can't work that one out either)! One lady wrote in and asked me not to crack my 'one-liners', because their fatuousness embarrassed her entire family, whereas everywhere I appeared in cabaret or as a speaker, people begged me to include more of my 'funnies' in the programme. The jokes stayed in, but they weren't allowed to detract from the seriousness of the questions

John Clarke comments: 'While avoiding jokes, as such, he always tried to write links that seemed engaging.'

Most of the programmes were recorded three months ahead, and despite a ban on such activities, one paper splashed its town's victory across the front pages, weeks before the show went out. Viewers were sometimes invited to take part in competitions. In round 5, for example, they were asked to *Hunt the Heritage*, by identifying mystery mansions and other landmarks.

Offbeat jobs seemed to follow me: a promotional evening for Lada Cars, with swimmer, Sharron Davies; a film for a London taxi firm (my contact lenses were playing me up, so I arrived wearing glasses. In bright sunlight the lenses turned black and I was told I looked like a 'hit-man' for the Mafia). A training film with another comedian, who said to me: "They've teamed this old biddy up with me as my wife. Have you ever seen mis-casting like this? I'll go over and stand by her and you can see." I looked at him, posing, permed hair, shirt open to the waist, gold medallion, rings on every finger, gleaming bracelets, and by his side, a plain, middle-aged lady with grey hair – and they looked exactly the same age!

During the making of 'Know Your Place' I discovered there hadn't been any books published about Birmingham during the Second World War. After a chat with Clive Hardy, I decided to see if the Birmingham Mail would be interested in publishing a scrapbook of events. Clive had already published 'Derby At War', so with that as a template, I was sure we could do a good job. I approached the paper and over a period of six months, they turned me down, time and time again. Then the Falklands War happened.

Chapter 17 -

ALTON AT WAR

"Charlie, I haven't seen you for a long time. Where have you been?" "I've been in the army." "Did you get a commission?" "No, just a flat wage."(Well, it was new in 1940)!

The whole country was fired with a spirit of patriotism, as the Falklands War came to a successful conclusion. The 'high-ups' at 'The Birmingham Mail' decided - you might think a touch cynically - that it was the perfect time to produce our Second World War book, 'Birmingham at War'. Mind you, I planned the launch for the day after Remembrance Sunday, so my middle name could be 'Exploitation'!

On the day Alton's first 'nostalgic' book was published, 12 November 1982, the Mayor of Birmingham received the first copy at the Council House and later that day Alton was featured on ATV's *Midlands Today*, talking about it.

Within forty-eight hours, the publishers covered their costs. No one can comprehend the thrill of seeing a shelf of your own books. So Jo and I, very much the novices in the book world, went to view our pride and joy at Hudson's Bookshop, in Birmingham. Nothing could have prepared us for the shock in store, however! Standing across the other side of the shop talking to the assistant, and with no one else around, we were shocked to see the entire display fall towards us. With literally thousands of titles in the shop, it was just our books that toppled off the shelf, as if a ghostly hand had given them a push.

Hudson's also featured in an incident in the life of a friend of theirs, the actor, Frank Marlborough. He was playing the Frankie Howerd role in *A Funny Thing Happened on the Way to the Forum*. The show came to the *Alexandra Theatre*.

This was Frank's first visit to Birmingham and the very first shop he went into was Hudson's. Within seconds of entering the shop, a tiny letter bomb went off on a bottom shelf. He suffered singed hairs on his legs, scorched trousers and the biggest shock of his life! The management insisted on replacing the trousers, but from that day onwards, the rest of the cast dubbed the show, 'A Funny Thing Happened on the Way to Birmingham'!

On Boxing Day, Jo and I drove to Sidmouth, where I'd been booked for the second consecutive Christmas, to appear in cabaret at the 'Riviera Hotel'. Afterwards, a man with a strong guttural accent said to me: "I vud like to purchase one of your books." I said, tentatively: "Where are you from?" "I am from Germany." I said: "Well, I don't think you're going to like the outcome – our side won!" He patted me on the shoulder: "I vas born in Smethwick!"

June Lowndes recalls going into W.H. Smith's. "It must have been one of Alton's first books. It sold extremely well. They were all piled up in a circle at the front, with quite a few people milling around. He had a good idea really, didn't he? Because he's got a memory and he digs things out. Like a reporter – really."

Which I wanted to be as a kid!

Ken Windsor recalls: "Just as I was giving up the cabaret-compèring, because the venues decided to switch to disco, Alton and people of his like were beginning to see exactly the same thing - the venues were drying up. This is why I admire the guy, to be honest. Alton and Jo turned round and said, 'Hang on a minute – in another six months we're going to be casualties. I'm sorry, but that's not going to happen to us!' They had the 'get-up-and-go' to say, 'What else can I do? What else have I got a talent for?' So, about six years after we first met, he started his writing venture, and he's never looked back." His previous experience as a journalist, scriptwriter, playwright, and so forth, meant that he had a wealth of writing experience to draw upon; with hindsight, it was a natural progression.

Within the first week of publication, 4,000 copies of *Birmingham at War* had been sold, and a second print run ordered. The book was a largely pictorial account of life in the city between 1939–1945. It contained approximately two hundred captioned photographs, reports, historical notes, stories, memories and anecdotes of Birmingham life, during that period. The *Evening Mail* reported that Alton, whom they described as 'Comedian, quizmaster, actor, author and after-dinner speaker', was "... over the moon and absolutely thrilled by its early success."

Presenting prizes to the winners of the West Bromwich Building Society's competition, based on "Know Your Place", 1982.

Clem Lewis, writing in the *Mail*, described the book as 'a unique record of the city at war.' Readers were able to order a copy, by completing a coupon printed below the article. Its author continued: 'This very special book will stir many memories, vividly illustrating an important part of the city's past.' It was suggested that this was not merely a book for the over forty-fives, but would also stimulate the interest of many others, including schoolchildren. Alton, Jo, Gordon Stretch and Clive Hardy, it was explained, had driven all over the city, meeting people with stories and pictures. Clem Lewis quoted a passage of Alton's, taken from the book:

'My thoughts, as I travelled the streets, were of marching men and women, devastation, mugs of tea, comradeship, heroism and above all, of wonderment that the human spirit could survive and triumph over anything (even some of those mugs of tea!).'

When Alton entered the book world, he was impressed by Clive Hardy's basic approach, of producing clear, uncomplicated books.

I liked that idea: books that weren't difficult to look at – that weren't 'arty-farty' books. But I wanted to take them a stage further. I wanted to make them more of a scrapbook. I looked at what he'd got and they were mainly pictures, with maybe an odd poster or advert. But I wanted them to have far more of a scrapbook feel, bearing in mind that somebody could look at our book and enjoy it, then six months later, look at it again and think: 'D'you know – I haven't seen half of this book before!'

Although he's essentially a highly organised person, I wondered if Alton had intended to create an informal style in his books – so that the contents didn't appear too set?

I don't know whether I ever thought of it like that, but I didn't want it to look like anyone else's book – that's the only way I can describe it really! I always thought that one day I would produce a book called 'The Birmingham Scrapbook', but Jo has always been against it, because the word 'scrap' can mean 'junk'.

When you look at our books, they're pictures, they're posters, old adverts, cartoons – they're a mixture of everything; they're not just photographs in a book. Quite a lot of people, like Ed Doolan from Radio WM, have latched onto that – and they like the 'fillers' rather than the photographs.

Whether it's showbusiness or the world of books, one of Alton's principal aims has always been to add *variety*:

All my life I've been conscious of holding the audience – not keeping too long on one theme; always twisting and turning slightly – and throwing people off balance a bit – which is what every good comic does. He takes people down a road and then suddenly turns a corner - that they're not expecting. I've tried to do that with almost everything, be it elements of surprise with the band, or with the books, or my act – everything I've ever done. I've tried to give a twist to it.

So nobody's ever bored: they're all wondering what's coming next?

Yes – exactly. I'm always conscious about boring people, although oddly enough, boredom isn't an emotion I've ever experienced myself.

Groucho reveals his other self, for the Christmas card market.

More diverse jobs came in - a shop opening in Oldbury and one in Handsworth - compèring a national computer quiz, although at that stage, no one would ever have described him as 'technologically-minded'.

Returning to early 1983, Alton was asked to deliver a speech for the *Book Club* in Wolverhampton, with the instruction that, in keeping with tradition, formal attire must be worn.

The only person who came improperly dressed was the sole-surviving founder member. I also attended a charity concert at the 'Library Theatre' in Solihull, where I gladly gave my services for free, only to find that everybody else had been paid!

However, it was the annual dinner of the Rubber Industries where my favourite story cropped up. Feeling quite pleased at the reception my speech had received, I stood at the bar, waiting for further plaudits. A woman came over and said (confidential whisper): "Mr. Douglas, we've had all sorts of speakers, sportsman, actors, writers, trade unionists – the lot. But I can honestly say that you are the worst speaker we've ever had!" Absolutely crushed, I just stood there, stunned, as she walked away. A committee member rushed over and said in the most apologetic voice: "I couldn't help overhearing that, please ignore her. That woman's a complete and utter fool. All she ever does is go around, repeating things that everybody else is saying!"

There was even a beauty contest, with the film actor, Victor Maddern – no he didn't win! I was completely out of my depth, attempting to commentate for a version of 'It's A Knockout', at the 'Old Edwardians Rugby Football Club'. I'd never even seen the television show that it was based upon, and although Don Maclean had recommended me, on this occasion, I wasn't worth the recommendation.

Alton then recorded a small part in the TV series *Angels*, as a consultant.

I also filmed a 'short' called 'The Villagers' - again - with my pal Dave Mitty, in Loughborough.

At the University of Birmingham, I was the guest speaker at a dinner for colostomy patients. At the interval, instead of announcing the customary short relief break, the chairman clapped his hands and said: "OK – everybody change their bags!"

Alton proposed the idea of a regular big band programme to the M.D. at Beacon Radio, Peter Tomlinson.

We'd been colleagues during my days at ATV, where Peter was a continuity announcer. He and the programme controller, Bob Pierson, decided it would be a good idea. 'Beacon Swing' went out every Thursday, at 8 p.m. >>> *Today, Peter is the M.D. of Saga 105.7.*

Alton was involved in recording a radio commercial for BRMB Radio, when Shaw Taylor, of *Police Five* fame, asked him to fly out to Sardinia, to entertain leading members of the car industry and their customers.

At the bandcall, I discovered that not only could the band not read a note of music, but they also couldn't speak one word of English! That night, as I was introduced, a director fell backwards out of his chair, and had to be carried out unconscious, a fight developed between two factions, and the microphone functioned so badly, I sounded like a man speaking in Morse code. It was absolute bedlam! The next morning, a badly 'hung-over' and bleary-eyed rep said to me: "You should have been here for the dinner last night. We had a smashing comic!"

Sometimes if I drove to a booking, a long distance away, I'd pull short of the place, about ten miles or so, drive into a lay-by, and put the seat back. If it was six o'clock and I'd got to be on my way by 6.30 I'd tell myself to wake up at that time and it was never ever a problem to do that. I could go straight to sleep, them wake up in half an hour; I've always had that capacity, from the days at Catterick railway station, when I could go to sleep on a table, with all the noise going on around me. To this day, I can sit in the front room and say I want twenty minutes sleep, go out, then wake up, re-charged – just like Winston Churchill did.

I hadn't fully realised, until I came to research this book, what an industrious little devil I'd been at this period. Because all through 1983, I'd been working with Clive Hardy, Gordon Stretch and the indefatigable Jo, on the books, Birmingham at War Volume 2, and Coventry at War – and what a fund of anecdotal treasures they produced!

STAMFORD FESTIVAL COMMITTEE PRESENTS
A TOMMY LAUGHTON PRODUCTION

THE

NAUGHTY NINETIES
MUSIC HALL
SHOW

STARRING
ALTON DOUGLAS
T.V COMEDIAN FROM THE GOLDEN SHOT.
KNOW YOUR PLACE. Etc

Souvenir Programme

STAMFORD ARTS CENTRE BALLROOM
JULY 12th and 13th 1983

Chapter 18 -

LORD HA-HA

*Conceited? My uncle tried to join the Navy so that the world could see him!
Being overweight, the Senior Service turned him down. They said they were
alright for anchors. However, they did say they would reconsider, if they started
a naval blockade!*
*It used to be said that the Second World War was started by Vera Lynn's agent.
More recently someone said it was my dad.*

"Right from the outset we made a decision that at no time would we actually
publish any books ourselves," explains Jo. "Our mutual feeling was that, if
we put all the hard work into the preparation of the material, 'Money
people' should look after the financial side – a philosophy we have followed
to this day."

It's amazing how many good stories emanate from the most dramatic
period in people's lives. As research progressed on their two forthcoming
books, people queued up to relate wartime tales:

*I was interviewing an elderly lady, in connection with 'Coventry at War'. She
said: "I do remember one incident. I don't know if I should tell you?" Naturally, this
was the one story I had to hear. So after a moment of hesitation she said: "I was
pushed up against this static water tank by an American serviceman, who said: "Are
you going to let me make love to you?" I said: "Certainly not!" He said: "If you don't
let me make love to you, I'll throw you into the static water tank!" I waited for her to
continue and when she didn't, I persisted: "Well go on then – what happened?" She
paused, then looked at her feet, and said very softly: "I still can't swim!"*

Then there was Jo Ault, who in 1940 was out celebrating a hen party with
her friends. On the way back, they were giggling noisily along the street,
when an ARP Warden rushed up to them shouting: "Will you girls please be
quiet. I can't hear where the bombs are falling!"

*The singer, Frank Ifield, whose biggest hit 'I Remember You' is still played today,
told me: "My dad, Dick Ifield, came over to England from Australia before World
War Two, to get British Industry to promote and develop some of his brilliant
inventions. He settled in Evenlode Crescent, Coventry. One of his inventions was a
very high efficiency hydraulic pump, which came under scrutiny for a highly secretive
aircraft engine – the Whittle Gas Turbine."*

The engine was named after its designer, Frank Whittle. Dick Ifield's fuel
pump was selected for high priority development.

Its secret was that by employing accurately-balanced high-pressure bearings, it could use the actual fuel it pumped as a lubricant, and so reduce the weight and bulk of the pumping unit and control gear – something that had never been heard of before. Frank and his mother, who was over from Australia at the time, came over for tea. I'd worked with him at the 'Cresta Club', which as you'll recall was in Solihull. Now Brummies always pronounce it "Sew-lee-hull," but everyone else called it "Solly Hull". Dickie Valentine used to say it sounded like a Jewish agent!

Neighbour Dave Mitty recalls: "I asked Alton where the number on his post had gone. He replied: "Frank Ifield knocked my gatepost over, when he backed out of the drive in his Rolls Royce." I thought, 'Oh yeah? Pull the other one!' But sure enough, he'd been down here. He must have thought a lot of Alton, because he'd come all the way over from Coventry, with his mother."

Frank drove all the way up to West Heath Hospital, by mistake. He rang me from there: "Where the hell are you?" I was further down the road, whirling like a dervish, to catch his attention!

>>> Alton was invited to chat with Frank, on the *Ed Doolan Show*, broadcast from Australia, on Sunday 15 September 2002, to celebrate Frank's fifty years in showbusiness. He began by mentioning Frank's visit, in the Rolls Royce:

AD: What type was it? Could it have been a *Silver Cloud*?

FI: It was – yes.

AD: We had a lovely afternoon and you gave me the story about your dad's wartime invention, which must have come under the *Official Secrets' Act*. Do you remember?

FI: Yes I do Alton, and it's lovely to talk to you again; I can't wait to tell my mum that I've spoken to you. I remember that day very well indeed (laughing) because it made a nasty scratch on my car!

Further details of their conversation are in our closing chapter.

The enthusiasm of the amateur was demonstrated to me by actor John Taylor. He explained that when he was an apprentice for 'Chance Brothers', an ex-First World War major instructed him on how to make knobkerries out of steam pipe, with a solid spike screwed into the end, in order to repel any would-be invaders!

Coventry at War was published on 18 November 1983. It was launched by the Lord Mayor of Coventry, Councillor Joe Thompson, one of scores of people who had provided personal memories and photographs for the book. Alton consulted George Hodgkinson too; he was mayor of Coventry in 1944.

On 11 November, exactly a week before *Coventry at War*, a second volume of *Birmingham at War* reached the bookshelves, published once again, by *The Birmingham Mail*. The first volume had been a runaway success, having sold over 10,000 copies, during the previous year. Readers responded by sending Alton more photographs of their wartime lives. A selection of these was subsequently included in Volume 2, together with illustrations from archives of Birmingham firms, and others from Birmingham Reference Library. In addition, there were pictures of houses, shops and cinemas, wrecked in the blitz, plus photographs of morale-boosting events, such as special charity shows and factory concerts.

Amongst the most evocative pages were advertisements from wartime copies of the *Post* and the *Mail*, such as *Your ABC of ARP,* and *What to do About Gas.* There were instructions about obtaining ration books and investing savings in *Birmingham's Warship Week.* Culinary tips for making the best use of food were also included. Alton concluded his Foreword to the second volume with the words:

'My involvement with these two books has made me wish I could climb to the top of the Town Hall. Once there I'd proclaim to the world that I was proud to be a BRUMMIE.'

Meanwhile, his radio programme, *Beacon Swing with Alton Douglas,* was being broadcast regularly for two hours, every Thursday; the listening figures were quite good, and, according to the press, the programme attracted letters from a wide area. John Slim, of *The Birmingham* Mail, wrote a substantial article about it, on 17 July 1984, describing Alton as Beacon's *King of Swing.* Alton is pictured, seated on his lounge carpet, surrounded by part of his record collection. The music was mainly Glenn Miller, Artie Shaw, Benny Goodman, Tommy Dorsey, with vocals from good quality singers, and every so often a feature on a lesser-known orchestra.

I was stopped in the street by a young girl, who enquired, "You're Alton Douglas, aren't you?" I confessed to being guilty as charged. She excitedly exclaimed to her parents: "This is Mr. Douglas, mum and dad. He's the chap I told you about that plays that 'old-fogey' music!"

Neil Allen, area manager of a plastics company, was relocated in 1980, from a plush city centre office in Manchester to his firm's Oldbury factory. "To say the least, I was unhappy," explains Neil. "Furthermore, our social life was minimal and the house move had coincided with our youngest going off to university, so my wife was turned from a busy housewife to a lonely one.

If you were cynical you might think this was a publicity shot for my radio programme.

"A young colleague in the Oldbury office said: 'Hey Neil, what do you listen to on your way into work?' I replied: 'I dunno, probably Radio 2 or Radio 4.' He said, 'Try Beacon Radio – there's a real idiot on there,' (Gordon Astley). Next day I listened, and one of the 'commercials' featured a trailer for *Beacon Swing*, for that night. Alton had a very personal style, playing requests from listeners and advertising new issues and events: 'December 1983 – *Glenn Miller Society Christmas Party* – only 75p – *Old Crown Hotel*, Broad Street, everybody welcome.'

"I went to the party and found myself sitting next to Alton . As it was a first visit for both of us, the regulars thought that I'd come with him. It wouldn't have mattered – we hit it off straight away. For many months I enjoyed his company at *The Glenn Miller Society* and subsequently, *The Syd Lawrence Music Society*."

Major Mills, another fan of *Beacon Swing* recalls: "I was drawn into the music of the big band era, in the 30s and my favourites were Tommy Dorsey and Benny Goodman. When I was stationed in Bridlington I bought Goodman's *Six Flats Unfurnished*, from Woolworth's. Tuning into *Beacon Radio* in the mid-80s, I heard Alton's programme and sent in a request for the number and it was played for me. I then began recording the programme every week, purely for my own pleasure, and still have every one of them on cassette. It's become a regular ritual that every Friday the tapes come out and I listen again to his shows from the 80s."

A delightful part of that year was spent assembling 'Joe Russell's Smethwick', which was a collection of photos by the well-known local photographer.

Although already a fan, through the *Swing* programmes, Neil Allen wasn't familiar with Alton's first series of books. Only when *Joe Russell's Smethwick* was published, on 1st May 1984, (Neil and his wife were born in the area), did he discover Alton's 'other life'. He explains: "I was able to nip out of work and photograph the presentation to Joe Russell, in front of Smethwick Council House (with Alton and Jo in the frame). I was the only photographer and using a spare copy, was able to introduce myself to Joe Russell and together with my wife, got him to show us some of the three thousand or so photos which didn't get in the book."

Photography was engineer Joe's hobby. His collection comprised a unique sixty-year record of the changing face of an area, which has famous associations with James Watt, Thomas Telford and Matthew Boulton. Joe was seventy-seven when the book was published. It took Alton nine months to reduce the collection to just over two hundred photographs, for the eventual one hundred-page book, published in conjunction with Sandwell council. Many pictures were paired as 'before-and-after' shots of pubs, churches, streets, etc.

We launched the book on Ed Doolan's Radio WM programme, as we did with many of our titles. During the chat, a call came through from Dennis Moore (if you remember, he'd been part of the 'Know Your Place' Wolverhampton team) telling me that he'd retired early and that he was available if ever I needed him. We met for lunch, got on famously, and that was the start of eighteen very happy years, working together. Dennis also doubled as our rep in the Black Country. By this time we'd tried various methods of selling our books, and eventually whittled it down to doing our own 'repping' and organising deliveries ourselves.

Former bank manager Dennis explains: "Alton was talking to Ed Doolan and they mentioned the war years. As it was a 'phone-in' programme I reminded Alton and Ed that during the Second World War, Hitler had a penchant for giving his particular raids rather obscure names. The big raid on Birmingham, he called *Operation Umbrella*. This was a snide remark to do with Neville Chamberlain, who was Mayor of Birmingham at one stage, and was Prime Minister at the time, who always went everywhere with a rolled up umbrella.

"The big raid on Coventry, he called *Moonlight Sonata*, because he'd done his homework with his 'met' people, and they said it was going to be a fine moonlit night. Wolverhampton got off very well: we didn't have any big air raids at all, but he did plan one, and he called it *All One Price*. This was for the simple reason that he couldn't separate the word 'Wolverhampton' from the word 'Woolworth's'. They always sold their goods, in those days, for nothing over sixpence in the store. So everything was the same price.

"So I called in with this information and Alton said: 'I tell you what we'll do – I'd like to meet you for lunch, because I want to discuss a book about the Black Country.' So Ed Doolan chipped in: 'Hey – now – if there are any free meals going, I want to be a part of it!' Alton and I worked together on *The Black Country at War*." It was published by Beacon Radio, in November 1984. >>> By 2002, when his conversation with the co-writer took place, the grand total for the entire series had risen to thirty-five.

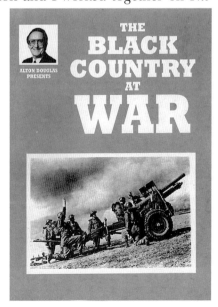

Clive Hardy, after agonising for an hour about what logo to use for our series of books, had decided that as I was getting quite a lot of exposure on TV, we should use my head. So when 'The Black Country At War' came out, Dennis and I were signing copies at the 'Black Country Museum'. A man picked one up, squinted at the photo of me, top left, front cover, and said: "My God Alton, this picture was taken a few years ago, wasn't it?" I must have been feeling a bit grumpy that day, because I couldn't resist replying: "Well, unfortunately, most of us do age through the

years. Not like you! I don't think you've aged one jot in half a century!" This chap, whom I never clapped eyes on before, looked at me with gratitude and said: "It's very nice of you to say that."

Jo was instrumental in producing the fourth book in the series, entitled *Celebrity Recipes*, published by a different company, *Streetly Printing*, in the same month as *The Black Country at War*. "That was a big challenge for me," she explains, "because I'd never had a cookery lesson – not even at school; we never did Domestic Science. We needed a change from the war side, to a lighter subject.

"So we approached several celebrities that Alton had worked with or had contact with in some way, including President Reagan, Liberace, Bob Hope (through one of his cousins that he knew), and many others. I spent hours converting the American recipes into recognisable British measurements. I can honestly say that we tested every meal, and as a belt and braces, we got the chef from the *Rainbow Club*, Manolo J. Benavente, to double-check."

*Jo had a phone call one morning, with a query: "I'd like you to include my favourite recipe, but can you say that Lord Longford likes fish cakes?" The author Jack Higgins, ('The Eagle Has Landed', etc) was so pleased with his inclusion that he rang from Jersey, and despite being a millionaire several times over, asked if he could have a discount, if he bought multiple copies. He could! Barbara Cartland also bought several, including one she wanted signing 'To Diana' – we wondered many times if it was **that** one.*

On several occasions Jo was mistaken for Jo Douglas, from the TV programme *Six Five Special*. (Her namesake was the co-presenter with Pete Murray).

"As we have progressed with the book side," Jo continues, "I am amazed how I could ever have entered this phase; my grandfather wouldn't have a book in the house. My dad never read a complete book (only car manuals) – the reason being, they were a very practical, hardworking family, who thought it was lazy to read – no time for relaxation. Also, I failed the entrance exam for the Grammar School (the only one of my cousins not to pass).

"My experience of secretarial work, typing minutes of meetings, etc, working on accounts, has given me an aptitude for research – which I absolutely love. As the years and the books have escalated I have become involved in collecting material, apart from the research side – and over many cups of coffee, we put together new ideas – yes, I think we work well together. (So many people have said to me 'I could never work with my partner.') We have our differences of opinion, but it seems to work out successfully. So I became the co-author. We find the best contacts for material is our network of existing contacts – just as some of the best customers for our books are our existing customers!

"All my life I have been a magpie – I hate throwing things away. (I wonder whether being a war baby has anything to do with it?) But by golly has it helped with the production of our nostalgic books!"

Alton's friend and fellow actor, Raymond Mason, recalls, "Above all, I shall be grateful to him for giving me back such a large part of my childhood! I was born in Great Bridge, near West Bromwich, and until the age of eleven, when my family moved to London, I lived in the Black Country – Wednesbury, Darlaston and Tettenhall. And in Alton's books, there it all was – photographs and captions which took me back immediately to days half-forgotten. My parents had a tobacconist's shop in Trouse Lane, Wednesbury, and there was a photograph of Trouse Lane, grainy, and taken on a wet afternoon, around the time we were living there (five Woodbines in a paper packet and two matches – one penny – or possibly tuppence!) And so many other places I had known – I once got lost in Walsall Arboretum. I feel that Alton's vast and definitive books have captured and preserved a way of life that has changed almost beyond recognition, over the past century.

"I've been trying to think of something to stem this tide of adulation. The awful thing is, I can't think of anything. In fact, I'll go even further – if you ever have the good fortune to be invited to chez Douglas, you'll be entertained royally, and Alton and Jo, do the most marvellous spaghetti bol! Another of Alton Douglas's Celebrity Recipes?"

Neil Allen and Alton continued to meet quite often until Neil volunteered "… to become Chairman of *The Syd Lawrence Society* and we couldn't sit and joke together, so eventually Alton dropped out. We miss him a lot with his wealth of repartee, anecdotes, and of course knowledge of the big band scene." They haven't seen much of each other over the past eight years, but, as Neil explains, "… we speak almost every Sunday morning and swap ideas and insults. I have had an enormous number of postcards from him: some rude and all offbeat – God knows what our post-lady thinks! We have swapped tapes and CDs – far more for me than *from* me, I might add. As Alton isn't exactly a technocrat, I usually have to sort out his electronic problems and record bits of daytime jazz for him, when he's out.

"Indirectly, he has *hugely* influenced my life – due to the friends we met at the music societies, my wife and I don't have any time to ourselves. Since I retired in '89, life has been hectic – all due to a chance remark, leading to Alton and *Beacon Swing*."

For Channel 4, I filmed a drama called 'Property Rites', based on the famous Birmingham murder of Mary Ashford. Wing collars, frock-tail coats, very uncomfortable under hot lights, but great fun to be a 'luvvie' for a while! In the middle of filming, I had to go to Newcastle-upon-Tyne, to speak at Garden Links' Annual Dinner. The chairman, sitting next to me, stopped me dead in my tracks by saying: "How are you getting on filming at 86A Park Hill, Edgbaston?" I did my

impression of a landed fish, and he said: "It's alright, I'm not psychic, the house happens to belong to a friend of mine!"

My life seems to have been peppered all the way through, with the most extraordinary coincidences.

By now, cabaret work was beginning to tail-off, as the effects of the breathalyser took hold, along with the advent of video recorders, the six-pack and so-called 'fun pubs'.

At one of those I was asked to do my act, standing on top of a table. I refused. Nightclubs closed almost every week, but because I was involved in so many things, it didn't become obvious at first. The only problem though was, because of the shortage of cabaret work, the wrong types of comics were turning to 'after-dinner speaking'. Organisers were becoming very wary of speakers who turned out to be 'dirty' comics. Instead of trying to adapt to a different type of audience, a great many of them thought they could get away with their club acts, rather than realising that a different approach was required.

By this time, I'd established a good connection with several 'speakers' agents, so along with RAF and other army officers messes; with Lance Percival, Janet Brown, Bert Weedon, and so on, and at private functions with Henry Cooper, Karen Kaye, Don Maclean et al, I still had a busy mix of activities.

Alton worked on *Starting A New Business*, for BBC 2 - an instructional film for the *Open University*. It was shot at Jackfield near Ironbridge. Instead of a script, they were given the gist of the story and told to improvise on dialogue.

On a hot June afternoon, I sat on the edge of the river, waiting to be called, and fell fast asleep. Two hours later, I could hear them calling me. I staggered to my feet, totally unprepared. Rushed on to the set, dropped a tray, stumbled over a chair, then gibbered a few lines. We got it in one take. The director said: "That's what I like – book pros who can deliver the goods – and by the way – I loved the comedy bits at the beginning!"

My Aunty Ivy came up with a request, to stage a little show for her pensioners' club. So one afternoon in December, Dave Mitty and I and a pianist sang our songs, told our jokes and generally 'acted the goat' for two hours. Part of Dave's act was a hilarious bit as Bing Crosby, singing 'White Christmas'. To give it a novel twist, he puffed at a pipe with a smoke capsule in it. Unfortunately, in such a tiny room, with the windows closed, in seconds the entire audience was enveloped in a dense White Christmas fog.

Alight Christmas.

Standing half in the doorway, Alton watched, in disbelief, as the audience was herded out, coughing and spluttering, and cursing – none too quietly – while Dave spiritedly battled on.

One old chap staggered past me with his zimmer-frame, muttering something about Dave's parentage. Another struggled to open the windows, but through it all, Aunty Ivy sat stoically, all alone, in the centre of the front row, with tears streaming down her face!

In February 1985, Jo's dad passed away. As readers may recall, he'd sworn that in the Great War, because of shortages, they'd given him a transfusion of horse's blood, and was told that he wouldn't make 'old bones'. He lived until the day before his eighty-ninth birthday.

The symmetry of it would have appealed to him and reminds me that his oblique humour is very much missed to this day.

Alton was featured in Malcolm Stent's TV series *The Barmaid's Arms*. It was a great opportunity to renew his acquaintance with George Melly and *John Chilton's Feet-warmers*. Back in his West End days, he'd been a regular customer at John's Bloomsbury Bookshop.

One night I appeared in Stratford-upon-Avon and got a big laugh from an all-male audience with: "I stopped a policeman on the way here and said: 'Can you tell me where the 'Falcon Hotel' is?' He said: 'Which falcon hotel are you looking for?' "

On the fortieth anniversary of VE Day, Central TV asked me to film an appropriate piece. I had the unique opportunity of going back to my old house in Heather Road, where I was made so welcome, by the incumbent Asian family. Then with our old next-door-neighbour, Mrs. Fletcher, still in situ after sixty-two years, we looked at the Anderson Shelter, which she'd continued to use as a shed. We went down to Digby Park, where the barrage balloon had been tethered, and then back to try to recreate some of the atmosphere of that period.

Just after that, at a Forties Night Alton was compèring at *The Grand Hotel*, Birmingham, he managed to meet up with one of his idols, bandleader Joe Loss.

When he knew that I was connected with George Bartram's office, he invited me to spend the whole of the interval, nattering about the old days. That night, the Guest of Honour should have been Princess Margaret, but the organisers foolishly contacted her office, a few days before the event, to say that as it was an evening in aid of a cancer charity, it might be an idea if she didn't smoke. They hurriedly had to find a new guest!

The same week, through his trade union, *The Society of Authors*, Alton won the *Brighton Festival of Short Story Competition*, despite the fact that there were over seven hundred other entrants, with *That Day Anne was Twelve*.

There seemed to be a spate of Ladies Luncheon Clubs coming my way. They are probably the best audience of all, for a male speaker, and just as importantly, by this time, they queued up afterwards, to buy our books. The ladies of Pedmore provided me with a smashing story! Usually there'd only be one male guest, the speaker. But this time the mayor was also invited. The organiser explained: "Well we thought it was a shame, you being the only man - and he can take you to the toilet!"

Women's bladders are often good indicators as to your success. For some reason, if females laugh a lot, they have to go to the loo. (Don't ask me to explain – I don't understand the mechanics). So a big queue outside the Ladies meant that you were a hit. The broadcaster, Basil Boothroyd, told me that once, when he had a speaking engagement in the Welsh Valleys, every so often a man in a white coat would stand framed in the doorway, and call out someone's name. They would disappear, then shortly afterwards, the whole exercise would be repeated. When he queried it, the secretary said, "Well as we're out in the wilds a bit, I thought it would be a good opportunity for the ladies to get their feet done!"

At one 'do' in Shrewsbury, Alton was advised to keep his speech short, because the ladies had to collect their children from school. Gazing out at the veritable snow-scene before him, he realised that no one in the audience was under sixty!

During the 80s, he was asked to commentate on an art exhibition. Sadly the interview was excised, because he had the audacity to complain about their not being a single *white* face, in an exhibition labelled *Birmingham Photography*.

All my life I've hated bigotry and racism, from whatever quarter, so I couldn't let that pass unmarked; it was just black faces. It had to be said by somebody, because the people at home would be thinking: 'Well, they're panning round this and we haven't seen a white person!'

A TV series called *Anything Legal Considered* may not ring any bells, but it was the working title for *Boon,* in which Alton played a substantial part with Michael Elphick.

Neil Morrissey, later to become famous in 'Men Behaving Badly', was in it, along with my old chum, Raymond Mason. I met Michael Elphick at a football dinner party in Henley-in-Arden, some years later, and he told me that when they finished a series they'd look at the 'out-takes' and they always included me at the very end of it, poking my head over the bar. There'd been a confrontation and I'd said ('anaemic' voice): "I'd have given you a hand Mr. Boon!"

Then I was offered a wonderful part as a drunken butler in 'Bergerac', on Jersey, but because of a prior commitment, I had to turn it down. The commitment was to commemorate the Fortieth Anniversary of VJ Day, at, of all places, Brierley Hill Police Station. Now by one of those strange, amazing coincidences that seem to dog me, the part of the butler was eventually played by an actor named John Rutland - the name of the character I played in 'Muck and Brass'.

In *Murder of a Moderate Man*, for BBC TV, Alton was an immigration officer, boarding a plane at Elmdon, and offering two of the occupants a lift, in a vehicle waiting for them on the tarmac - a Black Maria.

As we've mentioned, cabaret venues were closing at an alarming rate, coupled with the fact that Alton was enjoying that type of performing less and less. He began to feel that he was, perhaps, becoming 'rusty', which subsequently led to long and hard thinking about his future.

In March 1986 I made one of the most momentous decisions of my life. At 'Penn's Hall Hotel', with a very strong floorshow, the audience treated us with utter contempt. I'd long decided that when the pain exceeded the pleasure, I'd get out. I stood on the cabaret floor, looked at a 'tanked-up' audience, and remembering Lenny Bennett's: "There's nothing more undignified than a forty-five-year-old comic who hasn't made it," I decided that with so much work on the book front, after dinner speaking, voice-overs, and radio and TV work, 'enough was enough'. I no longer wanted to be a 'turn'.

The following morning I rang around all the agents and told them about my decision, and cancelled the few jobs that I'd got in the book.

The decision couldn't have come at a more opportune time, because I was about to embark on a new branch of radio work – and our biggest-selling book was just around the corner.

Jo and I help to launch my uncle, Victor J Price's book, "Birmingham Cinemas", 1986. Aunty Veronica has already bought her copy.

Chapter 19 -

PLAY AND WORDS

I'm tired of old TV programmes. I saw a film the other night that was so old, Henry the Eighth was played by Henry the Ninth. It was followed by a western, where the Indians attacking the wagons meant it! I don't mind old films, but when Thora Hird gets the man…

Part of *Big Deal*, the gambling series starring Ray Brooks, was filmed in a north London hospital. The BBC's chuck wagon was too big for the car park, so it was parked in the street.

We queued up for our food on a nice summer's day, some of us still in pyjamas and dressing gowns, with fake blood on our bandages. A resident edged nervously up to me and intoned: "What's going on 'ere luv?" I said: "It's part of the government cuts: they're having to use outside catering!" She stepped back and with her shopping bags pumping up and down yelled: "That fackin' Mrs. Fatcher!"

One of the actors, Desmond McNamara, complained during the filming that he couldn't always remember what position he was in on the bed at the end of each take. For continuity purposes, it's essential that all the different camera angles match up. I suggested to him that he should just lie flat on his back. He fell fast asleep and got the bollocking of his life from the director. My fault mate!

Hedli Niklaus, (currently playing Kathy – her third role in the series, 'The Archers'), having worked on several 'voice-overs' with me, in the early 1980s, suggested that I should audition for BBC Radio Drama; Dave Mitty had also made the same suggestion.

Dave explains: "A group of us auditioned, and Philip Martin said that he'd definitely use me, because he wanted to form his own little repertory company for Pebble Mill. I told Alton about it. Philip said: 'I think I'll give him an audition piece.' Anyway, the next thing I know is, Alton went down there and got the job as well."

I did it, but not having the faintest clue how you go about these things, I read an extract from 'Chips With Everything', changing voices as often as I could and generally behaving like a prat. The director, Philip Martin, wrote to me to say that it was one of the most impressive examples of vocal dexterity that he had ever experienced, but unfortunately, it didn't give him the faintest clue as to whether I could act or not!

Philip decided to take a chance and in June 1986, (the year that *Inspector Morse* first hit our screens, and the exact month when one of Alton's jazz heroes, Benny Goodman, passed away), booked Alton for a play called *Mr.*

Peabody and the Beast, by Ray Jones. The play was subsequently broadcast in Radio Four's *Thirty Minute Theatre*, on 3 February 1987.

It turned out to be Don Henderson's first radio play too. He played the title role of Mr. Peabody, a mysterious all-in wrestler, and I played almost everyone else! Once again, I felt completely at home in a new media.

"I did about twenty-odd radio plays altogether," recalls Dave. "Alton did some on his own as well, using his voice to advantage with lots of characters, including a memorable 'Brummie' accent." Two or three of the other plays that Alton and I were involved in, were about a woman detective, played by Rosemary Martin," he continues. "She died about four or five years ago – a lovely actress."

Philip Martin checks as AD gets to grips with Don Henderson. This was a special photograph taken because of an impending visit to the Pebble Mill studios by Prince Charles.

191

Dave recalls a particularly memorable joint venture, called *Troupers*; he played the role of Wilcox and Alton was cast as Larry. Written by Ron Hutchinson, the play, set in wartime Crewe, was broadcast on 7 June 1988. Its central theme was the problems that ensue when three professional artistes refuse to share a programme with local amateur talents.

In 'Troupers', Larry was a camp ventriloquist, dying of TB, and in the award-winning 'Guernica', I played a Spanish workman. Philip Martin, after he'd won the 1990 'International Radio Festival Gold Medal Award' for the play, wrote me a letter saying how well it had turned out, and that he particularly treasured the very English swear word I'd uttered when a painting was dropped on my foot! (It was actually a very heavy door we carried, to create a realistic sound effect – and it hurt!)

Alton performed in seven radio plays over a period of approximately four years, from 1986 to November 1989. A comprehensive list of his radio and TV appearances is included at the end of this book.

"We went down to Pebble Mill one morning," explains Dave. "Alton was always telling me that showbusiness is two separate words: you do the show and you *must* look after the business. It was quite funny that we sat down at this table, before we went in. We were surrounded by all the other actors and actresses, and we introduced ourselves to each other. Everyone was nervous. Alton put his briefcase on the desk, opened it up and inside were about twelve of the books that he'd compiled. They said: 'What are these?' He reacted as if he didn't know. He said, 'They're my books: I always carry them round with me,' and he was handing them out. I thought: 'I know what he means now – that's show - *and* business!'

"I used to drive around with him in his car quite a lot, working on his books," Dave continues. "If he wanted to know *exactly* where a house or shop was, on a street, I'd go with him. I'd stand on the spot. He'd walk backwards and say, 'Well it must have been there' - he gets everything perfect.

"I fell off a ladder at home and broke my leg and my foot. So I was sitting in the back garden – couldn't do anything. The bell rang and Alton came in – asked me how I was. Then he got quite annoyed: 'What are you doing, sitting here with your foot up? You should be utilising this time!' And he really meant it – you know? I said, 'How d'you mean? I've got my foot in plaster-of-Paris and I'm sitting here relaxing.' He said, 'You should be writing a book, or some sketches and ideas. You can't just *sit* there!' And that must be how *he* works - 'If I've got five minutes, I'll do something.' "

I was also invited to conduct 'vox-pop'-type radio interviews for a new brand of mints. In the Grosvenor Shopping Centre in Northfield, I asked a woman to try one and give an opinion. She replied: "Oh ah, they'm great – they bring the wind up – both ends!"

Three more films followed. The first was for the Manpower Services Commission, in which Alton played a Black Country shopkeeper, who takes a chance on stocking homemade chocolates.

It was filmed in Robinson's shop in Short Heath, and I came away with yet another outlet, to sell our books. The following week, I was involved in a training film for British Gas. They found it actually cheaper to film in a gas employee's house, than build a set. So we found ourselves in Seaford Road, Ward End. As part of a safety check, they tested for gas, and we had to stop filming for half a day, when they found a leak! In 'Moneyspinner', for Channel 4, I was a businessman, caught up in a 'High Noon' confrontation, in the main street in Worcester – umbrellas drawn at six paces and a very peculiar piece of filming, with the camera, for some strange reason, situated in the region of my crotch!

Alton's books were coming off the presses at quite a rate, with Beacon Radio agreeing to publish the Black Country titles, and the *Birmingham Mail* still actively marketing *their* list. The latest was *Memories of Birmingham*, which was launched in November '86, and has, over the years, been their biggest seller, with sales of over 50,000 to date.

I received a letter from a lady called Olive Pocius, in Safety Harbour, Florida, to say that she recognised a picture of me, as an eighteen-month-old, on page three of 'Birmingham At War, Volume 2'. As Olive Underhill, she'd pushed me around the local park, many a time, having only lived four doors away in Heather Road.

After marrying a GI she'd gone to live in America, but as with so many ex-pat Brummies, nostalgia featured heavily in her life. The outcome was that she came over

AD, Jo, Lady Mayoress Mollie Martineau, Lord Mayor Dennis Martineau and Dennis Moore at the launch of "Memories of Birmingham".

we had a big reunion with her, her husband, Joe, and another ex-Brummie, Marge Tassone, and her husband, Frank – another delightful bonus from our books.

Readers may recall Olive's account, in our opening chapter, of how she helped Dorothy to care for Alton as a small boy. Forty-five years later, in summer 1985, she and Alton were featured in a press article, which also included two photographs, the most prominent involving role reversal. When Alton was a small boy, Olive used to bounce Alton on her knee: in the press photograph, *she* is seated on his! There was also a group photograph featuring Olive's family, the Underhills, with two-and-a-half-year-old Alton in the centre. Olive had flown over from Florida to Britain, for a seven-week holiday. Having been reunited, the former neighbours went on to a show.

A charitable event that Alton particularly enjoyed, marked the tenth anniversary of Dave Poole's hairdresser's, in October 1986. The shop is still situated on the right, as you come from King's Norton, under the railway bridge in Colebrook Road, Shirley. Almost two hundred customers packed into the premises for a free celebratory glass of wine. The £150 raised by the event, for the charity of which Alton was a patron, was used to help partially-sighted and other handicapped people keep in touch with the latest news. Dave, who used to play the club scene and who's singing act was featured on local radio, decided to hold the event for the additional purpose of thanking his customers for their loyalty, over the decade.

They raised money for 'The Birmingham Tapes for the Handicapped', and I proudly accepted the cheque on their behalf. A lady came up to me and said: "I remember you in cabaret at 'Holimarine', at Burnham-on-Sea, in the early 70s. We've followed your career ever since. We love that TV comedy series of yours, 'Fresh Fields', with Julia Mackenzie." I said: "That's Anton Rodgers." She said: 'I know, it's so good, that programme." I said: "It's Anton Rodgers!" She said: "I know, we wouldn't miss it for the world!" I said: "IT'S ANTON RODGERS!" She said: "I know. Will you give Julia our best wishes when you see her?" I said: "OK."

At the end of the following January, in 1987, Groucho died. Sadly, he'd been suffering with rheumatism for some time.

I discussed it with our vet, who told me: "He'll tell you, when the time comes," - and he did. I watched him struggling to his feet, to go down to the park, and I realised in that second, that life was no fun for him. I rang the vet, he came round, we spread Groucho's blankets on the kitchen floor – and in seconds it was all over. As we carried him out of the house, his ear flopped out, and I wept buckets. Don't let cynics tell you that it's not as bad as losing a human being. After twelve years of so much love, it almost destroyed Jo and I.

Groucho, over the months, had been the inspiration for several nonsense verses and I found myself writing more and more in that genre, until I had a collection of over four hundred. A literary agent, Dianne Coles, who was also the librarian on the

QE2, fell in love with them, and tried desperately over several years, to get them published. But humorous verse is a terrible field to break into, and she had no success. However, our list of titles was growing, with the 'Coventry Evening Telegraph' now involved and three books on the city resulted.

After a lunchtime engagement at the Porsche factory in Reading, Alton was given a guided tour of the site.

When we returned to the service bay, the manager took off his white overalls and rolled across the floor in his suit, to show me how completely free the area was of oil and grease. It was – totally!

In 'The Bretts', for Central TV, I was completely mis-cast as a Society MC at 'Quaglinos'. Ironically, although I'd appeared there with some success in the late 1960s, the part called for someone more 'upper-crust' than his society audience, and the director made it clear, right from the start, that I was not 'it'.

The *Birmingham Mail* then suggested that as it was the Centenary of Birmingham becoming a city, Alton should compile another book for them, and so *Birmingham Remembered* was born.

The phone rang, the week after it was launched, in October 1988, and I heard an Irish accent:

Man: Hello there!

AD: Hello.

Man: D'you recognise who this is?

AD: I'm sorry, I don't.

Man: I'm the man in the middle of the Stock Exchange, in the photograph on page twenty-five of your new book!

AD: Pleased to speak to you.

Man: But it's not me!

AD: Sorry?

Man: It's not me – I've never been to the Stock Exchange.

AD: Perhaps it someone who *looks* like you?

Man: No, it's definitely me!

AD: Well if it's not you, but it looks like you, who is it?

Man: It's me! Do you ever stick people's heads onto other people's bodies?

AD: Certainly not! Why would I put the head of someone I've never met, onto the body of a person I don't know, when I've not even got a picture of the man in the first place?

Man: Pardon?

AD: I'm sorry, but I've had enough of this!

Man: Shall I send you a photo of me?

AD: No, don't bother.

Man: Why not?

AD: I'll only go and stick it on somebody else's body!

Dennis Moore recalls: "When *Birmingham Remembered* was published, we did a signing session at Snow Hill Tunnel, when it was re-opened for use. We went home with money *stuffed* in our pockets; it was in our socks, our wallets – up our armpits!"

In just six weeks, *Birmingham Remembered* sold 18,000 copies in hardback, easily enough for it to qualify for the best-selling lists, so Alton went into action:

I contacted the people responsible for compiling the charts and was told that it did not include local books. Why not still amazes me. We have to compete with national authors, so why not?

Traditionally, Alton writes the introductory page to each book. "He always does the 'here we are again' type of page – and very well indeed. You must remember that this wasn't his principal trade," says Dennis. "So really, he came from nowhere with this, and his success has been absolutely *phenomenal*. Of course, each book we did, as time went on, got better and better and we learned from any mistakes we made. It's really gone from nothing to absolutely everything!"

According to Dennis: "Alton's never used a swear word in any of his work - I'm told," (except perhaps for the accidental one in *Guernica*!) "Also, I understand that whenever he did his plays for the BBC or the ITV, or whatever, he was known as 'One take Alton'. He saved them a lot of money; you don't have any of these 'out-takes', where they get it wrong, or they swear and they've got to bleep it out. 'One take Alton' – and you've got it. He was there on time, did his work, 'Goodbye Alton, cheque's in the post.' Now that's wonderful, from an employer's point of view.

"He totally knows where he's going – no doubt about that. I'm pretty sure that if he decides that he's going to do a book, whatever he's going to do it on, he's already got this plan. He can be dissuaded from one or two things, and sometimes he's come to me to help with the proof checking. If Jo and he have done something, they can be too close to it, and he's come to me and said, 'I'd like you to do this for me, if you don't mind?' I've found one or two odd little spelling mistakes, which they've passed time and time again – or a little bit of grammar that's gone wrong – or commas have given the wrong impression. You can be sure that, at the beginning, he knows *where* he's going – and you're eighty per cent on the way then.

"We have never ever fallen out. I might say: 'How about … Alton?' Or - 'No, wait a minute – what are you talking about?' That sort of thing – but we never ever fell out, at all." Like many others who've assisted with our book, Dennis finds it difficult to identify Alton's weaker points. "I don't think he tolerates any wasting of time. He might phone me perhaps, when I've got the 'nosebag' on here. I come to the phone and I'm chewing away. He'll say: 'Well I'm sorry, you'll have to give me – oh you're eating are you?' "

His present co-writer has had the same experience: he's *so* enthusiastic, gets carried away with many ideas – and it's difficult to break the flow!

In the evenings Alton was still pretty busy as a guest speaker.

At one or two of the more select dinners at which I was booked, audiences were often quite small, sometimes just the directors, their wives and a few guests. So instead of standing up to give my speech, I'd remain seated and just natter to them informally. I remember one at Ettington Park, near Stratford, that must have been so informally successful, afterwards one of the guests said how lucky they were to have had such a humorous guest, as it must have saved them from having to book a speaker!

After recording another of Philip Martin's plays, *The Family that Plays Together*, broadcast in October '88, Hedli Niklaus, who was playing 'Beth', the leading role, said that she'd recommended Alton to a television producer friend of hers. The BBC was using a lot of actors in *Crimewatch*, and it was proving to be a useful source of income.

I was offered a part in a reconstruction of a crime involving a man who'd been molesting schoolgirls. The casting agent thought my voice was too 'light' for the part (whatever that means). It was probably a good job, as a close friend of mine told me that he'd never have been able to respect me again if I'd accepted!

By this time 'Birmingham Remembered' was selling at such a pace, that the printers couldn't keep up with the binding, so it went into paperback. By Christmas 1988, 24,000 copies had been sold. Due to the ensuing publicity, I was approached to become the Video Archives and Stills consultant for a film entitled 'Made in Birmingham'. Again, one of those amazing coincidences cropped up. After years of impersonating him, and singing his hit song, 'If I Were A Rich Man', I found myself actually working for Chaim Topol's company, 'Mentorn'.

During Christmas 1988, showbusiness lost one of its 'behind-the-scenes' heroes. Ironically, during a period when Alton was doing particularly well, George Bartram died at the age of sixty-four, following a long illness.

Born in Handsworth, he looked after countless stars, and always in an unassuming and highly professional manner.

Fred Norris, writing a December 1988 obituary about George, in the *Birmingham Mail*, quotes a comment, which Ernie Wise made to him: "George is one of the best. He is part of the Morecambe and Wise story. He was looking after us when nobody seemed to know us." George told Fred, prior to his illness: "I have a great life and I have always enjoyed my work."

To me, he was more than just a publicist, he was a friend. The one minor piece of comfort was that I was invited to take part in a radio tribute to him. I reminded the listeners of how much George prided himself on his reliability, and of how he thoroughly deserved his chosen epitaph: "He always rang back."

We closed the programme with "Au revoir G.B."

Chapter 20 -

SING SOMETHING, SIMPLE.

I can sing you know, people say I've got a voice like a bird - have you ever heard an ostrich? Talk about the voice that could shatter glass - mine would open a tin of pilchards!

Although, by now, I'd given up appearing as a comic, I did agree to a request from Sandwell Hospital Radio to compère a charity concert, in July 1989, at West Bromwich Town Hall, featuring the 'All Ohio State Fair Youth Choir'. I was glad to repeat the experience for the two subsequent years. Meanwhile, in April 1990, the committee awarded me the distinction of becoming their first Honorary Member.

The full choir comprised some three hundred singers, aged between sixteen and nineteen; approximately a third of their number embarked on a tour of Great Britain and Europe each summer, performing free of charge, in aid of worthy charities. Clive Reeves' publicity release for the 1989 event, included the following paragraph:

'The compère for this wonderful evening of entertainment was local showbiz personality Mr. Alton Douglas, who also gave his services free of charge, and made a donation to Sandwell Hospital Radio, from the sale of his books, during the interval.'

In a short period of time, several more friends passed away. Tom Mennard left us, on 2nd November1989. He once gave me his card, which read: 'Tom Mennard - juggles with live geese'. After years of being acknowledged as a 'Pros' comic', he achieved recognition late in life, in 'Coronation Street'. The image of him carrying his dog around in a bag, is one that still conjures up smiles today! Tom had a beautiful cottage, down in the south, with clocks in every single room. When you stayed there, it used to drive you barmy. There was also a local pub where the barmaid was so old, you went and served yourself and put the money in the till!

That same month, *Memories of Dudley* and *Memories of Walsall* were published within a week of each other. In a *Walsall Observer News* article, dated 17 November 1989, Alton commented:

'Although Walsall probably hasn't the amount of history of some of its neighbours, it is nevertheless a fascinating place, if not least, because of its wonderful leather industry and manufacturing past.'

We discover from the article that the photographs in Alton's books were now being reproduced more clearly, because of a new printing system. Alton, Jo and Dennis were pictured alongside the Mayor and

Mayoress of Walsall, Councillor and Mrs. Ray Farrell.

Just a week later, the Dudley press carried similar articles and photographs, showcasing *Memories of Dudley*. The three co-writers were featured again, on this occasion, with the Mayor of Dudley.

*We launched 'Memories of Dudley', at the Mayor's Parlour. Councillor Sam Davies turned out to be one of the most jovial people that Jo and I had ever encountered. His enthusiasm was contagious and we all sat around, chuckling at his reminiscences. Eventually his secretary popped her head round the door, saying: "Don't forget you've got another appointment in twenty minutes." "OK, I won't." Then: "Just ten minutes to go!" "Alright, I'll be with you!" And finally a very impatient: "Mr. Mayor, you can't keep the **Queen** waiting!"*

Pete Lindup's dad, Rowland, who was responsible, as scenic artist for the Blackpool Pleasure Beach, for some of the most humorous illustrations in the world, departed shortly after Tom Mennard, in January 1990. He'd also painted a mural depicting a hundred of the top comics who'd appeared at the resort, which had received great acclaim.

Alton has a video of Rowland, in which he recalls: "I was no'but a lad when I drew my first mural...."

The actor, Edwin Richfield, died in August 1990, aged sixty-eight. Alton had the unforgettable experience of acting with him, in several radio plays:

I should explain that when crowd noises are required, everyone 'mucks-

Jo, Dennis and I pretend not to notice as the Mayor of Dudley takes the eye, November 1989.

Edwin Richfield.

in' and supplies appropriate sounds – not Edwin! As an act of defiance, instead of making the expected cries, Edwin would go off into a cacophony of peculiar effects and dialects. I once overheard Philip Martin saying to him: "Edwin, will you be giving us your Turkish carpet seller today?"

Dave Mitty drew our attention to Alton's maxim that showbusiness is made up of two words – show and business. In earlier sections of the book, Linda Grant and others, have made a similar point, stressing the importance that Alton places upon, not only developing one's talents to the full (whatever they happen to be), but also, of supporting this with sound business practice. Edwin, it would seem, took a similar view; although he put years of effort into becoming a well-established and respected character actor, he also allocated sufficient time to his business – he and his wife had a home-brewery shop in Shrewsbury.

Edwin was best known for his portrayal of theatrical agent, Steve Gardiner, in the 1960s serial, *The Odd Man*, and appeared earlier with Robert Shaw, in *The Buccaneers*. His first love, however, was the theatre; in the late 1970s, this saturnine-featured actor became a stalwart of the *Royal Shakespeare Company*.

During the 80s, Jack Douglas, one of the stars of the *Carry On* films, was taken ill and Alton was asked to speak at a dinner in his place.

Unfortunately the booking agent failed to tell me that he'd sold me to the company as Jack Douglas's cousin. For two hours before my speech, I had to 'flannel' my way through questions about my famous relative. By the end of it all, I'd built up a completely fictitious family history and my neck was sore from imitating his Alf Ipititimus character – "Whahey!" That was in Stratford, at the same stately home venue where they threw custard and trifle at the expensive tapestries, as a way of finishing the evening.

Life was getting pretty hectic by now, because, to add to all other activities, we were being invited to take part in more and more signing sessions.

Alton's co-writer can relate to the experience of book signings (having participated in several, with Pat Roach – as his biographer). "You do have some problems," elaborates Dennis, "for example, with spelling different versions of the same name; the one that *really* foxed us was Mary – 'Mairhi'. Names are an absolute minefield! But it all adds to the fun."

Alton's brother, Maurice, recalls one particular launch: "Somebody went up to Alton and said: 'I don't consider that you're a proper author.' (I was standing right with him you see). So he said, 'I'm not – I'm an entertainer. But just ask your wife there; she's sat there for an hour-and-a-quarter with my book. That's what I do – entertain!' "

In January 1990, totally out of the blue, he received a letter from Piotr Bakowski, a teacher from Skarzysko Kamienna, asking if he could possibly have a damaged copy of one of Alton's books, to show his pupils.

The problem was, he couldn't send hard currency out of the country, to pay for it. So I was happy to forward him a mint copy of 'Birmingham Remembered', not expecting anything in return. However, I received by return of post, the badge of his trade union, the now disbanded Solidarity ('Solidat' in Polish) - another treasured memento.

In the *Birmingham Mail*, Alton quipped:

'I have no idea how he knew about the book, but I think there may now be a market for "Memories of Poland!"'

The same book disappeared behind the Iron Curtain, when leading Russian scientist, Dr. Natalia Kotelnikovia decided to take a copy back with her, as an exhibit for the Soviet Museum of Science.

Alton was guest speaker for a medical fraternity dinner, at Edgbaston Cricket Ground.

After the meal, I was sitting with our old family practitioner, Doctor Bamford, and watched in horror, as a guest, with all the studied concentration of the true lush, staggered across the floor, spilling beer as he went. He eventually subsided into a chair, raised a half-empty glass to an imaginary confidante, and Doctor Bamford said: "I wouldn't mind, but he's operating at eight o'clock tomorrow morning!"

On Burns Night, held annually to honour Scottish poet, Robert Burns, our intrepid hero arrived at a dinner, to find that the agent had been given strict instructions to send a speaker along who could perform the 'Addressing the Haggis' ceremony. It includes that immortal second line - 'Great chieftain o' the puddin' race...'

Not only could I not perform it, but I'd never seen it performed. The organiser was distraught. I could only apologise and explain that it was the first I'd heard about it. Tearing out hair time! Then I spotted Pipe Major Vic Humphries. Explaining the predicament, I said: "Just give me a few minutes and I'll see what I can do." Vic said: "Don't worry, I can recite it in my sleep." I said: "Don't – do it while you're awake!" I wrote it on a card, and then I waited for my cue. Sitting there, I remembered Joan Mann in the 'Fol de Rols' saying to me: "Alton, when you're a bit unsure, just go at it." The cue came and I launched into the spiel, with enormous gusto and my best Scottish 'burrr'. At the end of the address, I stabbed the haggis with such enthusiasm that it spurted all over the lady sitting at the next table, and she promptly fainted! The general consensus of opinion was that it was the best Haggis Ceremony that anyone could remember!

As if the unpreparedness of the Burns Night wasn't enough, I walked into a Yachting Club dinner, just in time to see someone being pinned to the wall, whilst members methodically spread butter, all over the back of his jacket. At another dinner I was informed that it was 'infra-dig' to go to the toilet, until after the President had decided to relieve himself. I ignored the edict, quite convinced that the man had had a catheter fitted! Then at a trade union dinner in Rochdale, the other guest speaker was the Liberal MP, Cyril Smith. My speech was received with rapturous applause; a pleasant change from some of the northern reactions that I'd experienced. I saw him looking across at me several times and a lot of muttering went on. Eventually, he got to his feet and slowly walked towards me. I thought, 'He's going to congratulate me. It probably means a booking at the Liberal Party Conference. Maybe I'll be recommended for a knighthood?' He towered over me (Lancashire accent): "Young man, would you mind moving your car?"

By the early 90s, Alton had virtually decided to finish with the performing side of his life. As with the cabaret scene, external forces were coming to bear, which would curtail a lot of the work.

People with full-time jobs were prepared to go out and speak at dinners, just for the meal and a pat on the back, and fees started to dry up. More and more 'turns' and professional speakers were moving into the cruise world. But with all my book commitments, plus the fact that we'd started a mail order side, (in those days the forty-eight-hour delivery of books was unheard of and people outside the Midlands couldn't find our titles), I didn't want to be away for long periods. At much the same time, sadly, Philip Martin's little radio repertory company disbanded, as he moved on to conquer pastures new, and 'Beacon Swing' had ended, with the appointment of a new programme controller.

So with new titles appearing and an ever-expanding back catalogue, Alton decided to devote himself to the book world, and set about promoting their titles at Open Days, Book Fairs and signing sessions. A complete list of his publications, up to and including the year 2003, may be found at the end of this book.

At W.H. Smith's in Dudley, surrounded by copies of the towns' book, and with photos and cuttings all around us, a man asked: "Are there any Dudley pictures in this book mate?" I couldn't resist it: "No, I'm sorry, the printers have got it wrong – it's filled with Walsall photographs." He threw a copy back onto the table: "Well it's no bloody good to me then!"

Many of our titles had been re-published by a local firm Streetly Printing Ltd, but in early December 1990 I had a panic call from the MD to say that they were in financial trouble and the bailiffs were moving in! Although it was a disaster for them, it was pretty calamitous for us too. Having virtually burned all my boats and committing myself completely to books, it could have been the end of the road.

As in so many instances, positive thinking came to the rescue - and a man called Alan Brewin entered, to act as yet another important bookmark in the pages of our story.

Dennis Moore and I, sporting a nice variation in military ties, prepare to raise money for charity, Wolverhampton, 1990.

Chapter 21 -

WHAT'S BREWIN?

My publisher's preoccupied with wealth. He's the sort of fellow who smokes a cigar at Christmas and wears the ash all the year round.
Gold fillings in every tooth. On his way home last night, he was mugged by a dentist.
Conceited? The police took his fingerprints and he ordered a set of enlargements for all his friends.

Bang in the middle of our 1990 Christmas rush came the news concerning the demise of 'Streetly Printing Ltd'. Jo and I agonised all night over our next move. Then we remembered meeting with Alan Brewin, some years previously. We'd been struck by his patently honest and straightforward approach to business and had said at the time that he was the sort of person we'd like to deal with. I rang him, met within hours and quickly reached an agreement that 'Brewin Books' would take over the publication of most of our titles.

Our judgement has proved to be pretty sound in the years since. Oh yes – and despite my gags – he's the most unassuming person. (Now if that isn't 'creeping' enough for Alan, tell him he's not in the book!)

With everything settled, they plunged headlong into the book world. Dennis Moore and Alton attended a signing session at *Fagin's* in Merry Hill. The week before, the *Express & Star* had taken a photograph of Dennis. So he ordered a copy to put in the shop window.

The photo didn't arrive until the morning of the signing. Running a bit late, Dennis grabbed the envelope from the postman, on his way out. As he tore it open, Paul, one of the shop's owners, saw his face drop, as a photograph of the Wolves Centre Forward, Steve Bull, emerged. "Don't worry Dennis," he said, " stick it in the window, it will sell more books!"

Dennis describes Jo as, "… a lovely bubbly blonde. My wife likes her very much indeed. She and Alton have a wonderful relationship. She knows all the jargon, and the way he thinks: that's important; he doesn't have to *explain* what he wants, because she's got it. She usually does all of the typing – because if you've seen Alton's writing… Perhaps that's one of his faults? Poor writing! I used to guess at what he was saying, but I can now read his letters, and so forth – I'm pretty good at it."

Alton has an idiosyncratic way of using language, reflecting a rather intricate personality. Dennis mentions Alton's expertise and attention to detail: "You don't have to query his grammar or his punctuation, because it's such a joy to read what he's put. Captioning pictures can be boring for people, but he finds a different phrase to explain things. He'll say that so-and-so is 'sitting centre stage', when it isn't a stage at all, and describe 'a ghostly backdrop', to something. He's got that turn of phrase. When he does corrections for the printers, you wonder if they're ever going to read them, because as you know, proofreaders have this special cryptic language; and then there's 'Altonese' as well – but they get the message, and they do it for him."

Living proof that you can survive marriage.

Quite often, instead of organising a formal signing session, shops would ask for signed copies to be delivered. I deposited some of them on the counter, paused to talk to the manager, then we noticed a woman looking at them, in open disgust. The manager said: "Can I help you madam? Do you wish to buy a book?" She said, with great indignation, "No I don't want one of them: somebody's writ in it!" Another time, a lady recognised me in a bookshop and asked me to sign a copy. I wrote in my best copperplate: 'Good luck.' She squinted hard: "Does that say what I think it does?" "Of course." "Oh thank goodness. For a minute I thought you'd written 'Good luck'."

Family illness forced Clive Hardy to relinquish the job, after designing their books for over ten years. They scratched around, trying to find someone to take it on.

Suddenly Jo had one of her brainwaves (duck Alton)! : "Why don't you do it?" (Jaw hits floor, mouth sags open, stomach spins out of control). "Me – why me?" By this time she'd remembered some urgent ironing. I thought: 'I'll nip this in the bud, right away.' I grabbed a copy of one of our books and bad-temperedly worked out, in reverse, how Clive had reached his conclusions. From that moment onwards, I was Layout Man.

Alton was involved in fund raising at a 40s Night, held in the *Tower Ballroom*, Edgbaston, for the *Birmingham Mail Christmas Tree Fund*, (which was celebrating one hundred and one years of service to old people, needy families and children).

The Count Basie Orchestra provided the music. You can imagine the thrill when I signed books for some of my heroes: tenorist Frank Foster, trumpeter Irwin Stokes. It seemed like only yesterday when I was collecting their autographs as a lad, at Birmingham Town Hall.

At a coffee morning for cancer charities, Jo and I were standing behind a trestle table, covered with our books, when a lady said: "I'm a close personal friend of Alton Douglas you know." I said: "Are you? Perhaps next time you see him you'll give him my regards?" "Certainly, what's your name?" " Douglas." "OK Douglas. Next time I see him, I'll remember you to him."

Jo, by now, was becoming much more heavily involved in the production of our books, and it was only fitting that she should be credited as a co-author. It gave me a real buzz to see her name appear on the spines of our new titles. Her agency had gradually faded away in the 80s, due mainly to a lessening demand for cabaret artistes and dance bands, and also to the advent of the discos. She reluctantly attempted to book a few DJs, but with the exception of the ever-reliable Ian Sandy, they had proved to be a total disaster.

Ian is a mutual acquaintance of both authors and was a tremendous help with Pat Roach's book. Alton and Jo then set about raising funds for the *Birmingham Dogs' Home*, and, in 1991, put together *Dogs in Birmingham*.

In our ignorance we filled the book with almost every canine breed known to mankind, not realising that 'doggie' people only seemed to collect books about their own pet's breed. It did give me the opportunity to recount a true story. A few years before, I had to take Groucho to the vet's. The owner sitting opposite me was impressing on me how well behaved his Alsatian was. "If I say 'sit', he sits; if I say: 'lie', he lies, if I say 'stand' he stands." Just then the receptionist called the man's name. He stood up and said: "Right!" The dog - who must have been a bit hard of hearing - took a bite out of him!

Although Alton and Jo work side-by-side in the book industry, she has separate interests too. "I'm interested in anything to do with medicine," she explains, "aromatherapy, herbal remedies and acupuncture. I've been to most of them, for medical reasons. I have Raynaud's disease in my fingers and toes (the tips go white), which is a nuisance: for example, it was a damp day today, so I put something around my shoulders, to keep my back warm. Alternative medicine's something I've always been fascinated with. There are some wonderful drops you can take, Bach 'Rescue Remedy': if you're nervous, for example, they're great for calming you down. The only problem is, if you're taking alternative medicine, you have to be very careful about mixing it with traditional remedies: most doctors think it's taboo."

There's undoubtedly a link between her use of alternative medicine and her interest in astrology: they're both relatively uncharted, unconventional fields, and have an air of mystery about them.

We discussed Zodiac signs - Jo's a Leo and Alton's an Aquarian. Are the two signs compatible? "If you have a look at the chart I brought," she explains, "that's one of the partner combinations. It's a fire sign. I've always got on with other Leos; they're often either outgoing or bossy."

No biography can be truly accurate, without contrasting the subject's life, with the other side of the coin - the subtext of a wife, husband or partner; combine the two, and a far more interesting and broader picture emerges. Unfortunately, many biographies, for a variety of reasons, (some unavoidable) lack this additional insight. We are very fortunate that, in this case, Jo has supplied those all-important pieces of the jigsaw.

In the stereotypical showbusiness marriage of twenty years ago, there was an often-perceived image of the 'little wife', at home, maybe lonely and 'put upon' – perhaps ignored. Nowadays, however, when celebrities often marry one another, there are times when the situation is, perhaps, more balanced.

In Jo and Alton's case, she explains that they were never apart for more than two weeks, and were able to maintain regular contact with each other: "He would always ring me, tell me how the show had gone; how various people had perhaps gone in, to offer him work. At the same time I was getting more and more involved with his agents and getting work for him. When he was doing summer seasons and pantomimes, so many of the cast would go home and have no work at all. So if it was a summer season, they finished in September – but where was their Christmas work?

"If I went with him at any time, usually to help with the long distance driving, I would go and sit with people that he was working for – or whoever was with them."

Over the years, this evolved into a kind of showbusiness community; friendships subsequently developed between Jo and some of the artistes, and their families.

"At the same time I tried to switch myself round - to put myself in Alton's position: I didn't want him to see me standing at the bar, staring into space, with him thinking: 'Oh dear!' Because that would have put him off what he was doing."

The same would apply, of course, regardless of one's profession; in any relationship it's important that neither partner should feel either excluded or restricted. One obvious solution, as in Jo and Alton's case, is to develop separate interests, and retain a certain amount of independence. But difficulties inevitably arise when two partners have opposing lifestyles.

Jo makes it abundantly clear that life with Alton has been tremendously stimulating, and anything *but* lonely! "It could have been – had I *not* joined in, or not been interested in what he was doing, which a lot of wives aren't. You had to be careful as well, because perhaps during the season, the singer or someone had been going out with somebody else and the wife came up – and you knew; so you'd got to be careful about what you said." Affairs amongst the showbusiness community, are, notoriously, one of the more negative aspects. Jo comments: "If you're jealous in any way – forget it! I think jealousy destroys people - I don't have any time for it." The following old Chinese proverb seems to exemplify the *wisdom* of allowing a partner the freedom to express him or herself:

'The butterfly that flits from flower to flower is mine. The one that lies, struggling and dying in my net, is lost to me.'

Jo was alert to this need, right from the early stages of Alton's career. She agrees: "Married couples must have space." It's difficult to see how a showbusiness marriage or close partnership could work, unless the supporting partner has a similar attitude to her own, because, as she explains: "... they're going to be forced into the background, in lots of ways." From the performer's point of view, he or she might be prevented from focusing on the task-in-hand, due to anxiety about a partner feeling neglected or excluded, leading in turn, to feelings of guilt about pursuing their ambitions.

We discussed the fact that sensitivity is an integral part of Alton's personality. One is frequently conscious of not wanting to upset him. Even though he's more than capable of fighting his own corner, is very forthright in his opinions, has been tough enough to sustain a demanding career, and is very much his own man, the dichotomy remains. It's a strange contradiction, because he's more than capable of looking after himself, and is *certainly* not slow in telling you when he doesn't like something! These two contradictory sides of his nature are one of the elements that have made co-writing Alton's biography so intriguing.

Jo acknowledges: "Yes, he's so good-natured, that you feel you don't want to hurt or upset him." She wonders how he's managed to remain so even-tempered, considering the pressure he's frequently been under, during his career, but feels that, as they've known each other for most of their lives, if there was an intolerant side to him, she would have seen it by now. She explains: "I had an aunt, my dad's sister, who would argue at the slightest provocation. That's something I don't like. It frightens *me*. We both hate that. If I disagree with Alton, and there's perhaps an argument coming up, or something like that, he'll close ranks, whereas a lot of people would go on and on. Arguments escalate and divorces too – for the stupidest reasons." Several contributors have made a point of mentioning this special rapport between Alton and Jo - the fact that they seem very much in tune. She adds: "I think it also helps if both of you come from the same background."

Pete Lindup defines success as: '...being in the right place at the right time, and doing the right thing in front of the right people'. Luck *undoubtedly* plays a part - "...and hard work too," adds Jo. "Apart from child prodigies, I don't think there's any such thing as 'overnight success'."

It's been suggested that had Alton been a London or a Liverpudlian comedian, he'd probably have gone further. Birmingham, it must be said, has produced just a handful of successful comedians.

Only four of the best – Sid Field, Tony Hancock, Jasper and Don!!

People have described Alton as very loyal - he keeps in touch with his friends. Jo agrees: "He's like that, even with someone he's only met once or twice." She confirms that Alton is a 'man of his word': if he agrees to do something, you can guarantee that it will be done.

In 1993, Bob Monkhouse's first book was published. As part of his promotional tour he came to *Waterstone's* in Birmingham. Jo decided to buy a copy, as a surprise for Alton.

On seeing her, he darted around the table, hugged her, and despite a growingly impatient crowd, he insisted upon talking about the good old 'Golden Shot' days. He also inscribed the book, 'Happy Memories Alton and Jo. Now my life is in your hands. Your co-author, Bob.'

The following year, I was saddened to hear that Billy Wright had passed away. At one time I almost seemed to be living at the ATV Studios and I kept bumping into Billy. As everyone knows, he'd been England's football captain, but by this time he was Sports Controller at ATV. I've always thought that you can measure the worth of a person by the little things that they do. Billy always seemed to find time to stop and talk.

One time I was standing at the entrance to New Street Station and Billy came 'haring' around the corner. He saw me and sprinted the entire width of the concourse, just to grab my arm and pant: "Alton – sorry – I can't stop now mate, I've only got three minutes to catch my train!" – and he was off.

That reminds me that another character, who I used to meet frequently at ATV, was Noele Gordon's mum, known to us all as 'Jocky'. For some reason she used to find me excruciatingly funny, and would sit in the audience, just to watch my warm-up, and then leave before the actual show started. I committed another of my famous 'faux pas', talking to Noele about her, when I said I always knew when Jocky was in – as she had the heftiest clap.

Studio stories abound. Alton recalls a tale about the MP for Warley, Andrew Faulds, getting involved in a very heated discussion with a political correspondent at the BBC. It finished up with the two of them sparring up to each other. Eventually, they persuaded Andrew to leave. As they pushed him through the doors, he was heard to mutter: "It's a shame. If you'd let me hit him it would have been worth three thousand votes in Warley."

How about this for spooky? The same year, we were in Leamington Spa, when I said to Jo: "For some reason, I feel I ought to go to 'Tomes of Leamington'." They'd been the printers of our three titles for the 'Coventry Evening Telegraph'. I'd never been to their premises, had never dealt with them directly, and had to ask the way. We stood outside and looked into a deserted workshop. The only things remaining of the business were one piece of machinery and an enormous cardboard folder, containing film. You've guessed it – the film of our three books was the last item

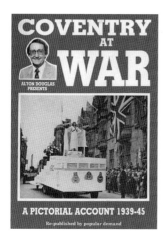 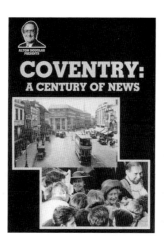 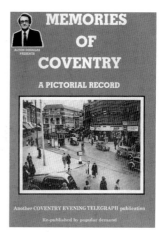

waiting to be collected for scrap. Thanks to a premonition, we salvaged them and with the Telegraph's permission, all three were republished by 'Brewin Books'.

At Christmas, Ken Dudeney, from Radio WM, invited Alton to take part in a three-way comedy radio quiz, with Malcolm Stent and Dave Ismay. Modesty forbids him from telling us who won – but it wasn't one of the other two! Typical questions were: "Who was the comedy star of *Lady in Red*, with Kelly Le Brock? It was Gene Wilder – that sort of thing. He won two *Morecambe & Wise* videos.

By now, the back catalogue of our titles was growing at such a rate, that if I wanted to check a shop's stock, I had to open a book and look at the list. Once again, although our sales were over the 350,000 mark, not everyone was satisfied. I was accosted by a very disgruntled man in a Garden Centre one day, who said he'd scoured our books for a photograph of his father's shop. I asked, "When did you send me one?" "I haven't sent you one." "Why not?" "I haven't got one." "Neither have I!"

Whilst I'm having a whinge, isn't it odd that people often assume that because you're reasonably well informed in one field, you automatically become an expert in other subjects? Over the years, I've found myself hopelessly miscast in various roles, including being asked to judge a dog show, acting as a TV critic at an art exhibition, voting on Easter bonnets, and sitting on the panel of countless beauty contests – (can I withdraw that last moan?).

Paradoxically, he's also signed books, proudly wearing his 5th Royal Inniskilling Dragoon Guards badge on his blazer, at air shows at RAF Cosford.

Commemorating the 50th Anniversary of VJ Day, 1995, at the Alexander Stadium, the sight of my badge was greeted with 'Ah – a 'donkey-walloper'"- (apparently an old army term for a Cavalryman).

Sometimes, central casting gets it completely wrong. During the following year, Alton visited Bournville Police Station, to collect a car security sticker.

The fellow in front of me presented quite a sight. He wore combat fatigues, size sixteen army boots, a cropped head – at the time when long hair was still fashionable, and I swear, even the tattooed figures on his arms had tattoos! "Can I help you sir?" The desk sergeant enquired. "Is there a problem?" "A problem – I'll say there is – I've just been mugged!"

Alton and Jo research photographs for the books separately: "You get loads of them, of course; you might have a couple of thousand. If you saw the way we work – which is all over the floor!" reveals Jo. "People would think: 'How confusing – how on earth do you do it?' "

Because they have so many regular readers, it's become almost like a family reunion: welcoming people home, with each new book; likewise with the annual mail shots that they send out. Alton and Jo are able to work successfully together on the books, whilst at the same time, enjoying it. "Things have just come together naturally, over a period of time," adds Jo, " but not because we've forced it."

Douglas Birt, Alton's friend from Heather Road, who kept him company during the traumatic period of Sidney's demise, had, paradoxically, only renewed his contact with Alton via a chance letter, written in December 2002. The key paragraph concerns a book that was first published in 1997:

'This is a long shot Alton, but could you confirm whether or not the contributor on page 47, *Birmingham in the Fifties Volume 2*, is the Douglas Price from Heather Road, Small Heath?

I have all your books and can honestly say they are amongst my most treasured possessions. Apart from living in five districts of Birmingham in the 40s, 50s and 60s, my working life as a driver salesman and eventually company representative for Pepsi Cola, gave me access to every type of business outlet, so *Birmingham Shops* was of great interest to me. *Birmingham at Work* was also unique in that in the 50s and 60s every factory had a canteen, so I recognise most of the contributions to the book, and *Birmingham at Play*, with its golf courses, bingo halls, dance clubs, and skating rinks. Thank you for so many hours of absolute pleasure reading your books.'

In a later conversation with the co-writer, Douglas expanded upon this: "To many people, if you just lived in Birmingham (you may have lived in one or two districts of Birmingham) you would be interested in those districts. But the job that I did took me into – I would say – without a lie – every *single* district and street in Greater Birmingham, within a fifty-mile radius, over forty years of working for the company."

From *Birmingham Shops* (1992) he recalls a photo on page 32, of Hingeston Street, in the Jewellery Quarter in Birmingham. "An aunt lived in this road and when we visited, I would watch the horse-drawn barges on the canal. Others are Lewis's, (page 123) in the centre of Birmingham. I had a long association with this department store. Civic Restaurants, also in the centre; there were loads of them at one time – and they're all featured in the book - I was selling to all of them."

With the second book, *Birmingham at Work*, (1993), factory canteens were familiar to Doug. "There was one canteen, which was in Alton's district – the Triplex canteen in Kings Norton. The factory next door to that, Burman's, had a huge canteen: we used to sell *oodles* of Pepsi-Cola – and they were all in the book. Kings Norton Green on page 100, represents places that still retain their village character. Edgbaston Street (page 13) always reminds me of a workmen's' café that opened around four o'clock in the morning, because of the wholesale market traders; their day started very early and they required a full English breakfast."

Birmingham at Play, (1994) covered the bingo halls, golf courses and dance clubs. "*Kings Nightclub*, Hamstead Road was once the coalminers' canteen. One of my favourites was the *Embassy Sportsdrome*, in Walford Road, Sparkbrook," explains Doug. "There were dance halls – *Tony's Ballroom*, in Hurst Street. I've got a 'claim-to-fame', that I've been in every golf club in the West Midlands, but I've never picked up a golf club!" (Alton later confirmed that, although he was there in a different capacity, in his case as a comic, he can probably make the same claim!)

During the spring of 1998, Alton suffered from a trapped nerve in his neck, which proved obstinately difficult to treat.

However, don't let anyone tell you that music doesn't have therapeutic qualities. I'd waited for forty years to hear 'The Dave Brubeck Quartet' in the flesh, and their visit to 'Symphony Hall' was a must for me. I can date my recovery from that magic October evening onwards. Thanks Dave, for half a century of wonderful jazz and for the healing. I always remember an eminent surgeon telling me how he envied those in the Performing Arts, because he could only help to heal the body, but we could heal the body and the soul.

>>> In 2003, The Brubeck Quartet came back to Symphony Hall, just in time to give him a health top-up!

It's a sentiment that Linda Grant entirely endorses: music therapy, plus working with choirs, and as church organist, has helped tremendously, in easing her osteoporosis.

Roy Hudd, in recent times, told me that he could never give up 'comicking' and he wondered how it had been possible for me to walk away from the performing side? I could only answer that I've missed being a comic greatly, but I've never, ever regretted giving up; I just knew when it was the right time for me to go.

I've also been asked whether I felt bitter about not becoming a household name as a comedian? Well, I think about my contemporaries: Alex Cochrane, Dev Shawn, Tony Cawley, Dave Ismay, Pete Conway, Tony Kent, Pat Tansey, Barry Lane – the list is endless – all excellent comics. You could have picked with a pin and made any one of them into a star.

I've been so fortunate that, when showbusiness fell apart in the mid-1980s, I was able to move into a field that I've always loved – the world of books. I'm so grateful that there's still a demand for what I have to offer – to this day. Our new titles still run off the presses at the rate of anything between one to three books a year, and our sales are now around the half million mark, and virtually all of our entire Back Catalogue is still in print.

I'm still setting myself goals and reaching constantly for the moon. After fourteen years of striving to get my Nonsense Verses published, Alan Brewin suddenly said: "Why don't we do it?" And 'Shocking Nonsense!' - a collection of dodgy dragons, stupid spiders and gormless ghosts, with glorious, full-colour cartoons by Clive Hardy, was inflicted on an unsuspecting public, in 2001. The book was designed by Alan's very talented son, Alistair.

Although not *really* a political animal, over the years Alton has had quite a few dealings with MPs, starting with lengthy correspondence to Edward Heath, when it was suggested that a charge be made for library books.

I then had a very stroppy exchange with Tom Litterick, after he was quoted as saying that naval guns should be turned on the Boat People. It culminated in him telling me that if I felt so strongly, I ought to go away and join the Quakers!

Incensed by the government's handling of red deer in the Highlands – it was reported that their antlers were being hacked off, and that they were left with blood streaming down their foreheads – I complained to Anthony Beaumont-Dark, who said that he was perfectly satisfied with the way the problem had been dealt with. I responded by telling him that he was there to pass on my disquiet. In reply I received a letter apologising for any offence caused, but unfortunately our correspondence had been mislaid, and he had no idea what it was that we were arguing about! We forgave him, and even went on to raise funds for his re-election.

Although from a Tory-inclined family, Alton has found that some of his happiest dealings have been with Labour MPs.

Peter Snape, then the member for West Bromwich East, invited Jo and I for a tour, and tea on the terraces at Westminster. Our current MP, Doctor Lynne Jones, has kept me informed, every step of the way, in a lengthy two-year battle against graffiti. Which reminds me that when I first voted, at the age of eighteen, the ballot papers did not include the name of the candidate's political party. Nervously I entered the polling booth, repeating the name of the Conservative hopeful under my breath. The next morning, checking the results, I found ninety-eight other people had also voted Communist!

As part of our mail order promotions over the years, we've given away souvenir bookmarks, coasters and once our publisher brought out a limited edition Lledo model van, with 'Alton Douglas Books' on the side.

I had a letter of complaint from a man who felt that the latest book did not contain enough pictorial material. (It had five hundred and fifty items in it, for £7-99). I was able to tell him that, in twenty years, it was only the second letter of complaint we'd ever received; the first was from him!

Our mailing list, at present, includes a host of well known celebrities, four majors and a naval commander; seven reverends and three knights of the realm, as well as hundreds of other correspondents, who write in so frequently, they're welcomed as old friends.

In the autumn of 2001, the gymnasium, which Alton and Jo attended, closed. By that time they were in their 25th year of membership.

We'd always referred to it as 'The Corinthian', but over a period of time; it had suffered several name changes, eventually finishing up as 'Curves & Co'. Imagine a bunch of muscular individuals admitting to that! Bill Sharrocks, one of our circle, had been scoffed at frequently by a neighbour. One of his last exchanges went: "Oh, I see you're off to the gym again!" "That's right." "God blimey, how often d'you go there?" "Three times a week." "Good God – three times a week? Flippin' heck!" "Where are you going?" "Hospital."

Speaking of hospitals, Jo's friend, Rosemary, has a daughter, Nicola, who was a nurse. One afternoon, just as the doctor started his rounds, a patient developed a terrible urge to use a bedpan. The curtains were hurriedly pulled around, but as they lifted the patient up, an enormous quantity of air escaped. There was a stunned, embarrassed silence in the ward, until the doctor said: "There – I bet you feel a lot better now nurse!"

To complete the medical trilogy, for many years our doctor, who's sadly retired now, was Doctor Davies – a great character; the least pretentious person you could wish to meet and vocally, a dead ringer for Jasper Carrott. I had to go for an injection. He opened his fridge and said, with some annoyance: "Hey Alt, look at this. Why do people put empty cartons back in the fridge? I've got to go to Reception now and top it up." He got to the door, turned and looked at me, and said: "There's only me uses that fridge."

In March 2002, Dennis Moore woke up and suddenly realised that he was seventy-eight, and it was time to retire. We miss his contribution to our books, but we still meet up once a month and put the world to rights.

Signing sessions often seem to produce the unexpected. A West Indian handed me a book. When I asked ungrammatically, "Who would you like it dedicated to?" he replied with something that sounded like "Tarzan." "Tarzan?" "No – Tozam." I looked at Jo - Jo looked at me – we both shrugged helplessly. "Tozam?" "Yes, Tozam." "Tozam? How do you spell Tozam?" "T-o S-a-m."

A substantial number of their titles have been presented, by the various mayors, as gifts to distinguished visitors to the area. Only last year, when she was ordering stock, the mayor of Wolverhampton's secretary told Alton about a visit he'd made to a local school. It was his practice to talk for twenty minutes or so, about the office and various duties of the mayor, and then to invite questions from the pupils. A boy stood up and earnestly asked: "Mr. Mayor, I was wondering if you could tell me please? Who was that man in the black suit in *East Enders* last night?"

Over the years, doing research, I've been made welcome in the Midlands, in the houses of so many folks, such as Dennis and Mollie Martineau, part of the family that has provided Birmingham with a succession of mayors and lord mayors, and Neville Chamberlain's daughter, Dorothy Lloyd. Also, André Drücker, who was the owner of several well-known Viennese-type coffee bars in the city. He was quite a cultured man, played the piano and the paintings on the walls of his cafés were his work. He also wrote a novel that was set in Birmingham, entitled 'Little Man in a Blind Alley', and he insisted on me taking away a signed copy. I especially revel in his description of the ever-changing face of the city; climaxing with the memorable phrases 'worms harbouring under the asphalt skin.' And a final 'People have always survived progress.' Very apt today!

As I've roamed the country, I've chatted to characters as diverse as Ian Botham, Henry Cooper, Earl Mountbatten, Bert Weedon, Barbara Windsor, Professor Magnus Pyke, Victoria Wood, Norrie Paramour, Marty Wylde, Marty Feldman, John Inman, Lord Montague and many, many others.

Two of the sexiest people I've ever met were Katie Boyle and Maggie Moone. The least sexy were the drag artistes who propositioned me. One of the funniest was a drag artiste who didn't proposition me at all – Adrian Varcoe, from Bristol.

Roy Hudd takes centre stage for his final spot in our book, bringing down the curtains on our penultimate chapter:

"At last, having written about every possible aspect of life in his beloved Brum, from *Birmingham Under the Romans*, to the wonderful fantasy *Birmingham – Winners of the Premier League*, he has turned to autobiography – his own!

"I've been dying to know how he's got away with it all these years – now we've found out. The truth – from the man who's trombone was the West Midland's secret weapon. The man of whom Muffin the Mule said, 'The best of my older warm-up men.' The recording star whose 78s have been on the shelves for so long, the holes in the middle have healed up. Tell it how it was – and still is Alton - (Love from an admirer)."

Roy Hudd.

Chapter 22 –

TURN UP THE LIGHTS

All the world's a stage,
And all the men and women merely players:
They have their exits and their entrances;
And one man in his time plays many parts,
His acts being seven ages.

William Shakespeare,
'As You Like It' (1599) act 2, sc. 7.

Our show is ended. As the audience heads back to suburbia, a few remaining members of the orchestra file through the exit doors. In the dress circle above, chairs swing and creak, backwards and forwards, as rows are checked, in the nightly ritual of hunting for mislaid belongings.

A tall, solitary figure emerges from a side door, at the back of the auditorium, d.j. in plastic holder, slung over one arm and a solid black trombone case, held tightly in his right hand. He pauses for a moment or two, then sinks his lean frame into a seat, on the back row, for a brief rest. 'God – it's been a long week!'

Doors slam, as muffled engines splutter into life, in the nearby car park. He hums a refrain or two to himself, from the show, drumming his fingers on his right thigh, as he recalls the night's events: "I'm a bit of a character – dum-di-dum, di-dum, di-dum ..." Quite an evening really – playing to a packed house; the audience response really got his adrenaline going tonight – unlike some venues he could mention! He sincerely hopes that you enjoyed the performance... we *both* do.

Red velvet curtains, trimmed with gold, bedeck a stage, ablaze a few minutes earlier, with lavish costumes, vibrant songs and the glittering prizes of his past. And he remembers...

The Bard of Stratford-upon-Avon spent the first two acts of his life, just thirty or so miles away, from Alton's home near the Lickeys. Shakespeare likened life to a seven-act play: infant, schoolboy, soldier, professional (seeking a reputation), achieving a comfortable and respectable lifestyle (in this case, a judge, in Alton's an entertainer and author); the onset of old age and finally, dotage and second childhood, bring up the rear. Hopefully, we've covered all but the last two!

So what's it all been about – this 'show' of ours? The lights return to full power, illuminating every nook, cranny and spider in the musty theatre, (plus any personnel, who happen to have lingered). Devoid of wigs or stage make-up, lines that time has etched on the face of our Top of the Bill, plus a receding hairline, fall sharply into focus.

We've staged a pageant of entertainment and achievement that *anyone*, hopefully, would be proud of. As he closes his eyes, they become a little jumbled: Icky Todd rubs shoulders with Ken Dodd; Mrs. Crusoe takes tea with Bob Monkhouse; Vince and Groucho chase madly up the centre aisle; a cello begins to 'camp it up' again, and confused pensioners fight their way through a haze of smoke.

But behind every icon or performer is an honest-to-goodness living, breathing, human being, with fears and foibles like the rest of us. So – as they used to say on an old TV quiz show, when the co-writer was a mere slip-of-a-girl: "Will the real Alton Douglas please stand up?"

It's impossible to get the full measure of a comedian simply by reading his script, for delivery and timing (difficult to record on paper) can be *crucial* elements, separating a competent act from a brilliant one. By the same token, one can't adequately reproduce the one-to-one conversations with Alton, spanning well over a year. If you've been able to imagine him, sitting there beside you in your living room, having a chat, then we've come close!

There's a side of Alton that is very endearing, but difficult to convey, simply through writing a biography. It's the softer, more playful, 'clowning' side of him, which isn't always apparent, and can't be adequately portrayed by describing his achievements, or even via an amusing tale. It reveals itself every time he telephones as a different character - Donald Sinden, Max Wall, George Formby, Groucho Marx, and so on – the list is endless.

And again, during the course of our conversations, when this master of linguistic humour suddenly makes an 'off-the-cuff' comment or an ad-lib 'play-on-words', based on something we've just been discussing. It's the flip side of the more business-like, sophisticated Alton – but an equally important part of him. I've been tempted, on more than one occasion, to simply 'tape' him during these more informal moments - and slip a copy in with the book!

In considering Alton's success, four key elements emerge. Firstly, an insatiable curiosity, about everyone and everything. Secondly, (a natural extension of the first), the ability to make a quick-fire assessment of what makes a particular person tick, then get the best out of that person, to their mutual benefit:

I get so cross and frustrated when people don't exploit their full potential (it's always someone far more naturally talented than me). Also, I feel that in the main, we are responsible for our own destiny (the realisation of that terrifies some people - and you can quote me!)

216

Thirdly, there is his talent for innovation, and - last but not least - a finely tuned instinct for keeping 'one step ahead of the game', which doesn't preclude sensitivity, but rather, demands it.

Both Jo and Alton are skilled communicators; Jo qualifies this: "Alton is, but withdraws, *perhaps*, a little more than I do. He can't bear to watch children or animals being harmed, on television, *hates* anything to do with hospitals, and is terribly squeamish with injections – or anything like that."

Several contributors have described Alton as 'impractical'. "He can't even put a screw in," confirms Jo, "if he tries to, it's crooked! I wonder whether it was because he didn't have a father from the age of ten? There was just his mother, so he didn't have – like fathers do – 'Oh, come and help me repair this shelf' - it *might* be that. He hates getting his hands dirty – he can't stand it! He won't do gardening; on rare occasions, he's mowed the lawn, but he'll do it very quickly."

Dave Mitty comments: "He's very practically minded – but not in the sense of *fixing* things. I don't know whether he's told you this, but if he bought something like a radio or a record player, I doubt if he could get it out of the box! Jo has to do all of that. We're all different aren't we? I'm not very practical either. I went round to Alton's the other day. He said: 'Isn't it hot?' I said: 'Well turn your fan on!' He said, 'I don't know how to do it. It's brand new – I can't find the switch! When Jo comes back, she'll turn it on.'

I just bent down and happened to see the switch: it was left to right. He said: 'How did you do that?' That's very typical. Jo does all the practical work in the house: fuses, lamps, mends things, moves furniture. She said to me, 'You know something? If I can't work it out, I stand and I say: 'Go on dad!' Her dad was an engineer you see - he could work anything out. I suppose Alton's so determined and single-minded, if he wasn't he wouldn't be in the position that he is today. But *she's* everything to him: his wife, secretary, mate… And I tell you what – she's very, very proud of him – I know that."

Ken Windsor observes: "Often the 'unsung heroes' are the wives. Now, when he first came to do the cabaret show I was compèring, he brought Jo. Normally, I was used to having all the comedians' wives down there, and they didn't want to know *me*. I was a single man, on my own, without anyone tagging on, and the wives wanted to socialise with those who mattered: which was usually couples, who were high up in the social scene. But Jo came up to me that night: 'Ken,' she said, 'I'm on my own. I *hate* being on my own. Can I sit with you for the night?' And that was it – she was a human being – and she's always been like that as far as I was concerned. I think that's often something that goes unnoticed: the fact that behind every good performer – there's always a good wife."

Alton has always been ultra-practical, dynamic and 'go-getting', in terms of furthering his career, and, in that respect, could never be accused of lacking in drive and physical energy. At the same time, he's an intellectual who becomes engrossed in thinking things through – a 'deep thinker' - contemplating theories and a range of ideas.

Jo agrees: "He's very much like that. There's so much in there; he's *very* talented, although he'll say: 'No, I'm not.' It sounds as if I'm perhaps prejudiced, but it's a shame, because there are so many things he could do, that he's not doing - writing plays, writing musicals. If someone says to him: 'I want an idea for such-and-such a thing,' he'll walk away and come back again – and it's done – he has a very quick mind."

Although astute in terms of human relationships, she adds: "There *are* certain things that people will say to Alton, which I get really hurt about, but he doesn't. But it hurts me, because I don't think they should be saying it about him. People are sometimes very *jealous* of him. (I suppose - anybody successful ... and somebody who has an ordinary job...). I think men are far more critical of each other – and far more hurtful."

Being forthright, Jo will discuss any concerns with him. "He'll say: 'You're reading far too much into it.' From what I can see, he's far tidier than most men - his mind is tidy - he's very tidy in himself; when he was on stage, he was absolutely immaculate... and yet he hates looking for praise."

The Alton who emerges from the pages of this book, in some respects, fits the stereotypical profile of many successful individuals; he is, without doubt, a multi-talented, highly accomplished person – a man of many parts. An engaging personality who is kindness and encouragement personified, with both friends and colleagues. Don Maclean observes: "He's never been a bitter bloke, has he? He's never been one of those blokes who said: 'Oh I don't think much of so-and-so.' He's always been very generous towards his contemporaries." Pete Lindup, in Blackpool, comments: "He's a good mate actually; we've kept in touch for thirty-four years, which has got to be a record. We correspond, but very rarely telephone: he does all the talking anyway, so I'm not paying to listen to *him* – (he'll like that!)"

John Clayton comments: "He looks after me really well. I have all of his books – signed; he usually

Don Maclean.

218

sends me them, every Christmas. I've got the *whole* collection, including *Celebrity Recipes* and *Know Your Place*. I've also got the 45 record he made - *Alton Douglas Sings?*

"When he used to work for the Britannic, we'd often visit each other's houses." John moved to Cornwall over seven years ago, having retired through ill health about three years before that; despite losing much of the use in his left leg and arm, he still manages to do landscape paintings.

John's sold three paintings, in America, via the Internet. (I told him, I consider that a hell of an achievement).

"If a person needed some sort of favour I'd say - 'Well he's the best bloke to go to.' Although he's done well for himself, it's made no difference – as far as that goes. Alton's always been a good friend," John continues. "When he gets on the phone to me (he phones me, more than I phone him), I say: 'Oh, I was just going to phone you.' He says: 'Everyone says that!' He'll always ask how I'm getting on. If anybody's ever been a friend to him – I don't think he ever loses touch with people he's met. He'll say, 'I met so-and-so today. I haven't met him for years.' You can bet your life, if he meets somebody, he'll be contacting that person again."

Conversely, several contributors have described Alton as a perfectionist, who refuses to settle for 'second best'. Mike Gancia explains: "Alton can be difficult. He's got his own ideas about how he wants a thing to be done. For instance, a show: if we went to a place and it didn't look right, or the staging or lighting didn't look right, he'd kick up a fuss. He's too much of a perfectionist - in some respects. He comes across as a friendly person, but you don't cross him – or he becomes a very unfriendly person. He's got his own ideas. He's temperamental, but I always think – and my wife will confirm this – that if an artiste is a perfectionist – they *are* temperamental."

Regarding Alton's highly professional approach to whatever he does, Pete recalls: "...all of the material for his act was written down. I *think* he wore special clothes for different venues. He wore a white shirt with every suit and it had to be a certain make of shirt. Alton doesn't 'suffer fools' at all."

It's also a two-edged sword, because attention to detail has, on many occasions, produced very positive results for him; the following is merely one example:

A club in Portland was literally, just a long tunnel, with a stage at one end. I had the stage moved to the middle of the room. We played it like an umpire situated in a tennis match. The committee was absolutely livid, but the audience said it was the best night they'd ever had there! A friend went back there, some years later and the stage was exactly where I'd put it!

For the co-writer, the mark of a good comedian is that the humour appears to flow naturally. He's probably worked on it for ages, but it's the delivery - almost as if the next joke is something that has just occurred to him.

Mike cites Noel Briton, a relatively unknown comedian, as a case in point. "He does a thing called *A Bath Walk*. If ever you go to Bath – it's a comedy walk that goes on every night – you must go on it. This guy is *unbelievable!* The first time I saw him was at the *Playhouse*, Weston-super-Mare. He came on, and there was a lady in the front row with a baby – crying its eyes out. I mean – come on – you're in a theatre! He stood there and looked at it for a minute. Then he said: 'Oh, come on missus, take the batteries out!' And he got the audience – instantly!"

Alton's original brand of humour and creativity have been coloured throughout by a powerful predisposition to 'paddle his own canoe'- or 'plough a lonely furrow' (hence the dedication page quotation from Thoreau) - even though this reduced his chances of more widespread fame.

Mike quotes another comic who, like Alton, preferred originality to conformity: "There's an American comedian, Stephen Wright. He's got a unique style; no one had got an act like him. And it's purely words. He'd say: 'Do you know, last night I got burgled, and when I came downstairs, everything had been replaced with an exact replica.' It was really 'off-beat' stuff – terrific he was. But where's he gone? Where is he?"

Nevertheless, four years into the 21st century, our *Kaleidoscope Comedian* continues to create new books, touring the country, come rain or shine, distributing a wide range of publications. Ably assisted by Jo, he exhibits the determination, energy and enthusiasm of a man, twenty years his junior.

Two main factors seem to have contributed to Jo and Alton's successful partnership. She has helped Alton's career in a variety of ways. From a personal, psychological aspect, she's been prepared to stand back, shunning jealousy or possessiveness, providing peace of mind to continue. When one is the public eye, it seems essential that the wife, or one of the partners takes a back number; two strong egos, vying for position, yet still trying to maintain a stable relationship, seems a well nigh impossible situation to sustain.

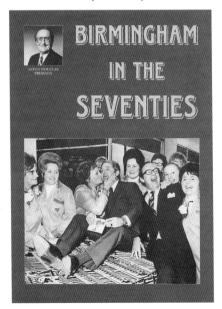

"I don't think that two successful people can 'gel', observes Jo, "there's got to be one of them pushing forward, trying to push the other one out. Alton had to have a strong ego, in order to achieve what he has done. For example, after compèring *The Golden Shot*, he had a high profile. Now if somebody came over to interview him, I would gradually backtrack away; if there were any photographs to be taken, I would be out of the way." She stayed sufficiently close to lend her support, but also knew when to make herself scarce – as in the Kenny Rogers song – The *Gambler*:

You've got to know when to hold up, know when to fold up,
Know when to walk away, know when to run.

"He probably wouldn't have even realised that I'd moved out of the way – that I'd gone. I found it quite easy to do that, because I'd never wanted to be on the performing side. I loved the theatre and the entertainment side, but I didn't want to be up there. I'd far rather be at the side of the stage." Jo's early experience of theatres and performers, (later extended into running an agency), fostered an understanding of performers and what makes them tick. This, combined with her *preference* for not being an entertainer, evolved to provide the kind of tailor-made support system, in which Alton's career could flourish. "It's gelled together - come gradually really," she observes.

Her outgoing personality and independent spirit have proved invaluable. She comments: "I think we both bring our own talents to bear – there must be no duplication (otherwise somebody is obsolete)." Alton refers to Jo's determination, and tremendous capacity for hard work. "We're both alike in that way," she explains. "Some people go to bed when they feel ill. I didn't come from a family like that." It's fortunate that they're well-matched, because Alton's always 'on the go'. As Dennis Moore observes: "...when Alton has something on his mind, he goes for it!"

Dave Mitty describes Alton as, "... a very likeable 'Brummie'; he's ambitious and very funny. I often say to people: 'You don't know the *real* Alton.' You get so many people in our business saying: 'I've worked with him,'- or her. It's all a load of 'bull' - half the time. But he's *really* worked with them. There's no 'bull' with him - he's so honest."

Occasionally I still get involved in the odd bit of radio. In Chapter 18 we referred, to Ed Doolan's broadcast from Australia in September of 2002, which included me, in Frank Ifield's 50th Anniversary celebrations. Having mentioned the day he and his mum came to tea, and how he managed to get his Silver Cloud jammed against our gatepost, reminds me - I must put it back sometime!

Alton congratulated Frank on his fifty years in showbusiness. He also referred to a mutual acquaintance of theirs, in the jazz world:

AD: Several years ago, I sent you a photocopy from Graeme Bell's book, *Australian Jazzman* – the best jazz book ever written. You didn't realise your picture was in it. Did you ever get a copy of that?

FI: Yes, I did actually. That was from the tour that we did together in New Zealand, at the time. I did the tour with a guy called Jimmy Little, who was a very famous man over here.

AD: I'm looking at a picture of him, right now. David Blakewell, a friend in New South Wales, sent me the book. He said: "I've not only got you a copy of this lovely jazz book, but I popped round to Graeme Bell's and got him to sign it!"

Alton concluded by reminding listeners that at one time, Frank had attended College Road School, in Moseley, Birmingham, when he and his family were living in Wake Green Road. Later in the programme Frank mentioned that he was hoping to do a tour of Britain in 2003, with new Australian talent.

Recently, I walked into a shop on King's Norton Green. The owner said: "I've just realised, you're the only famous person I know." I said: "I'm not famous." He replied: "I know that, but you're the nearest I'll ever get to Joan Collins!"

Frank Ifield.

Alton has always tried to find a new angle on whatever he tackles. With the band he introduced a visual aspect, creating a dance band that could be *watched*, as much as listened or danced to. Exactly the same applied when he became a comic. Most comedians were doing roughly the same act. There were one or two original comics – so he became one, writing much original material, sometimes aided by others, such as Gordon Stretch and Pete Lindup, designating himself - *The Original Alton Douglas* – our book's title. Never allowing himself to become bored with his career, he continues to *actively* seek variety. Every time there is any suggestion of coming to a dead end, or not succeeding, he changes course *before* it happens.

Yes, deliberately, every time, it's been me. Sometimes pushed by events, very slightly nudged, but in the main, it's been because I've wanted to change course. I think of my life as being about five lives in one really.

There's a dual analogy here, because Alton's entire *life* has been like a 'scrapbook', in the most positive sense of the word, or alternatively, the ever-changing kaleidoscope in our opening poem. Although now at an age when many are reaching for a pipe and carpet slippers, he'll kaleidoscope and change the existing picture, or present new material, in the same way that his scrapbooks do. Because of this constant, never-ending thirst for variety, he could never have settled for a 'nine-to-five' job.

Several of his friends have mentioned Alton's lack of technological expertise. However, all is changing! As this chapter takes shape, he is gradually becoming computer literate. Now able to send e-mails and 'surf the net', he regularly accesses his own website – www.altondouglas.co.uk designed for him, by Ken Windsor.

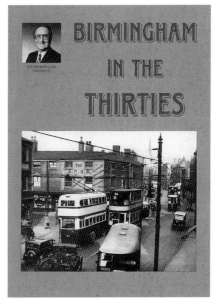

You've got to ensure that you're not left behind by events. The jazz tenor player, Zoot Sims, was obviously troubled by the same thought, when he mused: 'They've just landed a man on the moon - and I'm still playing 'Idaho'!'

Dennis Moore describes Alton as "A totally absorbing person. He will get you on his side, and you will be on his side very quickly and very easily. It's not that he wants to get a victory out of it. He *needs* what he wants from you, but he'll make you feel at ease and when you've left him you'll think: 'Well that's good – I really helped there.' He's brilliant like that – there's no doubt about it."

It's been a long journey for a shy lad from Small Heath. It's taken me into the Dragoon Guards, on to leading my own band. Then through twenty years as a comedian, playing virtually all the major theatres in the UK; to fronting my own TV series for three years and finally on into a life as the biggest selling author/co-author of local books, in the history of the West Midlands. Through it all, Jo and I are still happily together and still finding humour in most situations. Although, we don't always agree - as somebody once said, "If a couple are in total accord, someone's being bullied."

Incidentally, as well as the names mentioned, throughout the course of the book, I greatly treasure the friendships of so many people, too numerous to list, but too valuable to ignore. Thank you for putting up with my eccentricities!

Here's a final joke that I heard recently. A Jewish lady, in the street, is confronted by a flasher. He opens his raincoat – wide open. She stops, absolutely horrified, then says· "Huh – you call that a lining?"

By pure coincidence, the two co-writers both admire the poetry of Dylan Thomas. As his father, a former English master at Swansea Grammar School, lay on his deathbed, Dylan made the now famous heartfelt plea:

> *Do not go gentle into that good night,*
> *Old age should burn and rave at close of day;*
> *Rage, rage against the dying of the light.*

Alton has no intention of 'going gently': as usual, he currently has several new schemes and projects in mind.

And surprises still seem to lie around every corner. Even as we were completing this final chapter, Keith Ackrill, a retired television producer/director, sent Alton a CD copy of the radio programme he recorded in October 1976, with the Norman Dovey Orchestra!

So, this is not *really* the end of The Original Alton Douglas – there's life in the old Doug yet!

FAVOURITE THINGS

PERSONAL LIKES:

Jazz; cricket; reading; theatre; walking; early mornings; punctuality; Western films; bacon sandwiches; straight answers; friendship; the professional approach to anything and everything.

PERSONAL DISLIKES:

Parties; unreliable people; shilly-shallying; monstrous egos; car radios with the volume stuck on 'deafening'; most politicians (see monstrous egos); promos for TV plays and films that disclose the plot; sopping-wet towels; ditto people; houses without books, videos or music; drunks; manual work (especially gardening); traffic diversions; litter; liars.

FAVOURITE BOOKS:

The Magic of Believing, by Prof. Claude M Bristol; *Harpo Speaks,* by Harpo Marx; *Australian Jazzman,* by Graeme Bell; *The Penguin Guide to Recorded Jazz*; *Roget's Thesaurus*; *A Lot of Hard Yakka,* by Simon Hughes.

FAVOURITE COMEDIANS:

Jacques Tati; Bob Monkhouse; Jackie Mason; Robb Wilton; Jasper Carrott; Ken Dodd; Jimmy James; Laurel & Hardy; George Burns; Groucho Marx.

FAVOURITE FILMS:

The Third Man; *Casablanca*; *Monsieur Hulot's Holiday*; *The Tall Target*; *Zulu*; *The Fugitive*; most Randolph Scott, Audie Murphy and James Stewart Westerns.

FAVOURITE WRITERS:

Ogden Nash; Dylan Thomas; Dirk Bogarde; Steve Voce; Jo's husband.

CURRICULUM VITAE

TELEVISION DRAMA:

THE BRETTS
BIG DEAL
BOON
PROPERTY RITES
MONEYSPINNER
A SOFT TOUCH
START UP YOUR OWN BUSINESS
MUCK & BRASS
ANGELS
MURDER OF A MODERATE MAN
CROSSROADS

OTHER TV APPEARANCES:

NIGHTS AT THE SWAN (3 progs)
THE BARMAID'S ARMS
NEWSHOUND
KNOW YOUR PLACE (21 progs)
THE KNOCKERS
THE ORIGINAL ALTON DOUGLAS
THE GENTLEMAN'S GAME
SECONDS OUT
WATCH THIS SPACE
TODAY
MIDLANDS TODAY
TESCO commercial
LUNCHTIME WITH WOGAN (6 progs)
THE GOLDEN SHOT (5 progs)
CELEBRITY SQUARES
ATV TODAY

THEATRE:

THE MATT MONRO SHOW
(London Palladium)
WANTED ONE BODY
FOL de ROLS
Six Major Theatre Tours
Three Pantomimes
Five Summer Seasons

RADIO VOICE-OVERS:

Over 1,000

RADIO PROGRAMMES:

THE NORMAN DOVEY BIG BAND SHOW
OPEN HOUSE
RADIO WM/ BRMB/ BEACON RADIO
RADIO WYVERN/ MERCIA RADIO
(dozens of miscellaneous interviews)
BEACON SWING (3 years)

TV WARM-UPS:

THE GOLDEN SHOT (3 years)
SOME MOTHERS DO 'AVE 'EM
TERRY & JUNE
ARE YOU BEING SERVED?
CITIZEN SMITH
SECONDS OUT
THE DANA SHOW
UP THE WORKERS
LUNCHTIME WITH WOGAN
NEW FACES
CELEBRITY SQUARES
THE VAL DOONICAN SHOW
THE MAX BYGRAVES SHOW
THE GENERATION GAME
THE PEGGY LEE SHOW
MOTHER MUFFIN
HAPPY EVER AFTER
THE LENA ZAVERONI SHOW
THE GRACE KENNEDY SHOW
THE JIMMY TARBUCK SHOW

FOREWORD FOR:

THE TOSS OF A COIN by Maurice Bird
MURDER IN THE MIDLANDS by J.P.
Lethbridge
BIRMINGHAM CINEMAS by Victor J Price

INCLUDED IN THE SHORT STORY ANTHOLOGY:

SHORTS OF THE MIDLANDS

134,000.

RADIO PLAYS:

GUERNICA
THE FAMILY THAT PLAYS TOGETHER
TROUPERS
MR PEABODY & THE BEAST
SORRY. GOODBYE & GET STUFFED
YOU CAN'T JUDGE A BOOK BY LOOKING AT THE COVER
A CONFIDENTIAL AGENT (DETECTIVE ONE)

FEATURED IN THE FOLLOWING BOOKS:

MY LIFE AT CROSSROADS by Noele Gordon and Clifford Davis
CRYING WITH LAUGHTER by Bob Monkhouse
WHO'S WHO ON TELEVISION
BIRMINGHAM POST & MAIL YEAR BOOK & WHO'S WHO
THE YO YO MAN by Bill Maynard
BIRMINGHAM THEATRES, CONCERT & MUSIC HALLS by Victor J Price

VIDEO ARCHIVES & STILLS CONSULTANT:

MADE IN BIRMINGHAM

PATRON:

THE BIRMINGHAM TAPES FOR THE HANDICAPPED

INDEX

Index Notes: AD = Alton Douglas; JD = Jo Douglas; MP = Maurice Price. Page numbers in italics refer to photographs and their captions. Biographical details are listed chronologically.

A

Ackrill, Keith, 224
Adam, Lawrie, *86*
Admiral Crichton, The (musical), 48
Alhambra Theatre, Bradford, 142
All Ohio State Fair Youth Choir, 198
Allan, Johnny ('Farmer Jim Allan'), 170
Allen, Neil, 181–2, 185
Allyson, June, *33*
Alton Douglas Quartet, The, 53–5, 56–7, 58–61, *61*
Alton Douglas Sings?, 135
Anchor public house, Small Heath, 4
Andrews, Eamon, 136
Angadi, Darien, 172
Ansell, Lieutenant Colonel, 46
Arnold, Desi, 63
ARP, Small Heath, 15
Arthog, 5
Askey, Arthur, 116–17, 136, *136*
Astor Productions, 63–4, 71
ATV studios, Birmingham, 11, 117, 208
  see also individual television programmes
Atwell, Winifred, 75
Ault, Jo, 179

B

Bachelors, The, 138, 152
Badham, Jack, 31
Badham, Marjorie, 31–2
Bailey, Harry, 94
Baker, Hilda, 103
Baker, Kenny, 75
Bakowski, Piotr, 200–1
Balaclava Day (1957), *47*
Bamford, Doctor, 201
Barking Fox, Market Needham, 167–8
Barmaid's Arms, The (television series), 187
Barnby, Adrian, 58, *61*, 62
Baron, Bunny, 74, 82, 86, 99
Barrows, Ron, 121
Bartram, George, 43, 106, 131, 135
  death of, 197
BBC Midland Unit, 141–2
BBC, Pebble Mill Studios, 159, *191*
  see also individual TV and radio programmes
Beacon Radio, 182, 183, 193

Beacon Swing with Alton Douglas (radio show), 181–2
Beale, Colin, 156
Beaumont-Dark, Anthony (MP), 212
Bedder's Fish Restaurant, Birmingham, 3, 11
Benavente, Manolo J., 184
Bennett, Lennie, 105
Bennett, Tom, 162
Benton, Mary-Rose, 28
Berens, Harold, 67, 74–5, 101
Bergerac (television series), 188
Best Cellar nightclub, 64–5, 69, 71
Beverley, Anne, *132*, 133, 147, 148, *148*
Bexhill, 136–9, 141
Bexhill-on-Sea Observer, 138
Big Deal (BBC television series), 190
Bird, Maurice, 135
Birmingham, roads and streets
  Clark Street, Ladywood, 6
  Coventry Road, Birmingham, 3–4, 10, 11
  Heather Road, Small Heath, 18, 21, 28, 187
  Monument Road, Ladywood, 8
  New Street, 36
  Somerville Road, 3, 16
  St Andrew's Road, Small Heath, 4
  Wood Street, Ladywood, 5–6
Birmingham at Play, 210, 211
Birmingham at War, Vol 1, 10
  launch, 174–6
Birmingham at War, Vol 2, 180–1, 193
Birmingham at Work, 210, 211
Birmingham Dogs' Home, 205
Birmingham Hippodrome, 33, 38, 121
Birmingham in the Fifties, 210
Birmingham Mail, 135, 159, 163, 197, 201
  AD's book and, 173, 176, 180, 181, 195
  Christmas Tree Fund, 204
Birmingham Photography exhibition, 188
Birmingham Referees, 26
Birmingham Remembered, 195, 197
Birmingham Shops, 210
Birmingham Tapes for the Handicapped, 134, 194
Birt, Dorothy, 29–30
Birt, Douglas, 20–2, 24–5, 28, 210–11
  on sister and neighbours, 29–30
  Price family and, 20–2, 24–5, 28
Black Country at War, The, 183–4

Blackpool, 77-81, 102, 164
Bloomer, Diane and Freddie, 30
Blue Parrot restaurant, Blackpool, 102
Bob Hatch Memorial Trophy, 141
Boon (television series), 188
Boothroyd, Basil, 188
Borehamwood studios, 117
Borge, Victor, 121
Botfield, Chuck, 92
Bowen, Jim, 170
'Boy Robison' (singer), 85
Boys' Brigade, 12th Company, 27–8, *29*
Bramble, Wilfrid, 154
Bretts, The (Central TV), 195
Brewin Books, 209
Brewin, Alan, x, 203, 212
Brewin, Alistair, 212
Brigden, George, 45
Briggs, Bill, 46, 48
Bristol, 95, 100
British Beermat Collectors' Society, 133–4
BRMB radio station, 130
Bromsgrove, 58
Brookes, Peter, 148
Buckmaster, Michael, 62
Burton, Tommy, 147
Butler, Dave, 146
Butt, Ray, 161

C
Cadell, John, 172
Caesar's Palace, Dunstable, 71
Calvert, Eddie, *61*
Campbell, Christine, 29, *29*
Care, John T., 6
Cargill, Patrick, 87
Carmichael, Charlie, 46
Carrier, Sandra, 163
Carrott, Jasper, 135
Cartland, Barbara, 184
Casino Club, Port Talbot, 100
Castle Bromwich, 113
Castle Bromwich Aeroplane factory, 14, 17
Castle, Roy, 152
Catterick Army Camp, 39
Celebrity Recipes, 184
Central TV, 187
Charles, Hugh, 136, 137
Cheltenham, 162–3
Chuckle Brothers, The, 60, 151–2
Churchill, Winston, 17
Citizen Smith, 160
Civic Hall, Grays, Essex, 133
Clamp, Johnny, 133

Clapshaw and Cleave Limited, 1–2
Clarke, John, 141–2, 147, 150, 162
    on *Know Your Place*, 157–8
    on *Nights at the Swan*, 168
Clayton, John, 4, 10, 20, 28, *54*
    on AD, 218-19
    on Alton Douglas Quartet, 55
    works with AD in trio, *52*, 52–3
Cleasby, Paulina, 3, 10
Cleopatra's, Bristol, 75
Cleveland Court, Wolverhampton, 84
Close, Brian, 87–8
Cocks, Les, 123, 125, 128, 130
Coghill, Jimmy, 118
Cohen, Harry, 34
Commodore Club, Nottingham, 133
Congress Theatre, Eastbourne, 146
Conway, Pete, 123
Cooper, Graham and Reg, 129
Corbett, Harry H., 154
Corinthian gymnasium, Birmingham, 213
Count Basie Orchestra, 204
Couton, Jim, 103
Coventry at War, 179, 180
Coventry Evening Telegraph, 195
Coventry Road, Birmingham, 3–4, 11
    B.S.A. Works, 10
Crawford, Michael, 150
Cresta Club, Solihull, 76–7, 95, 98, 107, 122, 153
Crimewatch (BBC television series), 197
Croft, Peter, 99
Crossroads (television series), 129–30
Curves & Co, Birmingham, 213

D
Dair, John, 67
Daniels, Billy, 68
Daniels, John, 57
Daniels, Paul, 151
Darlington Band Club, 73–4
Dave Brubeck Quartet, 211
Davies, Councillor Sam, 199
Davies, Windsor, 132, 150
Dawson, Harry, 63–4, 68
Dawson, Johnny, 40–1
Dawson, Les, 135
de Courcey, Roger, 154
De La Warr Pavilion, Bexhill, 136, 138, *138*
Dennis, Johnny, *153*
Derby, 105
Derbyshire Diary, 126
Derbyshire Education Authority, 166
Derbyshire Miners' Holiday Camp, 60–1
Desmond, Lorrae, 43

Devoti's Ice Cream Parlour, Birmingham, 3,11
Dick Emery Show, The, 133
Dietrich, Marlene, 121–2
Diller, Phyllis, 169
Distel, Sacha, 120
Dogs in Birmingham, 205
Dollery, Tom, 27
Dominic Drive, King's Norton, 91, 92, 113
Donaghy, Aloysius, 58
Doolan, Ed, 180, 183
Doonican, Val, 117, 150
Dors, Diana, 76
Douglas, Alton
    on George Bartram, 197
    biographical details
        birth and infancy, 1, 2
        contracts diphtheria, 9
        during World War II, 10–11, 15, 16
        at infant school, 11, 17, 25
        love of books, 19
        meets Douglas Birt, 21
        father's death, 23–5
        sports, 26–8
        at grammar school, 30–1, 34
        first crushes, 29, 31–2
        signs of performer, 30–1, 33
        meets Jo Ward, 35–6, 38–9
        takes up trombone, 37
        National Service, 39–46
        songwriting and early broadcasts, 46–7
        demobilization and work as musician, 51–2
        forms quartet, 53–5
        as Britannic agent, 55–6
        performing with own quartet, 56–7, 59–61
        goes solo as comedian, 61–2
        Astor Productions and London's West End,
            63–6, 68–70
        touring experiences (1968), 66–8, 70–1
        Working Men's and Social Clubs, 72–4
        touring experiences and Blackpool (1969),
            75–6, 77–81
        first pantomime, Hastings, 82–4
        touring experiences (1970), 85–6
        Summer Season and marriage, 86–9
        as pantomime dame, Hastings, 99
        touring/boarding house experiences
            (1971), 100
        Blackpool season and clubs, 102–3
        as principal boy, pantomime, 104
        touring experiences (1972), 105–13
        friendship with Don Maclean, 105–6, 108
        Summer Season, ends clubbing, 108–12
        as television warm-up, 114–18
        Bernard Manning and, 119
    compères *The Golden Shot,* 122–6
    mother's illness and death, 127–8
    acting debut, 129–30
    doing voice-overs, 130–1
    performs at London Palladium, 132–3
    Presidency and Patronage, 133–4
    records EP, 135
    as principal comic, *Fol De Rols,* 137–4
    makes television documentaries, 141–2
    interviews, broadcasts, warm-ups (1976), 143
    Terry Scott and, 143–4
    recordings and broadcasts (1977), 146–8
    warm-ups and appearances (1978), 150–2
    writes column for local paper, 153–4
    Open House broadcast, 154
    Inland Revenue and a new house, 156
    works on *Know Your Place,* 157–60, 162, 173
    last warm-up, joins Media Players, 163
    performances and tours (1981), 163–4
    first book published, 166, 169
    compères *Nights at the Swan,* 168
    records *Muck and Brass,* 170–2
    launches *Birmingham at War,* 174–6
    appearances and projects (1983), 177–8
    launches *Coventry at War* and *Birmingham at War, Vol 2,* 180–1
    radio show *Beacon Swing,* 181–2
    works on *Joe Russell's Smethwick,* 182
    works on *The Black Country at War,* 183–4
    appearances and awards (1985), 187
    Olive Underhill makes contact, 193–4
    resumes acting, ends cabaret, 188–9
    performs in radio plays (1986-9), 190–2
    launches *Birmingham Remembered,* 195–6
    ends performing, focuses on books, 202–4,
        209, 210–11, 212–13
    Frank Ifield and Ed Doolan Show (2002),
        179–80, 221–2
    character and talents, 216–21, 222–3
    clown collection, 111–12
    comic experiences
        Roger de Courcey and, 154
        as Jack Douglas's cousin, 200
        being recognized, 173, 194
        bomb scares, 120–1
        booking agents, 156
        Burial and Cremation Authorities, 161
        dinner speeches, 177, 201
        in Glasgow, 149–50
        Guernsey masseur, 126
        mints, 192
        offbeat jobs, 173
        offbeat performances, 186–7
        at RAF Scampton, 155

at the vet's, 205
working men's clubs, 144
comic style, 84–5, 91, 92–3, 96, 106, 167
on giving up 'comicking,' 211
JD on, 206–8
on Bill Maynard, 98
on Tom Mennard, 198
on mother and father, 8, 9, 18, 20
on grandfather Price, 5–6
philosophy, 72, 169
photographs of
    as baby and infant, *2, 3*
    with Anne Beverley (1974), *132*
    at brother's wedding, *19*
    with Eddie Calvert, *61*
    with John Clayton, *29*
    and clown collection, *93*
    Coronation Party, *31*
    during *Crossroads* (1973), *129, 130*
    during time with Dragoon Guards, *41, 42,*
        45, 47, 48
    with *Express* and *Star* Personality Girl
        Contestants, *130*
    on stage at *Fol de Rols, 140*
    with Jack Freedman (1969), *78*; and Gerrie
        Raymond (1971), *103*
    compering *The Golden Shot, 124*
    with Jo, *204*; (1960s), *77*; and Groucho
        (1975), *13*
    recording *Know Your Place, 171*
    with Pete Lindup (1960s), *29*
    marching with Boys' Brigade, *29*
    with Philip Martin and Don Henderson, *191*
    at launch of *Memories of Birmingham, 193*
    at launch of *Memories of Dudley, 199*
    modelling knitwear, *161*
    with Dennis Moore (1990), *202*
    rehearsals, *Muck and Brass, 170*
    as pantomime dame, *83, 99*
    radio programme publicity shot, *181*
    with Jill Rogers, *78*
    as character John Rutland, *171*
    with Helen Shapiro (1971), *104*
    still from *A Soft Touch, 153*
    with South Staffs Townswomen, *167*
    still from *The Original Alton Douglas, 148*
    with cast, Temperance Seven Show, *109*
    and trombone, *37, 101, 145, 154*
    with cast at Weston (1970), *86*
    on stage, Weston (1970), *88*
    with West Bromwich Building Society
        winners (1972), *175*
    with Mike and Bernie Winters, *147*
    as young man, *34*

on police force (1900), 2
politics and, 212
on Price family, 7
on spiteful professionals, 146
on Edwin Richfield, 199–200
on Derek Salberg, 121–2
on 'Icky Todd', 12–13, 14
on Jo Ward, future wife, 38
on Ward family, 36
on Billy Wright, 208
Douglas, Dougie, 108, 112
Douglas, Jo (née Ward, AD's wife), 7, *77*, 117,
    122, *155*, 159, *193*, 199, *204*
on AD and marriage, 206–8, 217–18, 220–1
alternative medicines and astrology, 205
biographical details
    meets AD, 35–6, 37, 38–9
    during AD's National Service, 44, 49, 50
    courtship with AD, 51–2, 54, 56
    starts dance band agency, 58
    work and leisure, *69*, 69–70
    travels to see AD in Blackpool, 80
    as booking agent, 84, 165
    Terry Scott and, 87
    marries AD, 89–90
    visits AD at Bexhill, 140–1
    tries acting, 153
    as book producer, 184–5, 204, 205, 210
Drake, Ted (footballer), 59
Drücker, André, 214
Dudeney, Ken, 209
Dudley, 202
Dudley, Mayor of, 199, *199*
Dulay, Peter, 117
Duncan, Lindsay, *170*
Dunstable, 71
Dyer, Charles (formerly Raymond Dyer), 163, 164

E
Earl, Roy and Yvonne, *86*, 87
Early Days in Small Heath, 4
Eastbourne, 146
Ed Doolan Show, 180, 183
Edwards, Roy and Joyce, 93–4
Egan, Peter, 87
Ellesmere Road, Shrewsbury, 5
Elliot, Paul, 103–4
Elphick, Michael, 188
Emery, Dick, 133
Emmanuel, Ivor, 101
Equity, British Actors', 166
Era Cinema, Bordesley Green, 32, *32*
Estelle, Don, 132, 150
Everything and the Kitchen Sink (sketch), 57

F

Fagin's, Merry Hill, 203
Family that Plays Together, The (BBC radio play), 197
Farmer, Mr., 11
Farnall, Geoff, 120, *120*
Farnon, Robert and Dennis, 126
Faulds, Andrew (MP), 208
Fellows Club, Dudley Zoo, 142
5th Royal Royal Inniskilling Dragoon Guards,
      39–50, 209
Flamingo Club, Naples, 68
Fletcher, Mrs., 9
Foenander, Alan, 170
Fol de Rols, Bexhill, 136–9, *140*, 141
Folkestone, 43, 48
Forbes, Hughie, 56
Forsyth, Bruce, 150, 157
Forum cinema, New Street, 36
Forum Theatre, Billingham, 104
Francis, Myra, 87
Freddie and the Dreamers, 153
Freedman, Jack, *78*, 102, *103*
Fury, Billy, 143
Fyffe, Jane and Robert, 68

G

Gancia, Mike, 63, 84, 141, 168
      on AD, 219, 220
      on performance, 106–7
Garbett, Arthur, 27–8
Garland, Judy, 56
Garr, John, 108–9
Generation Game, The, 150
George Harris Quartet, *53*
Gillard, Clive, 92
Gino's, Cardiff, 75
Glasgow, 148–9
Goddard, Mike, 80
Golden Shot, The (television show), 114, 118–19,
      122–4, 128–9, 131
Gordon, Noele, 130, *130*
Gotch, Ted, 56–7
Grace Kennedy Show, 160
Grand Hotel, Birmingham, 187
Grant, Linda, *96*, 211
      on AD, 65, 95–7, 101
      on Bob Monkhouse, 114
Grappelli, Stephane, 120
Gray, Eddie, 152
Green, Bertie, 63, 68, 71
Green, Hughie, 60
Groucho, AD's dog, 131–2, *138*, 141, 148, *155*, 177,
Guernsey, 126–7

H

Hall, Terry, 94–5
Hamp, Johnny, 117
Handley, Tommy, 22
Hankinson, Philip, 63
Happy Ever After (television show), 143–4
Hardy, Clive, 166, 173, 176, 183–4, 204, 212
Harman, Paul and Barry, 152
Harmer, Richard, 134
Harris, Anita, 120, 127, *127*, 128, 148–9
Harris, George, 53, *53*
Hartland, Norman, 21
Hastings, 82-4, 99, *99*
Hatch, Bob, 141
Haymes, Dick, 102
Haynes, Jimmy, 60
Hayward, Squire Ronnie, 144
Healey, Dennis, 164
Heather Road, Small Heath, 18, 21, 28, 187
      Coronation Concert, 30–1, *31*
Heatherton Grange, Taunton, 142
Henderson, Don, 191, *191*
Herbert, Trumpet Major, 43
Heyhoe-Flint, Rachel, 162
Higgins, Jack, 184
Hill's cobbler's shop, Birmingham, 22
Hill, Vince, 132, 142, 151, *152*, 164
      on AD, 151–2
Hilltop Social Club, West Bromwich, 72
Hinge and Bracket, 68
Hits & Mrs (BBC television programme), 152
Hobley, MacDonald, 104
Hobson, Derek, 150
Hockridge, Edmund, 103
Hodgkinson, George, 180
Holmes, Robert, 106, 135
Hooley, June, 120, *120*
Horseshoe Bar Casino, Blackpool, 78–80
Howell, Denis, 26
Hudd, Roy, 107, 112, 211, 214, *214*
Hudson's Bookshop, Birmingham, 174
Hull, Rod, 146
Hunt, Derek, 134
Hunter's Moon, Castle Bromwich, 113
Hutchinson, Leslie, 34
Huxley, Donald, 21

I

Ice Show, Blackpool, 80
If - The Pat Roach Story, x
Ifield, Frank, 179–80, 221–2, *222*
Isle of Wight, 108
Ismay, Dave, 105, 114, 211
ITMA (*'It's That Man Again'*), 22

J

James, Pete, 39
Jay, Ivor (journalist), 128
Jeans, Audrey, 155–6
Jenkins, Roly, 27, 142
Joe Russell's Smethwick, 182–3
Jones, Dave *see* Mitty, Dave
Jones, Dr. Lynne (MP), 212
Jones, John Paul, 117
Jones, Ray, 191
Jonsen, Junior, 95
Jorg, Julian, 62

K

Kanievska, Marek, 164
Kelly, Phil, 67, 73
Kemp, Alan (Lara), 69
Kent, Tony, 170, 211
King, Neville, 119
Kings Theatre, Glasgow, 148–9
Kingston Cinema, Small Heath, 2
Kinks, The, *61*
Knightstone Theatre, Weston-super-Mare, 86, *88*
Knockers, The (television programme), 144
Knott, Alan, 88
Know Your Place (BBC television series), 157–60,
    162–3, 168, 173
Kray, Ronnie, 66

L

La Rèserve, Sutton Coldfield, 96
La Rue, Danny, 80
Ladies Luncheon Club, Pedmore, 188
Lake, Alan, 76
Lamas, Rafael, 77, *77*, 77–8, 79–80
Lambert, Michael, 57–8
Lane, Sandy, 104
Laughton, Tommy, on AD, 60–2
Lawn for Spindlethrift, A (play), 57
Lawton, Ralph, 163
Laycock, Johnny, 100
Le Mesurier, John, 131
Leamington, 208
Lee, Peggy, 163
Leeman, Dickie, 123, 125
Lena Zavaroni Show, 160
Lewis, Clem (journalist), 176
Lilley, Les, 144
Lindup, Pete, 78–9, *79*, *109*, 137, 141, 207
    and AD at Bexhill Fol De Rols, 139–40
    on AD, 218, 219
    on end-of-pier 'spieling,' 110
Lindup, Rowland, 199
Lipman, Maureen, 152

Litterick, Tom, 212
Little and Large, 84
Little Man in a Blind Alley, 214
Lloyd, Dorothy, 214
Locke, Josef, 66, *66*, 67
Loss, Joe, 187
Lowe Street, Wolverhampton, 6–7
Lowndes, Billy, 54, 76–7, 114
Lowndes, June, 54, 76–7, 175
    on *Golden Shot*, 114, 115, 118, 120
Lucas, Jeff, 92
Lucas, Pete (Peter Price), 6
Lunchtime with Wogan, 117–18, 128
Lynn, Dame Vera, 152–3

M

MacDonald Hobley, 104
Maclean, Don, 49, 100, 119, 142, *218*
    on AD, 114, 218
    on comedy, 105–6, 108
Made in Birmingham (film), 197
Magic Of Believing, The (book), 169
Malpas, George, 82–3
Malston, Wally, 117
Mann, Joan, 137
Manning, Bernard, 119
Marlborough, Frank, 174
Marquis, Maxine, 73
Martin, George, 43
Martin, Philip, 190, *191*, 192, 197
Martin, Reuben, 111
Martin, Rosemary, 191
Martine, Ray, 74
Martineau, Dennis (Lord Mayor) and Mollie
    (Lady Mayoress), *193*, 214
Mason, Raymond, 172, *172*, 185
Massey, Mike, *147*
Mastern, Mildred (hotelier), 110–11
Matthews, Brian (historian), 3, 10, 11, 17
Maurice Price (AD's brother)
    biographical details
        during World War II, 15
        early married life, 22
        football refereeing, 26–7, 59
    on AD, 54, 58–9, 200
    on family house, 3
    on father, 14, 19, 23
Max Bygraves Show, The, 131
Maye, Audrey, 82
Maynard, Bill, 98
McCoig, Band Sergeant Major, 49
McDowall, Paul, *153*
McGlynn, Ian, 126
McMichael, Billy, *29*

McMichael, Christine, 29
McVay, John, 76
Media Players theatre company, 163
Melly, George, 187
Memories of Birmingham, 193
Memories of Dudley, 198–9
Memories of Walsall, 198
Mennard, Tom, 95, 104, 198
Mercer, Tony, *86*, 86–7, 88, 89
Merson, Bettina, 64, 80, 103
Michaels, Mr. (hotelier), 89
Midgley, Vernon and Marietta, 67
Millard, Sid, 53
Miller, Derek, 21, 24
Miller, Jenny, 168
Mills, Major, 182
Mitchell, Guy, 75, 77
Mitty, Dave, (Dave Jones), 170, *183*
    on AD, 165–6, 180, 192, 217, 221
    on BBC radio drama, 190–2
Moneyspinner (Channel 4), 193
Monkhouse, Bob, 92, 106, 114, 118–19, 122, 208
Monsell, Stella, 163
Moore, Dennis, 162, 168, 182–4, *199, 202*, 213
    on AD, 196, 203–4, 223
Morecambe, Eric, 70, 133–4
Morley, Ken, *153*
Motor Union Insurance Company, 35, 39
Mount Hotel, Tattenhall, 164
Mr. Peabody and the Beast (BBC radio play), 191
Muck and Brass (ATV show), 70–2
Mullins, Spike, 68
Murder of a Moderate Man (BBC television
    programme), 189
Murray, Chic, 94, *94*
Murray, Frankie, 138
Murray, Pete, 154
Music Hall Tavern, Bristol, 95

N
Nash, Robin, 150
Nelson, David, 173
New Faces (television show), 116, 117, 121
Nights at the Swan (BBC television show), 168
Niklaus, Hedli, 197
Norman Dovey Big Band, The, 143, *224*
Norris, Fred (journalist), 163–4, 172, 197
Northfield Messenger, The, 153–4
Norwich, 127
Nottingham, 133

O
O'Connor, Tom, 151
O'Hara, Tommy, 57

O'Reilly, Jack, 149–50
Old Brum, 4
Oldfield, Martin, *170*
Oldknow Road School, Birmingham, 2
Open House (radio show), 154
Opportunity Knocks, 60
Original Alton Douglas, The (BBC television show),
    147–8
Osler Street Infant School, Ladywood, 6
Owen, Jonathan, 163

P
Painting, Norman, 163
pantomimes
    Goody Two-Shoes, 104
    Puss in Boots, 99
    Robinson Crusoe, 82–4
Parker, Johnny, 57
Pasco, Ora and Cyril, 145
Patou, Jeanne, 57, *57*
Pavilion, Weymouth, 164
Pavilion Theatre, Torquay, 164
Pebble Mill Studios, *159, 191*
Peet, Polly, 5
Peggy Lee Show, The, 163
Penguin Club, Birmingham, 75
Percival, Lance, 150
Pertwee, Jon, 149
Peters and Lee, 152
Pipe, Emily (née Withington, AD's grandmother),
    6, *16*, 16–17
Pipe, Richard (AD's grandfather), 6, 7, *7*
Pipe, Victor (AD's uncle), 7
Pleasant, Dick, 171
Poole, Dave, 194
Porsche factory, Reading, 195
Port Talbot, 100
Portland, 219
Powell, Sandy, 99
Price family home, 3, 17, 28
Price, Bob and Ethel (AD's uncle and aunt), 6
Price, Dennis, 126
Price, Dodie, 9
Price, Dorothy Margaret (née Pipe, AD's mother),
    1, *9, 16*
    biographical details
        birth and infancy, 6, 7
        meets Sidney, 8–9
        ill with phlebitis, 16–17
        tea with Harold Berens, 75
        tea with Dickie Valentine, 97–8
        illness and death, 127–8
    character, 28
    sayings of, 18

Price, Douglas John *see* Douglas, Alton
Price, Gwen, (MP's wife), 6, 17, *19*, 20, 23
  on Era Cinema, 32
  on Uncle Ted, 24
Price, Ivy, 33
Price, Jo *see* Douglas, Jo
Price, Lucy (née Crutchley, AD's grandmother),
  4, 5
Price, Maurice (AD's brother), *19*, 160
  at *Lunchtime with Wogan*, 118
  grandson's project on, 7–8
  on family house and business, 3, 4–5
Price, Richard (AD's great-nephew), 5, 7
Price, Sidney Neville (AD's father), 1, 5
  biographical details
    apprenticeship, 8
    service, World War I, 12–13, *13*
    marriage, 9
    during World War II, 10, 14–15, 16, *16*
    later career, 20
    death and funeral, 22–3, 25
  character, 19, 21
Price, Tom (AD's grandfather), 4, 5–6, *6*, 8
Price, Victor J., 5
Prince Monolulu, 60
Princess Theatre, Torquay, 151–2
Pritchard, Ray, 30
Probert, Mr (History master), 34
Prowse, Dave, 150
Pryke, Rob, 58
Public Eye, The (television series), 67

Q
Queen's Tavern public house, Birmingham, 38
Quinn, Miss E.R., 9, 12, 17

R
RAF Scampton, 155
Randall, Alan, 164
Raymond, Gerrie, 102, *103*
Reading, 195
Reeves, Clive, 198
Reneè, Ricki, 69
Rhodes, Joan, 69
Richfield, Edwin, *199*, 199–200
Rivers, Roy, 164
Riviera Hotel, Sidmouth, 174
Roach, Pat, 154
Rogers, Jill, 77, *78*
Ronalde, Ronnie, 127
Russell, Joe, 182
Ryan, Paddy, 58, *61*

S
Sakata, Harold, 70
Salberg, Derek, 121–2
Saltley Grammar School, 26
Sanders the Great (song), 24
Sandwell Hospital Charity Concerts, 198
Sandy, Ian, 205
Savoy Hotel, Blackpool, 164
Scarborough, 43, 45
Scattergood, Len, *48*
Scott, Terry, 87, 143–4
Searchlight Tattoo, White City, 42, *42*
Seaton, Ray (reporter)
Seconds Out (television show), 161
Shakespeare, John, 30–1
Shanklin, Isle of Wight, 108
Shapiro, Helen, 104, *104*
Sharrocks, Bill, 213
Shaw, Dennis, 99
Shaw, Wilf, 62
Shelley, John, 42
Shelley, Win, 9
Sher, Stanley, 147
Shocking Nonsense! (poems), 212
'shop window' events, 63–4, 85
Shrewsbury, 4–5
Sims, Zoot, 223
Singleton, Johnny, 94
Slater, Rob, 92
Slim & Slam, 1
Slim, John (journalist), 181
Small Heath, Birmingham, 1–4, 15
  Heather Road, 18, 21, 28,187
Smart, Keith, 91–3, 123
Smith, Cyril (MP), 201–2
Smith, Derek, 146–7
Smith, Mel, *170*
Snape, Peter (MP), 212
Soft Touch, A (ATV sit-com), 152
Somers, Patti, 152
Somerville Road, Birmingham, 3, 16
South Shore Casino, Blackpool, 77–8
Spencer, Garrie, 102
Spinning Wheel, Westerham, 136
Sprenger, Cyril, 166
St Benedict's Infant School, 9–10, 11, 12, 25
St John's Church, Ladywood, 6
St Pancras Reform Club, 63
Staffordshire Society for Brain Damaged
    Children, 129
Stage, The, 159
Stanshall, Vivian, 110
Stars and Garters (television show), 74
Stent, Malcolm, 187

Streetly Printing Ltd, 184, 203
Stretch, Gordon, 115, 147, 152, 164
   on *Know Your Place*, 159–60, 168, 169
   on *Muck and Brass*, 171–2
Styles, Kay, 163
Summerfield, June, 17
Sunday Mercury, 160
Sutton Coldfield, 96
Swan Theatre, Worcester, 168

T
Talk of the Midlands, Derby, 105
Tarbuck, Jimmy, 77
Taunton Hospital Radio Service, 142–3
Taylor, Derief, 26
Taylor, John, 121, 180
Temperance Seven, The, 108, *109*, 110, 112
Tennant, Mr., 11
Terry, George, 33
Tesco advertisement, 170
That Day Anne was Twelve, 187
Theatre Royal, Norwich, 127
Thomas Aleksandr Publishing, 166
Thompson, Brian, 69
Thompson, Councillor Joe, 180
Thompson, David, 31
Thompson, Geoffrey, 112
Thompson, Shirley, x
Three Merry Macs, The (act), 29
Today (ATV television programme), 136, 159
Todd, Dicky ('Icky Todd'), 12–13, 14
Tomes of Leamington (printers), 208
Top Gear (television series), 146
Torquay, 164
Tozer, Sheila, 156
Trimmer, Ted, 159
Trinder, Tommy, 100–1
Troupers (BBC radio play), 192
Truzzi, George, 95

U
Underhill, Olive, 2–3, 193–4
Underhill, Reverend Robin, 2–3
Urquhart, C., 4

V
Valentine, Dickie, 73, 95, 97–8, 180
Varcoe, Adrian, 214
Vaughan, Frankie, 105
Vaughan, Norman, 122, *122*, 123
Vince, Mr. (Band Master), 48–9, 50

W
Wade, Andy, 119

Walker, Stephen, 159
Wall, Max, 131, *134*, 134–5
Walsh's Bedsteads, Birmingham, 8
Wanted - One Body (play), 163
Ward, Cecil and Elsie and family, 36–7
   Cecil's death, 187
   Elsie's death, 147
Ward, Jo *see* Price, Jo
Ward, Roy, 92
Warwickshire West Midlands Star, 157, 158
Way to the Stars, The (film), 22
Wayne, Carl, 152
We're Just Good Friends (song), 57
Webbington Country Club, Weston-super-Mare, 82
Wells, H.G.(*War of the Worlds*), 1
West Bromwich, 72
West One Agency, 59
Westerham, 136
Weston-super-Mare, 82, 86, *88*, 161
White City Tattoo, 42–3
White Rock Pavilion, Hastings, 99, *99*, 132
Whitmore, Dennis, 52, *52*
Whittle Gas Turbine, 179–80
Wick, Denis, 37
Wiehenstroh family, 45
Wilkes, Rosemary, 38
Williams, Charlie, 123, 129
Williams, Robbie, 123
Wilson, Les, 67, 170
Windsor, Ken, 142–3, 151, 175, 217
Winter Gardens, Weston-super-Mare, 161
Winters, Mike and Bernie, 38, 147, *147*
Wise, Ernie, 133–4, 197
Wogan, Terry, 117–18, *118*
Wolstenholme, Ralph, 14
Wolverhampton, 6–7, 84, 162, 177
Wolverhampton, Mayor of, 213–14
Wombles, The, 131
Wood Street, Ladywood, 5–6
Wood, Roy, 92
Worcester, 168
World War II, 10–11, 15
Wright, Billy, 208
Wright, Katie, 173
Wright, Stephen, 220

Y
Yarwood, Mike, 107

Z
Zaraeda, Ozzie (hypnotist), 66–7